Change Matters

Critical Essays on Moving Social Justice Research from Theory to Policy

EDITED BY
sj Miller and David E. Kirkland

PETER LANG
New York • Washington, D.C./Baltimore • Bern
Frankfurt • Berlin • Brussels • Vienna • Oxford

Library of Congress Cataloging-in-Publication Data

Change matters: critical essays on moving social justice research
from theory to policy / edited by sj Miller, David Kirkland.
p. cm. — (Critical qualitative research; vol.1.)
Includes bibliographical references and index.
1. Education—Social aspects. 2. Social justice—Research.
3. Educational sociology. 4. Educational anthropology.
5. English language—Study and teaching.
I. Miller, sj. II. Kirkland, David E.
LC71.C47   370.11'5—dc22   2009042670
ISBN 978-1-4331-0682-8
ISSN 1947-5993

Bibliographic information published by **Die Deutsche Nationalbibliothek**.
Die Deutsche Nationalbibliothek lists this publication in the "Deutsche
Nationalbibliografie"; detailed bibliographic data is available
on the Internet at http://dnb.d-nb.de/.

FSC
Mixed Sources
Product group from well-managed
forests, controlled sources and
recycled wood or fiber

Cert no. SCS-COC-002464
www.fsc.org
©1996 Forest Stewardship Council

The paper in this book meets the guidelines for permanence and durability
of the Committee on Production Guidelines for Book Longevity
of the Council of Library Resources.

© 2010 Peter Lang Publishing, Inc., New York
29 Broadway, 18th floor, New York, NY 10006
www.peterlang.com

Printed in the United States of America

Change Matters

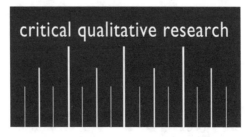

critical qualitative research

Gaile Cannella & Shirley R. Steinberg
General Editors

Vol. 1

The Critical Qualitative Research series is part of the Peter Lang Education list.
Every volume is peer reviewed and meets
the highest quality standards for content and production.

PETER LANG
New York • Washington, D.C./Baltimore • Bern
Frankfurt • Berlin • Brussels • Vienna • Oxford

This book is dedicated to all those people and living creatures who do not or did not have the voice or courage to speak up in the face of oppression, and for all those who speak out against social injustice. We celebrate and honor their lives with you.

This book is also dedicated to the life of Howard Zinn, whose words resurrected and honored the lives of the would-be forgotten.

You can't be neutral on a moving train.
—Howard Zinn

CONTENTS

SECTION 3: THE POLITICS OF SOCIAL JUSTICE REPRESENTATIONS:
RIGHT-ING AND RE-SEARCHING

SECTION 4: SUBJECT OF THE TRANSFORMATION: POLICY AND POSSIBILITY

Foreword

Glynda Hull

Some forty years ago, in an historical analysis of documents related to the teaching of English from the 1800s to the 1950s, Stanley Zehm (1973) discovered striking patterns in the labels given to poor performers in English classrooms. In particular, he noticed how the labels that were used to account for the academic difficulties of such students changed in parallel to shifts in the American zeitgeist. Characterologic labels were dominant early on—"shirker," "sleepy-minded," "reprobate," "loafer"—reflecting the moral and religious sensibilities of the time. The nature of the labels shifted with the advent of the IQ movement and efforts to scientifically determine developmental and intellectual normalcy. Poor performers were then designated as, for example, "one-talent" children," "dull-normal" and "undergifted." Such lists and terms now seem odd and dated, to be sure, the remnants of less enlightened times, offensive to modern sensibilities. Yet it does not require much reflection to realize that different but still problematic labels replaced and continue to replace and reflect these old ones, even in more recent reform-minded social science research. Zehm lists the following labels through the 1950s, for example—"culturally different," "non college students," "the bluejays" (for remedial readers); and from subsequent years—"bonehead English," "basic writer," "underprepared." Today we might add "struggling readers," a term that has catalyzed the subfield of adolescent literacy, and "disconnected youth," a recently invented demographic category for youth who lack both diplomas and jobs. The power of labels, Cuban and Tyack (1988) tell us in their discussion of Zehm's telling study, is that they suggest both an explanation and prescription. A child who is a "shirker" might be admonished toward industry and piety and demanded to develop a "spelling conscience," while a child who is "undergifted" might receive a less demanding curriculum—different if poor solutions both. The propensity to label directs us toward particular explanations and prescriptions, it appears, and away, far away, from others.

I read Miller and Kirkland's edited volume as a substantial and important effort to shift the explanatory discourse of education, to move from one long-entrenched kind of account for the failure of schooling in the United States to live up to a democratic vision of equal opportunity for all learners, to an explanation that is attuned to the more inclusive and democratic traditions in the U.S. rather than its exclusionary and elitist ones. In so doing Miller and Kirkland hope to clear some obstacles from the path of current and future generations of English educators and researchers, making it possible to imagine new participant structures for pedagogy and for research methods alike. What a hopeful and necessary project, and what a tall order, to be sure. The labeling example is but one reminder of the unexamined cultural biases, the unreflective habits of mind—our national educational habitus, if you will—that prime us to seek explanations for difficulties in schooling solely within individuals and then to imagine educational solutions that are similarly individually focused and deficit oriented (today, test and accountability driven), rather than, as Miller and Kirkland urge us, to locate recalcitrant problems within nested legacies of oppression instantiated in multiple social contexts and to imagine solutions and seek redress that targets multiple contexts, institutions, and conditions.

How do we shift our standard lens, to ask the question as Rose (1989) did two decades ago? How do we educate, how do we research when our goal is to reach and to raise the "full sweep of our citizenry" (p. 205)? How do we imagine our work as researchers and teachers such that we can most powerfully, actively, and effectively transform, reshape, and revision U.S. education to respect central human rights and capabilities (Nussbaum, 2006)? These are the questions that many critical literacy researchers have sought to answer over the years. The approach of Miller and Kirkland, and one of the achievements of this volume, is to highlight the importance, not only of theorizing schooling as potentially a democratizing space but of instantiating associated values and attendant practices in the official policies of relevant professional organizations and government-sponsored legislation. They thereby address a central dilemma in much social justice-oriented practice in the past—the hard fact that classroom-based solutions to social inequities, though of course essential, have proven insufficient. Classroom and school-based reform must be accompanied, they argue and I would agree, by changes in educational and social policy that index shifts in values and understanding, in the allocation of resources, and in the alterations of systems.

It is significant that Miller and Kirkland locate their project in the English curriculum and in English Education or that branch of teacher education that focuses specifically on the preparation of language arts teachers. To be sure, a social justice orientation can inform, and should inform, the entire curriculum, and Miller and Kirkland's volume can profitably be read by educators across grades and subject matters and outside of formal schooling too. But the language arts classroom perhaps takes pride of place among those educational spaces that can best potentially foreground the relationship of language to power and recognize the importance of a critical consciousness toward language use. Such a stance does not, it is clear, automatically obtain, since differences in language use, themselves referencing differences in race, ethnicity, socioeconomic class, and other social categories, are and have long been interpreted pejoratively as signaling almost insurmountable differences in ability, being, and worth: "Shirker," "One-talent child," "culturally different." Yet in our increasingly global world, the ability to communicate, understand, and respect across differences in culture, ideology, geography, and language is among the most crucial of habits of mind and heart. It is surely then the case that the language, literacy, and literature classroom has special import, indeed a major role to play, in fostering interpretive and critical skills and identities for an increasingly contentious world. Philosopher Kwame Appiah (2006) has written post-9/11 of the importance of dialogue even when difference seems most alienating and mutual understanding least likely, advocating a critically-turned "cosmopolitanism." Where better to explore such a conception of dialogue and such an identity as belonging both to local and global communities than an English classroom oriented toward equity and quality educations for all students as speakers, readers, writers, and communicators? Where better to focus the energies of our intellectual projects than in understanding how English teachers-to-be can best develop a moral and ethical vision for language practice and pedagogy?

Miller, Kirkland, and their colleagues show us the way toward imagining, sustaining, and institutionalizing such classrooms. Their achievements are several and substantial: the conceptualization of the need for a turn to policy as well as a continued focus on the practice of social justice approaches to education; the provision of an historical and theoretical framework on social justice approaches; an emphasis on reflective research methods that join serious approaches to scholarship with a focus on the ends of the research rather than merely its means; and the illustration of a compelling variety of scholarship, work various in genre, data, method, and forms of argument. They correctly argue that multiple differences frame our students' identities, and these should be afforded respect; the same can be said for researchers' identities and their approaches to conducting their work. There was a time when critical work on education appeared clubbish and required membership in and dues paid to particular discourse communities. That time, as Miller and Kirkland's volume well illustrates, is past, and thankfully so. Were Zehm's (1973) study to be carried out today, it would find a place at Miller and Kirkland's social justice table. The more that researchers and teachers from different traditions can join forces—those variously working for quality educations for all and redress for those who were in the past denied—the greater the likelihood of change at the policy levels that Miller and Kirkland hope to lead.

Hope circulates through this volume, nowhere more prominently than in the writings of the editors. I join Miller and Kirkland in emphasizing the necessity, in social justice work, not only of working for but expecting positive outcomes, of not only critiquing what falls short, as necessary as such critiques are, but in rejoicing even when the victories are small. In the field of critical pedagogy there have long been calls for a language of possibility as well as a language of critique, but our answers have too often been provided *sotto voce* or not at all. We have such a distance to go, as is made apparent even in this hopeful volume, in significantly changing matters, but let us not forget the range of achievements that the U.S. educational system represents, as well as the hard-won successes of those educational advocates who against big odds have managed to leverage resources and opportunities, imperfect though the system remains. Geoffrey Canada and the Harlem Children's Zone (www.hcz.org) come to mind as a recent example; we can take heart from the full-service community schools movement this work has made visible and inspired. Such examples, examined, cultivated, and as appropriate celebrated in the social justice literature, these juxtaposed to the all too apparent failures and challenges, can go some distance in reorienting the education of our teachers-to-be. Such teachers-in-waiting understandably feel ambivalent when we, in effect, ask them, primed by a social justice orientation to be resolutely critical, to abjure the very profession that they desire to join.

As they insist upon a hopeful cast for social justice orientations, Miller and Kirkland also make clear the necessity for the work to be informed by a vision that is morally and ethically alert. This, I believe, is one of the best and most intrepid achievements of their editorial apparatus. They not only confront directly the non-neutrality of the social justice enterprise, a gesture that is now customary, but in laying claim to these particular terms and values, they point the way toward an appropriation and re-creation of an important foundational discourse. We are unaccustomed, even in English education, where beliefs, judgments, and values are part and parcel of literary study, to tracing seriously the implications of thinking in terms of ethics and morality in our daily dealings with students, our structuring of schooling, and our articulation of educational policies. And so it is for most educational disciplines, where disciplinary interest lies in the inculcation, demonstration, exercise, and evaluation of skills and knowledge, which are usually assumed to exist outside value systems. Yet, Miller and Kirkland would position us differently, and in so doing, they join an array of scholars in disciplines such as sociology (e.g., Touraine, 2000), philosophy (e.g., Appiah, 2006; Benhabib, 2006), and media and communication (e.g., Silverstone, 2007), who of late have issued urgent calls for the development of moral spaces for communication that promote ethical understandings and acknowledge in an attempt to reach across, differences in ideology, geography, and culture (cf. Hull, Stornaiuolo, & Sahni, 2010). I see Miller and Kirkland's volume as prompting something similar, and something similarly crucial, in its forthright emphasis on the moral and ethical face of a social justice orientation.

Such an orientation was never more needed than now, when our zeitgeist centrally includes an uneasy awareness of the negative impacts of globalization. To be sure, we are awash in great shifts, challenges, and opportunities brought about by political and economic strife and realignment, environmental concerns and crises, unprecedented migration, and new forms and patterns of interaction, connection, and disconnection. In the same way that larger social arenas and particular national legacies primed the teachers and their curricula that Zehm (1973) studied to respond in particular deficit-oriented ways to students marked as different, our own historical moment primes us to respond in relation to perceived risks and challenges (Hull, Zacher, & Hibbert, 2009). One necessary response to conditions of globalization, long associated with critical theory and critical pedagogy approaches, is to reload our critical arsenal in order to call out ever more pointedly and clearly the injustice of inequalities: the corruption of international corporations, the neglect of whole regions of the world resulting in genocides, the pillaging of resources for the wealth of the few. Another crucial and necessary response focuses interpersonally, considering anew the skills, dispositions, identities, and values that position individuals to fashion ethical and moral responses to the construction of their own lives in relation to those of others (e.g., Hansen, 2010; cf. Comstock, Hammer, Strentzsch, Cannon, Parsons, and Salazar, 2008). How can we best prepare new generations of youth who are coming of age in a global and interconnected, but fearfully riven world? A third response, and this is Miller and Kirkland's call to action, takes up the challenge of institutional dialogue and change, assuming, demanding, that seemingly unbridgeable differences need not and must not divide us, especially at the level of policy. As we take up their call, we will need also to take care that longstanding and unproductive habits of mind about who is and who is not able, the remnants of legacies best shed, do not blunt our best intentions as educators and do not limit our constructs of reform. We will also want our social justice imaginaries to include global rights and responsibilities, thus, loosening their current geographic and national fetters. Let us each, inspired by the example of this book, locate the context for our own best work in a newly invigorated social justice agenda in our ever more interconnected world.

Bibliography

Appiah, K. A. (2006). *Cosmopolitanism: Ethics in a world of strangers.* New York: W.W. Norton.

Benhabib, S. (2006). *Another cosmopolitanism.* Oxford: Oxford University Press.

Comstock, D.L., Hammer, T.R., Strentzsch, J., Cannon, K., Parsons, J. & Salazar, S. (2008). Relational-cultural theory: A framework for bridging relational, multicultural and social justice competencies. *Journal of Counseling & Development,* 86, 279–87.

Cuban, Larry, & Tyack, David. (1997). "'Dunces,' 'shirkers,' and 'forgotten children': Historical descriptions and cures for low achievers." Conference for Accelerating the Education of At- Risk Students. Stanford University, 1997.

Hansen, D. T. (2010). Cosmopolitanism and education: A view from the ground. *Teachers College Record, 112*(1), 1–30.

Hull, G., Stornaiuolo, A., & Sahni, U. (2010). Cultural citizenship and cosmopolitan practice: Global youth communicate online. *English Education,* 331–367.

Hull, G., Zacher, J., & Hibbert, L. (2009). Youth, risk, and equity in a global world. *Review of Research in Education, 33,* 117–159.

Nussbaum, M. (2006). *Frontiers of justice: Disability, nationality, species membership.* Cambridge, MA: Belknap Press

Rose, M. (1989). *Lives on the boundary: An account of the struggles and achievements of America's educationally underprepared.* New York: Penguin.

Silverstone, R. (2007). *Media and morality: On the rise of the mediapolis.* Cambridge, UK: Polity.

Touraine, A. (2000). *Can we live together? Equality and difference* (D. Macey, Trans.). Stanford, CA: Stanford University Press.

Zehm, Stanley. (1973). *Educational Misfits: A Study of Poor Performers in the English class 1825–1925.* Unpublished Dissertation. Stanford University.

Acknowledgments

Change is happening all around us at the speed of light. This journey has impacted each of us to think differently and in far-reaching ways about social justice than we could have ever imagined. There are many people who we both want to acknowledge in our efforts in seeing this project to form. We are thankful to Glynda Hull for her *Foreword*, a thinking piece and provocative conceptual vision to kick off our book; to each of our contributors for their passion and commitment to creating change through a social justice lens; and to Peter McLaren for his inspiring, powerful, and summative *Afterword*. We are also grateful to Sonia Nieto, Keith Gllyard, and William Ayers for their kind and generous endorsements of our book.

It would be inconsiderate and flawed to not thank our mentors. I, David, would like to thank Geneva Smitherman, who has worked with me since I was an undergraduate at Michigan State University. I also thank Anne Haas Dyson for her inspiration and encouragement throughout the production of this book. Both professors Smitherman and Dyson have long worked the vineyards of justice, paving the way so that we could bring this volume to you. I also thank my social justice colleague sj Miller, who is one of the most determined and disciplined intellectuals I know. Indeed, there would be no book without sj's persistence and fortitude. Finally, I would like to thank my family, who daily reminds me why change matters. I love you!

I, sj, want to personally thank the Social Justice Policy strand participants of CEE who worked so diligently and tirelessly on the thinking and drafting of the Social Justice Beliefs statement in English education. What happened in our weekend together was politically and intellectually transformative. In particular, I am personally indebted to my social justice mentor Todd DeStigter, who has challenged me to refine and reflect my thoughts around social justice. Thanks also go to Ethan Bach for his inspiring cover. I thank my grandmother Esther Lassen, whose spirit keeps me going even in the darkest of hours, and to my family who lost their lives in the Holocaust—for having the courage to be themselves. Most importantly I thank my co-editor and friend David, whose indefatigable spirit flies high and long distances, even when he's at rest and for which this project has been able to find its wings, traveling beside, and not too near the sun.

We close with the infallible words of James Baldwin, who reminds us to be relentless in our efforts to move forward in being socially just: "The paradox of education is precisely this—that as one begins to become conscious one begins to examine the society in which he [*sic*] is being educated."

—sj Miller and David Kirkland

Glossary of Terms

Action Research In education, action research is research undertaken for the purpose of advancing an educational issue, practice, or policy in order to challenge and change existing practices/policies of educational inequity, discrimination, or endangerment. One of the goals for conducting action research is to help practitioner researchers develop a deep understanding of issues and problems plaguing education and to amass data to support efforts toward educational reform. Action research has a long and diverse history, ranging from practical applications in fields such as nursing to upholding more political purposes in fields such as environmental studies. Action research in education builds from these fields and their traditions.

Agency The concept of agency has a variety of histories in the academy. Taken primarily from philosophy and sociology, agency in education refers to the capacity of a person to act and create change in a given context. Agency includes the human ability to choose and make other kinds of enacted decisions that govern one's own well-being and the well-beings of others. All people who think, choose, act, or love for themselves have agency.

Change In education, change generally connotes improvement (as opposed to decline) in educational conditions, performances/practices, structures, etc. However, more generally (and perhaps more precisely), it refers to a transformation or alteration of something (e.g., injustice, oppression, etc.) into something else (e.g., justice, liberation, etc.). In this way, change can be seen as the act of becoming transformed or altered, usually due to some kind of external pressure or outside intervention. Change can also occur from within an individual and inside a group. Many religious and feminist thinkers believe internal change, or transformation, precedes external change. (See also **power**.)

Counter-storytelling Counter-storytelling is a method borne out of critical race studies, which offers critical analysis and presentation that seeks to decenter the authoritative, master narratives of the elite by centering the alternative narratives of the masses. This play on perspective highlights the performances of power (over) that exist in the "storytelling" process. It embodies the spirit of the African proverb: "Until the lion learns to write history, the story of the jungle will forever glorify the hunter." (See also **critical race theory.**)

Critical Discourse Analysis Critical discourse analysis is a transdisciplinary approach to research concerned with describing, analyzing, interpreting, and critiquing discourse, the social and cultural consequences of language, as a form of contested social practice. Critical discourse analysts examine the ways in which social and political domination are manufactured through various kinds of language use (e.g., spoken and written). Their approach to analysis reveals the sources of power, domination, inequity, and bias to shed light on how these sources are initiated, maintained, reproduced, and transformed at multiple levels of inquiry (e.g., linguistic, sociocultural, and politial) and various sites of struggle (e.g., social, economic, and historical). (See also **discourse.**)

Critical Ethnography Critical ethnography is an evolved approach to cultural inquiry, which applies critical theory to ethnography. In doing so, it challenges the belief that ethnographies and the ethnographer are neutral. Instead, it suggests that all research is politically slanted and all researchers express, either implicitly or explicitly, a politically specific agenda in the research they take up. Hence, critical ethnography is honest about the hidden ideologies that inform ethnographic studies, and the laden biases that may result from such ideologies. It is from this place that critical ethnographies seek to make sense of issues of power, domination, inequity, and oppression, in a bounded cultural situation. It takes as data the cultural practices and participation structures of individuals within groups. It also aims to highlight how individuals within groups discuss and derive meaning from things, such as oppression and liberation, inequity, and fairness.

Critical Ethnography of Discourse Critical ethnography of discourse is a phrase coined by David E. Kirkland that blends critical ethnography and critical discourse analysis. By blending the two approaches, it seeks to capture complementary cultural and linguistic data that can be helpful in proving context and meaning for a variety of critical issues that social justice researchers have long examined. While critical ethnography provides methods for collecting cultural data, including language, critical discourse analysis provides a way of deepening cultural analysis by focusing on various states of language in practice. Hence, a critical ethnography of discourse looks at language, society, power, and the complex relationship among them to represent knowledge capable of healing wounded worlds.

Critical Pedagogy Critical pedagogy is a teaching philosophy grounded in the tenets of critical theory. The critical practitioner, therefore, does not view class instruction as politically innocent. Rather, she or he acknowledges the ways in which instruction is capable of promoting justice or reinforcing injustice by reifying the status quo. Critical pedagogues attempt to raise students' awareness about critical issues, dominant myths, and habits of minds that sanction oppression. In critical pedagogy, students and teachers act as co-learners who engage in active and ongoing processes of problem posing about society and self, in ways that allow them to interrogate knowledge and ideologies to seek new knowledge and resolutions as a process of challenging domination. This process follows the logics of praxis (see below), the dialectical coupling expressed in the reflection/action sequence.

Critical Race Theory Critical race theory is an intellectual movement initiated primarily by law scholars interested in studying and transforming the relationship among race, racism, and power in the globe. Critical race theorists embrace a "race-consciousness" that challenges the various constructions and representations of race in our society and the social structures (like law and education) that define it. By extension, critical race theorists conclude that racial ideology is an invisibly normal rather than aberrant feature of American society. Moreover, racist assumptions are not only deeply prevalent in our everyday social landscape but in the various social systems that constitute that landscape. Critical race theory has been applied to education to analyze educational inequities associated with race and racism. Critical race theory in education is a social justice paradigm, devoted to combating racism as part of a much larger goal of ending all forms of human oppression and subordination.

Critical Theory Critical theory is the Marxist-influenced movement initiated by the social and political philosophies of members of the Frankfurt School, a group of thinkers associated with the Institute for Social Research in Frankfurt, Germany. Drawing specifically on the writings of Marx and the psychoanalytic teachings of Freud, critical theory maintains that the chief purpose of philosophy, social thought, and corresponding research is to understand oppression, social conflict, and societal chaos to help overcome the structures that dominate and oppress people.

Discourse The term discourse has a variety of meanings in educational contexts. For some it simply means talk, what James Gee terms small "d" discourse. It has come to represent the ways that meaning gets expressed through other social practices (e.g., behaviors, values, ways of thinking, etc.), what Gee terms big "D" discourse. Other philosophers, including Foucault and Bakhtin, have regarded discourse as systems of representation that signify things—real or imagined. Once signified, those things take on a life of their own and guide all existence. We view discourse more simply as the consequences of language. (See also **critical discourse analysis**.)

Hegemony Hegemony is the success of some dominant group, class, perspective, or interest in projecting its beliefs, values, and dispositions upon the masses whereby the masses consent to their own oppression. In education the concept has been used to speak to ways in which people generally work against their own interests.

Ideology A mystification of truth that serves class purposes. False consciousness. Lies.

Power Power is the invisible force that compels things to happen. It speaks to the ability of one thing to control or influence another. While in social justice circles power carries a negative connotation, not all forms of power are negative. We think of power as related to the prepositions that follow it. Power over connotes domination, or a state where power is used to oppress. There are other versions of power, which are less deterministic. Power with connotes a collaborative force, whereby people jointly influence or control things. Power within connotes an internal force where one finds personal value and validation to control the things that are within them. (See also **agency**.)

Praxis The critical change that occurs within a teaching context, which results from an iterative process of critical reflection followed by action. In turn, each action informs further critical reflection, and so on.

Social Justice Social justice means that each student in our classrooms is entitled to the same opportunities of academic achievement regardless of background or acquired privilege. Although such a disposition will prompt various pedagogical responses depending on the context, we believe that social justice must be a central part of the rhetoric we educators use to conceptualize and carry out our work. Thus, it means that in schools and university classrooms, we educators must teach about injustice and discrimination in all forms with regard to: race, ethnicity, language, gender, gender expression, age, appearance, ability, national origin, spiritual belief, weight (height and/or weight), sexual orientation, social class, economic circumstance, environment, ecology, culture, and the treatment of animals.

Social Justice Methodology Social justice methodology has dual purpose: as research and as classroom practice. As research methodology it presupposes a transformational outcome and grounds itself within theoretical social justice perspectives, it examines topics related to social justice or injustice, draws upon data analyses that are dialogical and discursive, and represents the data in ways that authenticate the experiences of the individuals. As classroom method it is reflected in choice of texts, construction of social space, discourse, classroom design, placement of artifacts, and pedagogy.

Social Justice Pedagogy Social justice pedagogy presupposes that all students are worthy of human dignity, that all are worthy of the same tenets in an education, that the contract they enter into in schools must honor their sociocultural advantages and disadvantages, that it must seek to offer the same educational, sociocultural, and psycho-emotional opportunities to each student in order to help them meet and obtain a (determined) basic threshold that is mutually beneficial to each party who enters into the school space. Social justice pedagogy strives for equity for all students, supports the affective, corporeal, and emotional growth of individuals and recognizes that students bring inequitable histories, and in spite of that strives to bring each student up to their capability threshold. Social justice as pedagogy also embraces the paradox of its conflicting principles and acknowledges its own flaws.

Social Justice Theory A grounded theory for social justice is premised on reflection, change, and participation. It presupposes that all students should be treated with human dignity, that all are worthy of the same tenets in an education, that the contract they enter into in schools must honor their sociocultural advantages and disadvantages, that it must seek to offer the same educational, sociocultural, and psycho-emotional opportunities to each student in order to help them meet and obtain a (determined) basic threshold that is mutually beneficial to each party who enters into the school space. Our theory also recognizes that efforts to move policy forward must bear in mind that *not* all students have the same essential moral, physical, and intellectual capabilities due to the historical inheritance of oppression and class status.

Subjectivity Subjectivity speaks to one's sense of self and one's perception of possibility and action.

Threefold Theory of Social Justice A grounded theory for social justice that includes: (1) reflection, (2) change, and (3) participation. *Reflection* refers to unpacking personal truths from people, ideologies, and contexts to help explain how hegemonic hierarchies are oppressive. *Change* refers to becoming more socially aware of how power and privilege that arise from within institutions, in relation to social class, ethnicity, culture, gender, religion, national origin, ability, sexual orientation, gender expression, political beliefs, marital status, and/or education, can be oppressive. *Participation* teaches how action, agency, and empowerment can be used to transform ideas and contexts, and may even lead to systemic change.

Bibliography

Conference on English Education Commission on Social Justice. (2009). CEE position statement: Beliefs about social justice in English education. *First Biennial CEE Conference*. Chicago: CEE.

Teaching Social Justice

sj Miller & David E. Kirkland

Theories of social justice should be abstract. They should, that is, have a generality and theoretical power that enables them to reach beyond the political conditions of their time, even if they have their origins in such conflicts. (Nussbaum, 2006, p. 1)

We began writing this book in early 2009, a moment of change in the history of social justice. President-elect Barack Obama was to be inaugurated as the forty-fourth president of the U.S. His election marked a milestone in the social justice crusade—the first Black president of a major Western nation, a progressive who promised to invest—like no other president before him—in the human liberties' projects of universal healthcare, global environment justice through clean energies reform, and education. As a country, each of us became part of history in the making, spilling into streets and promoting the righteous cause of hope and new beginnings. As we look back, we understand how given to romance the moment had been. Indeed, the forces of injustice have proven ardent, and, as we have well learned, change requires more than just fleeting solidarity.

Though as a country divided even still, we can try to change some of the injustices that hold us back from maturing into a more perfect union, a more connected U.S. The potential for change is all around us. Hope and optimism surround our work. The horizon whispers through the breeze; we can make a difference if we persevere. Now, more than anytime in history, is a good time to gird our loins to pursue changes for the betterment of all students regardless of social categories that might mark them for future failures. Though we acknowledge that the struggle will continue to be fierce, all we can do is try. All we can do is put our best effort forward, an effort motivated by good faith and love for the people who, more than change, matter.

Desire for social change and equitable schooling opportunities inspire us to write. As researchers and teachers and teachers of teachers, we have found ourselves hungry for the meat of critical ideas, yet left starving in the barren fields of our profession—a profession we find receding from the urgency of the moment. Indeed, reclaiming justice in education is our goal, and promoting social justice as a schooling practice is our aim. Ultimately, we hope to formulate social justice theory, practice, and research that can move us toward social justice policy. Without influencing policy, we well understand that social justice, like so many other catchphrases, will be as marginal as the populations for which we advocate.

This book features a collection of short essays written by leading scholars committed to social justice in English education. It aims to provide researchers, university instructors, preservice and inservice teachers, and those interested in critical research in social justice in other disciplines, with a framework that pivots social justice in theory and action toward policy. In doing so, the chapters in the volume detail rationales for generating social justice theory in what Freire (1970) calls "the revolutionary process" through essays that support research for social change. The spirit of the essays directs us toward the significance of enacting social justice methodologies in the intellectual work we do.

In the spirit of social justice thought, the book does not offer a panacea. That is, neither we nor our contributors are interested in participating in the intellectual performances of politically angled critique impenetrable to the unknown masses, offering impractical and utopian solutions. Neither do we purport to have access to the silver bullets capable of slaying the dark dragons of injustice that conspire, with their hidden fires, to hold captive educational equity. Indeed, if we felt these habits of thought were useful or even available, we would feel, out of a deep sense of love for the people, accountable to them. The fact is that social justice is as diverse as the populations it reaches toward and as vast as the issues it seeks to resolve. Therefore, some of the chapters included in this book may not look like other "social justice" writings. Many of them do not cling to flagellant arguments that strive for the sexy and sensational, the provocative and oftentimes petty. Rather, this compilation aims to broaden what can be considered social justice work, bringing together an exercise in pluralism as opposed to censorship. While we have sought to include a diverse range of conversations in this book, we have not excluded intentionally politically angled arguments most associated with social justice thought. In this book, a rich range of diverse writings converges around the topic of English education.

The text also privileges a variety of expository genres—from narratives to literature reviews. Therefore, when reading the chapters as we have thoughtfully collected them, we hope that readers will follow the implicit "meta-storyline" that diversity in how we represent "scholarly" work is as much a social justice issue as the "scholarly" work itself. Hence by intermixing narrative essays and more scientifically written texts, we have hoped to capture the complexity of concepts in social justice theory, practice, research, and policy. And while these means may seem different, their ends have been quite the same—to allow for a thoughtful conversation on how to move social justice from the borders of mind to the stages of performance, from the dalliance of research to the core of policy. All essays do not travel the same distance or route; that is, while one essay may begin at theory, it may not end at policy, and vice versa. In this way, chapters can be read as steps that together lead toward some greater destination. Therefore, the book as a whole is meant to illuminate a path that leads from social justice theory to social justice policy as understood in the research and teaching of English.

Social justice, from our lenses as English scholars, views human experience as a by-product of context and belief constructs. It grounds itself in Dewey's articulation of freedom. In this way, we view social justice as seeking to unpack truths that challenge master narratives and unveils counter-narratives that often go untold or ignored altogether. We return to Dewey's proleptic vision of a Deliberative Democracy, wherein schools might act as designated spaces where learners could cultivate the ability to make workplaces more democratic (Dewey, 1915), and could foster "democratic habits of thought and action" throughout each American community (Dewey, 1987, p. 225). Dewey believed that freedom, in its varied forms, in relation to others' powerful attributes such as love, can improve social conditions. Such change was predicated on the habits of "open-mindedness, tolerance of diversity, fairness, rational understanding, respect of truth, and critical judgment" (Hursh, p. 153, as quoted in Olssen, Codd, & O'Neill, 2004, p. 269). Dewey's view of freedom within Deliberative Democracy is foundational to our work, and yet we recognize that to reach it is a slalom of communal effort.

We also define social justice uniquely, but consistent with feminist thinkers who examine the relative effects of social injustice on education and society (Bell & Nugent, 2001; Blume, 1990; Collins, 1986). For such thinkers, social injustice is expressed through the various deposits of pain that are inflicted in the human processes—creation, life, struggle, evolution, etc. As such, pain is one of the man-made by-products of human endeavors, usually the result of conflicts of interests and other moral derisions that complicate human harmony. As people compete for things—resources, power, space, attention, etc.—wounds are administered, though unevenly, based usually on one's proximity to power and privilege

(Bell & Nugent, 2001). That is, the more powerful one is, the more damage one can inflict on others. The converse is also true; the less powerful one is, the more damage one will sustain in life. If social injustice deposits pain, then social justice is a process of healing wounds caused by social conflict (Kirkland & Filipiak, 2008)—a process of depositing hope as cure and inventing change as remedy. It is also the custodial work of repairing a broken world, a dangerous world that in many ways promises that people—all people—at some point in their lives will sustain wounds.

Further, some of the work for this collection stems from the work of capability theorists, who come out of the tradition of social contract theories. Capability theories call for basic human rights that each person should have in order for a society to be decently just. In particular, sj references Martha Nussbaum, one of the world's most influential capability theorists who offers "the capabilities approach," which she notes as a politics of humanity. Central to her capabilities approach are ten critical basic capabilities to which each person should be afforded and entitled: (1) *living life* to a normal length; (2) *bodily health* (including reproductive health and nourishment); (3) *bodily integrity* (including shelter, freedom to experience sexual satisfaction, freedom from sexual assault); (4) *senses, imagination, and thought* (including the ability to use one's senses, to think and reason); (5) *emotions* (including attachments to things and people and to love and care for others); (6) *practical reason* (to be able to form a conception of good and to critically reflect); (7) *affiliation* (respect, dignity, thus nondiscrimination); (8) *other species* (including the ability to live with concern for animals, plants, and nature; (9) *play* (including laughter and enjoyment of recreational activities; and, (10) *political and material control over one's environment* (including the decision to participate in political choices, to hold property, land and goods, and to have the right to seek employment and to have work without being harassed) (Nussbaum, 2006, pp. 76–78). Nussbaum identifies the positionality of these ten capabilities as moralized and socialized from the start; however, she stresses that if a society fails to secure these entitlements for citizens, it violates basic justice.

Nussbaum's presupposition for the list is that each person's life is worthy and should be treated with human dignity. Her claims are transparent, as she forefronts the presuppositions of an approach, which presupposes that humans cooperate "out of a range of motives, including the love of justice itself, and prominently including a moralized compassion for those who have less than they need to lead decent and dignified lives" (pp. 156–157). She argues that the ten principles should be embodied in a list by the U.S. Constitution. Her hope is that these principles be bound by legislative and judicial action as they are in India, Germany, and South Africa—three vastly different countries with vastly different histories which frame basic human dignity in their constitutions. While we in the U.S. have much work left to do to take care of our citizens, Nussbaum sees a capabilities approach as a starting point, although she notes there are limits to the philosophy in that it is not a comprehensive moral doctrine.

As we craft a theory for social justice, it might include Deweyian Democracy, feminist pain theory, and Nussbaum's capabilities approach. Still, any theory of social justice must include reciprocity and an investment for the good of all. It must presuppose that all people should be treated with human dignity and that all are worthy of education. Therefore, we find it necessary to press within our field of English education a set of legislative truths: The contract we enter into in schools must honor the sociocultural advantages and disadvantages of each of us. It must seek to offer the same educational, sociocultural, and psycho-emotional opportunities to all in order to help people meet and obtain a determined, but basic threshold that is mutually beneficial to each party who enters into the school space. Such a theory for social justice is not parsimonious nor does it leave any child behind. Rather, it extends outward toward our highest reaches of altruism and human dignity, embracing all. If any child is left behind, the system has failed, no matter how well some may have succeeded. A system for all is implicit in its inception; *it is a system for all*. We write, because as we see our fellow citizenry in schools, the school contract is full of flaws, and students are treated inequitably and in many instances, without dignity.

The Reality Is This

We have hope for our work, but there are still difficult realities. While significant research has been conducted attesting to the powerful effects of social justice pedagogy (Cochran-Smith, 2004; DeStigter, 2008; Duncan-Andrade, 2005; McLaren & Fischman, 1998; Miller & Norris, 2007; Morrell, 2005; Nieto & Bode, 2008; Reed & Black, 2006), there is also great resistance to enacting a pedagogy for social justice in the public schools (Apple, 2002; Apple & Oliver, 1998; Deyhle, 1995; Kozol, 2005; Levinson, Foley, & Holland, 1996; McLaren, 2000; Spring, 2001, 2005; Zinn, 1980). It seems that this divide is likely to widen because it is extremely difficult to institutionalize conflicting principles or as Fish (1999) calls them "strong moral intuitions as to how the world should go combined with the resolve to be faithful to them" (p. 9). Through naming the unresolved disparity between conflicting principles and informing ourselves about oppositional stances about teaching social justice, we become better prepared to take steps toward building bridges and breaking down stubborn boundaries.

Alarmingly still, Kathleen Brown (2005) informs us: "The evidence is clear that various segments of our public school population experience negative and inequitable treatment on a daily basis" (p. 155). Still, non-White and White students from deprived socioeconomic backgrounds experience lower standardized test scores, teacher expectations, and access to resources than their middle-class

White counterparts (Brown, 2005). In fact, over 4.4 million second language learners are enrolled in the U.S. public schools and are expected to take (and do well on) the same standardized exams as first language students. It is our failure if we do not find it atrocious that such students are typically evaluated similar to students whose first language is English (Arce, Luna, Borjian, & Conrad, 2005).

Another barrier we see in moving social justice toward policy is that under the current U.S. Department of Education we still seek "evidence-based," "best practice" cure-alls (Mathison, 2009, p. 10), and are also seeking "measures" of student success that qualify such practices for entry into the What Works Clearinghouse (WWC) of the Institute of Educational Science (IES). Leathwood (2005) shares, "assessment is used to provide a rationale and legitimacy for the social structures and power relations of modern day societies" (p. 308). Although, as we are well aware, the tests students take for annual yearly progress (AYP) are neither culturally nor economically sensitive. Popkewitz (2006) urges us to study the scientific method so that we are better equipped to handle the debate between the quantitative and qualitative approach to testing.

Our critique of these tests, besides those already mentioned, is that they are a measurement of how well we assimilate students into hegemonic and neoliberal containers. In actuality, we are assessing our own moral standards and what it means to be a citizen in our fluid multicultural democracy. The collective results are often reinterpreted or skewed away from the raw data, to hide the shame of our own complicity. Because, as a society, we cannot bear to see our own failures in the public school sector, the testing community pushes toward homogenous outcomes. Some believe that these testing results are adequate measurements that mask gaping inequities.

Under the Obama administration, we question, if change is now possible. Is it conceivable to decentralize educational evaluation and return it to the public sphere? Unfortunately, this may not be likely since our new secretary of education, Arne Duncan, is a neoliberal who, as CEO of the Chicago Public Schools (CPS), both militarized and corporatized CPS. It is not coincidence either that ninety percent of CPS students were poor and non-White under Duncan, who received benefits because of this as part of the Renaissance 2010 initiative (Giroux, 2008). The act to delocalize regulations and the implementation of draconian policies brought outcries from angry parents and community groups who felt that they lost control over their childrens' educations. Giroux (2008) writes, "Obama has appointed as his Secretary of Education someone who actually embodies this utterly punitive, anti-intellectual, corporatized, and test-driven model of schooling."

Yet we still have hope even if Obama's selection for secretary of education is far from ideal. It may be that standardized testing is here for some time, feeding into an anti-intellectual and corporate-driven model of education, but change is inevitable: We are confident, especially when reviewing the staggering statistics about a long history of public education inequities that support our vision to move social justice into policy. Evidencing our belief in the possibility of change, we see empirical evidence that asserts that large populations of U.S. youth do not attend graduate school or attend college (Skrla et al., 2001). It is no wonder why we shriek when we read the statistics provided by Valencia (1997): "Millions of…minority students (particularly, African Americans, Mexican Americans, and Puerto Ricans) attend schools that are segregated, inequitably financed, vapid in curricula delivery, teacher centered, and are generally hostile in any sense of a learning environment" (p. 1). Sadly, fewer than ten percent of postsecondary institutions have currently adopted policies that challenge First Amendment principles (Tierney, 2006). Again, it is no wonder why we are faced with what it means to be socially just in schools.

The hierarchy of educational injustice does not spare any of its K–12 and higher education constituents. At the top, education-based policies are handed down from the government that impale universities (with expectations for accreditation) and their academics, who must comply, lest their students of education be "ill-prepared" for the demands of national and state standards. The education a teacher candidate then inherits, regardless of the time-based policy that is relevant during a given moment, means that they pass on those values and expectations to their secondary or elementary classrooms. Consequently, a critical issue we face with employing social justice in teacher education is that "promoting social justice in teacher education is anathema to the mission and traditions of the modern university, which is intended to foster an open intellectual atmosphere of free thought and speech" (Cochran-Smith et al., 2009, p. 633). Ironically, social justice threatens the hegemonic pillars that have sustained national institutions. Social justice, which seems to be about equality, access, and redress, has motivated the moral majority and the testing community to create disjunctive and culturally insensitive tests, and disharmonious agendas that block access to equitable schooling practices. Social justice ceases to be a concern for educational policy; instead, we see educational policy in the U.S. exclusively dominated by accountability issues at the national, state, and local levels (Linn, 2000; Olson, 1999; Popkewitz, 2000).

Both researchers and teachers have inherited from this politics of hegemony, an intentionally socially constructed system of duality: that of the socially, economically, and culturally disadvantaged and that of the privileged. Because the "system" as we know it is dependent on a "language we never made" (Butler, 1997, p. 26) and the power (Foucault, 1980) that came before, the subject is vulnerable to repositioning (or even subordinating) the self, as a coordinate, at the center of this dichotomy. Preservice teachers' subjectivities are especially vulnerable to perpetuating social and educational inequalities if they aren't made aware of or are actively involved in recognizing the power they hold in co-constructing students' identities (Miller & Norris, 2007). However, if preservice teachers are made aware of the sociopolitical context of history and the concomitant inequitable schooling practices that have ensued, perhaps they would be more likely to address it in the classroom. However, social justice pedagogy alone cannot address the insurmountable depth of inequalities that will still linger in spite of changes in teacher education. Social justice research and policy are also needed.

Research on student achievement confirms that classroom teachers are directly relational to "quality and equitable delivery of education and student academic achievement" (Ukpokodu, 2007, p. 8). Over ninety percent of teachers are White while over forty percent of public school students are African American, Latino, Asian, and Native American (Epstein, 2005). Further, the diversity of student languages, ethnicities, religions, and racial and cultural make-up continues to grow (Banks, 2004). Hence, while the teaching force becomes increasingly and predominantly White, middle class, and monolingual (Futrell, 2000; Kailin, 1999), one wonders about the lack of knowledge, skills, and dispositions to work within schools that have predominantly non-White populations.

Unjust schooling stems from a long history of inequitable educational practices, institutional racism, and overt yet faulty, gendered beliefs about student achievement. In the U.S. schooling is compulsory, and given that we have no social justice policy related to our schools, justice is not. Bottom line—we fail our students daily when we force them into a system that is not "really" set-up for their spiritual, emotional, psychological, or academic success (Moffett, 1994). We assert that this volume is far from neutral. How could it not be? It both challenges hegemonic practices and seeks to institute transformational philosophies that will positively alter the fabric of our thinking and change our schools.

Why Social Justice in English Education? Why Now?

This work joins the established body of scholarship on social justice education. However, it is unique to English education, defined broadly, and to those interested in researching and teaching language and texts and their processes, practices, and products. Generally the conversation on social justice in English education is about theory—reading and writing texts to transform lives. It is sometimes about performance—teaching and affirming texts that honor student locations. It is also about the kinds of inquiry that challenge the status quo. But rarely has it been about policy, shaping standards and rules that have at their base the goal of empowering people. As these items exist, more or less, as disparate entities in English education, or in some cases fail to exist at all, it seems quite natural to want to organize them to get a broader view of social justice in the field. English education is arguably the most evolved subdiscipline in educational studies that deals with social justice issues. Yet, in our own readings of the field, we feel that social justice thought in English education is not well organized nor is it inclusive of scholarship that promotes the liberation of people without hanging onto floating social justice signifiers.

To produce what we feel is a comprehensive portrait of social justice (broadly defined) in English education, we have organized the field across conversations on social justice theories and methods, research approaches and policies. These conversations are grounded in their transferability of theory into practice, and recognize and honor the relationships among language, knowledge, and power in the teaching of English and in the preparation of English teachers, particularly those relationships that help foster and maintain uneven social and educational outcomes. In this way, we ground this work in the belief that English teaching, English teacher preparation, and language and literacy research and policies are political activities that mediate relationships of power and privilege in social interactions, institutions, and meaning-making processes. Such relationships, we believe, have direct implications for how we achieve equity and access in English classrooms. We feel it is impossible to prepare English teachers or to engage in serious inquiry in English education without first meeting these goals. Hence, we see the challenge of English education research and practice as sustaining the critical dialogue necessary for developing and uncovering theories and practices in the teaching of English that foreground and promote respect across multiple social categories, including race, gender, gender expression, sexual orientation, ethnicity, language, national origin, spiritual belief, class, socioeconomic status, size (height and/or weight), and ability (Conference on English Education Commission on Social Justice, 2009). These subjectivities, or ways that individuals imagine themselves and their possibilities for acting, function together to determine how teachers in English language arts position themselves and others in everyday interactions, in institutions such as schools, and in society. This act of positioning delineates individual and collective opportunities for growth and social activism in the profession of English language arts—opportunities we feel can have a transformative impact on society.

Based on our understanding of English education, Social Justice Theory (re)conceptualizes a critical review of language and literature that supports social justice methods both in the classroom and through research methodologies. It includes creating new and drawing from current methodologies that speak to the languages and literatures that are juxtaposed with the counter-narratives of participants. Sometimes the distinction between methods and methodologies may be vast and at other times they may be one in the same because our methods can become our methodologies, and vice versa. It also includes (re)conceptualizing data within a framework that draws from this literature and its' methods. It includes (re)presenting data that values its constituents' perspectives as they challenge master narratives. Lastly, it includes the possibility of its efficacy becoming drafted as social justice policy for fair but effective education.

For this comprehensive volume written for English educators on critical re-search practices, we have invited experts in the field of English education (broadly defined) who live their lives disciplined by and committed to social justice causes. That is, each of our contributors enacts a concern for people in their research. To aid us in this volume, we share with you their expertise, along with our own. We are also inclined toward hindsight to unpack the socialized, classed, cultured, racialized, and gendered shortcomings of our predecessors. We cannot separate this work from the context out of which it grew, but we can recursively reinscribe a theory of practice by practicing theory, in this case writing to change something. Since "It is difficult to find social justice in education policy these days [and] school reform is moving rapidly toward test-driven policies that have detrimental effects on equal opportunity" (St. John, 2007, p. 77), we are met with an urgency to solidify our commitment to social change, particularly in English education, a field that seems to embrace the immediacy of this work.

Conclusion

We once again remind you that this book is unique. It is divided into four sec-tions based on broad topics: social justice theory in ELA, its application to Eng-lish education, its presence in language and literacy research, and its place/need in policy. Each section is divided into chapters that explore these topics. Each section includes an introduction and closing comments written by us. Hence, sections are meant to stand on their own with a beginning, middle, and ending and attempt to record what we feel are vital arguments for change in English education. The chapters featured in each section are authored and co-authored by invited, leading scholars and researchers in ELA and language and literacy studies. Each author has contributed an essay on a selected topic based on her or his ex-pertise. The goal of each chapter has been to bridge English education and social justice theory in ways that provide a pathway for rethinking ELA, a platform for priming the field for social justice policy.

Section 1 includes three chapters, which set the context for the book. It ex-plains the significance of having a seamless framework to authenticate and vali-date social justice research. This section discusses the current educational climate and possible changes that are on the horizon under the Obama administration, provides a working definition of social justice, and discusses inherent barriers to enacting social justice in school settings. In Chapter 1, **sj Miller** presents the historical roots of social justice teaching in schools, revisits key literature that has led to a social justice pedagogy, explores some of the barriers to teaching it, and provides new insights and directions for pushing English language arts research beyond the current visible and invisible boundaries that teachers face when teaching social justice. In Chapter 2, **Tara Star Johnson** personally reflects on how her position as researcher in relationship to power and access both opened doors and undermined the research process. She shares moving accounts of how her positionality helped her conceive of what social justice meant in the context of her research. In Chapter 3, **Mariana Souto-Manning** and **Peter Smagorinsky** introduce the work of Paulo Freire and Lev Vygotsky's in relationship to foundational research in social justice. The authors suggest that Freire's and Vygotsky's work independently, and in relationship to each other, have engineered more complex evolutions of Marxist-influenced language and literacy research. In doing so, they present key ideas on power and social class that have long undermined social relationships and classroom practice. They also teach us how to integrate Freire and Vygotsky into our research methods and provide suggestions for moving these scholars work into social justice policy.

Section 2 contains five chapters. This section examines current classroom methods and methodological approaches to English education. Often when we speak of methodology, we tend to locate it in the context of how we only conduct research. However, the authors approach methods/methodology dualistically: (1) as preparation and (2) as classroom practice. Social justice as a critical (transformational) methodology within English teacher preparation can lay a common framework whereby we measure, qualify, quantify, and assess preservice teachers. As we develop new bodies of research, we are also challenged to construct methodologies that authenticate and validate our findings and which can have long-standing efficacy and remain true to its complex dimensions. To this end, methods can grow from methodologies and methodologies can grow from methods.

In Chapter 4, **sj Miller** provides a scaffold that builds on other essays in this collection, and presents a developmental model for scaffolding social justice identity into methods courses through her "6 re-s": reflect, reconsider, refuse, reconceptualize, rejuvenate, and reengage. In Chapter 5, **Laura Bolf-Beliveau** and **Ralph Beliveau** discuss understanding the historicity of fragments and friction within texts as method. By examining scenes from the film *Half Nelson* and a paragraph from Barack Obama's March 18, 2008, speech on race, they teach us about rich (counter) narratives and identity politics entwined and deeply embedded between unfinished or incomplete story lines. Such texts, they argue, can be useful in preparing critical English educators. **Korina Jocson**, in Chapter 6, discusses critical multiculturalism as a lens for exploring the relationship between student writing across multiple media. She argues that such "epistemological shifts" in qualitative research represent new paradigms of thought capable of helping language and literacy educators think in transformative ways about today's youth. In Chapter 7, **Margaret Hagood** discusses ways that identities act as multimodal texts. For Hagood, it is important, then, to understand how literacy and identity inform each other. Doing so might give us new ways to represent data. Lastly, in Chapter 8, **Janet Alsup** articulates the problems of data analysis procedures that seem too closely affixed to political rigidity that complicates the teacher education process. She argues for more active methodological approaches that embrace narrative and rethink generalizability.

Section 3 contains six chapters. The authors explore various approaches to collecting, analyzing, and representing data. Each chapter speaks to another. In Chapter 9, **Arlette Ingram Willis** advocates for a critical conscious research process, which has as its goal raising awareness about the socially unjust structures that plague schools. While she admits the idea is not new, Willis insists that "critically conscious analysis provides an approach that engages the complexities and depths needed to move the critical project forward" (p. 150). In Chapter 10, **Jonathan Eakle** introduces the concept of "nomadology" to critical language and literacy research. To push creative productions into majority spaces across multiple lines of struggle, Eakle argues that the processes of movements and of closing of lines enable nomadic sciences to form zones for possible social and political change.

Chapter 11, by **David Bloome, Stephanie Carter**, and **Ayanna Brown**, provides a cutting-edge view of how bottom-up critical discourse analysis in educational research invites a close reflection of teacher and student interactions. Extending Bloome, Carter, and Brown's notion of discourse, **David E. Kirkland**, in Chapter 12, articulates a need to blend critical approaches to texts and contexts, in this case, critical ethnography and critical discourse analysis. In doing so, he argues that a new approach to culture and language emerges, what he calls "critical ethnographies of discourse," which are capable of capturing language data that are culturally contextualized and explained indigenously by local users. He concludes that a critical ethnography of discourse will not only help researchers deepen their analysis of linguistic data, it will also help them capture specific kinds of data more constitutive of the lives of participants.

In Chapter 13, **Bob Fecho** and **Janette Hill** explore the use of narrative in representing research. They see the world as always telling a story, where transactions between narrative and the research context happen continuously. For them, unless researchers find ways to bring such stories to the surface, certain riches in the lives and important details of those we research will continue to be ignored and, indeed, at our peril. Chapter 14 closes this section. Similar to Fecho and Hill, **Janet Miller** explores autobiographical narrative as a technique for reporting research. In the chapter, she conceptualizes autobiographical and narrative methodologies as "shifting spaces of negotiation" that constantly knead categories of separation. As such, the telling of one's own story represents an important way of telling research that is itself useful for presenting the complexities of our lives, but also for penetrating the rigidity of "harder" sciences.

Section 4 brings our book to a close and makes good on our promise to move social justice theory to policy. Hence, each chapter marks the last steps in a path that leads from conceptualizations of social justice in ELA, social justice in practice, social justice in research, and, finally, to policy. The section provides critical implications for future social justice theories, practices, and research agendas as they relate to moving social justice toward policy. The section also offers suggestions for researchers, policy makers, teacher educators, and others who seek to have a national policy for social justice in ELA. In the end, the goal of this work will be to "prime the pump" for moving social justice toward sets of national, state, and local policies for schools and classrooms.

In Chapter 15, **Marilyn Cochran-Smith** discusses her concern for the future of teacher quality as intimately connected to the social and economic inequities that we continuously perpetuate in the day-to-day lives of people. She draws our attention to who has ownership over teacher quality and social justice, the BBA or the EEP, which both have limited views of social justice and have ignored "the unjust distribution of broader access, power, and opportunity and—just as bad . . . the unjust omission from curricula and educational goals of the knowledge traditions and assets of diverse social groups" (p. 186). In Chapter 16, **Les Burns** examines the NCTE's role in shaping unjust language education policies. In particular, his analysis reveals ways in which national English language policies, such as those found in the Core Standards, to this day work to reinforce staggering cycles of inequity that promote educational injustices of millions of American children. In Chapter 17, **Mary Juzwik** and **Matt Ferkany** express the need for careful, systematic, and precise theorizations and definitions of what it means to "teach for social justice." In the process of defining social justice, they argue that researchers, discourse-oriented researchers in particular, benefit from expanding narrowly defined research agendas and from collaborating with nondiscourse-oriented researchers. In this expansion, critical research agendas are held accountable in ways that might make them more liberating for the populations they seek to serve. In the final chapter of the book, Chapter 18, **Gerald Campano** and **Lenny Sánchez** invite us to consider how embodying and appropriating Buddhist beliefs in practitioner research can help guide us toward more socially just research. In so doing, Campano and Sánchez offer examples through a four-part model: the needs to trouble hierarchical notions of policy; to regard everyone as a public intellectual; to foster multiplicity in the curriculum; and to create non-hegemonic educational alternatives within and alongside dominant structures.

We end by retelling a story of great importance to this work:

Once upon a time in England in 2000, a group of five-year-olds were given a test of skills in schools. One of the results showed that black students performance on the test were the highest achieving of all groups in the baseline assessments. Then as students progressed through schools, these testing results went down and white students scores went up. In other words, initially black students on the whole did better than their white peers before compulsory schooling practices. (Gillborn, 2006)

What does this say about inequitable schooling practices? If such results were presented in the U.S., we might ascertain that there would be an immediate paradigm shift around assessment. Is this the America we want to live in or the America to which we are headed? If the answer is to be no, then we must take up arms and fight against the visible and invisible forces of oppression. Join us! We welcome you.

Bibliography

Apple, M. (2002). *Official knowledge.* New York: Routledge.

Apple, M. (2006). Interrupting the right: On doing critical educational work in conservative times. In G. Ladson-Billings & W.F. Tate (Eds.), *Educational research in the public interest: Social justice, action, and policy, (pp. 27–45).* New York: Teachers College Press.

Apple, M., & Oliver, A. (1998). Becoming right: education and the formation of conservative movements. In C. Torres & Mitchell, T.R. (Eds.), *Sociology of education* (pp. 91–119). New York: State University of New York Press.

Applebaum, B. (2004). Social justice education, moral agency, and the subject of resistance. *Educational Theory, 54*(1), 59–72.

Arce, J., Luna, D., Borjian, A., & Conrad, M. (2005). No Child Left Behind: Who wins? Who loses? *Social Justice, 32*(3), 56–71.

Ayers, W. (1998). Popular education: Teaching for social justice (pp. xvi–xxv). In W. Ayers, J.A. Hunt, & T. Quinn (Eds.), *Teaching for social justice.* New York: The New Press.

Banks, J. (2004). *Diversity and citizenship education: Global perspectives.* San Francisco: Jossey-Bass.

Bannier, B. (2008). Education research in the public interest: Social justice, action, and policy. *Journal of Adolescent & Adult Literacy, 51*(5), 436–438.

Bell, D. C., & Nugent, B. (2001). *Sites of resistance.* Radical Pedagogy.

Blume, E. S. (1990). *Secret survivors: Uncovering incest and its aftereffects in women.* New York: Ballantine Books/John Wiley & Sons.

Bourdieu, P. (1977). *Outline of a theory of practice.* Cambridge: Cambridge University Press.

Bourdieu, P. (1980). *The logic of practice.* Stanford, CA: Stanford University Press.

Boutte, G. (2008). Beyond the illusion of diversity: How early childhood teachers can promote social justice. *Social Studies, 99*(4), 165–173.

Brown, K. (2005). Social justice education for preservice leaders: Evaluating transformative learning strategies. *Equity & Excellence in Education, 38*(2), 155–167.

Butler, J. (1997). *Excitable speech: A politics of the performative.* New York: Routledge.

Christensen, C., & Dorn, S. (1997). Competing notions of social justice and contradictions in special education reform. *Journal of Special Education, 31*(2), 181.

Clark, J. (2006). Social justice, education and schooling: Some philosophical issues. *British Journal of Educational Studies, 54*(3), 272–287.

Cochran-Smith, M. (1999). Learning to teach for social justice. In G.A. Griffin (Ed.), *The education of teachers* (pp. 114–144). Chicago: University of Chicago Press.

Cochran-Smith, M. (2004). *Walking the road: Race, diversity and social justice in teacher education.* New York: Teachers College Press.

Cochran-Smith, M., et al. (2009). Teacher education for social justice. In W. Ayers, T. Quinn, & D. Stovall (Eds.), *Handbook of social justice in education* (pp. 625–639). New York: Routledge.

Collins, P. H. (1986). Learning from the outsider within: The sociological significance of Black feminist thought. In M. M. Fonow & J. A. Cook (Eds.), *Beyond methodology: Feminist scholarship as lived research* (pp. 156-178). Bloomington, IN: Indiana University Press.

Conference on English Education Commission on Social Justice. (2009). CEE position statement: Beliefs about social justice in English education. *First Biennial CEE Conference.* Chicago: CEE.

Cribb, A., & Gerwitz, S. (2003). Towards a sociology of just practices: An analysis of plural conceptions of justice. In C. Vincent (Ed.), *Social justice, education, and identity* (pp. 15–29). London: Routledge.

Darling-Hammond, L. (1997). *Doing what matters in schools: Investing in quality teaching.* New York: National Commission on Teaching and America.

Davies, L. (2002). Possibilities and limits for democratisation in education. *Comparative Education, 38*(3), 251–266.

Deyhle, D. (1995). Navajo youth and Anglo racism: Cultural integrity and resistance. *Harvard Educational Review, 65*(3), 403–444.

DeStigter, T. (2008). Lifting the veil of ignorance: Thoughts on the future of social justice teaching. In s. Miller, L. Beliveau, T. DeStigter, D. Kirkland, & P. Rice (Eds.), *Narratives of social justice teaching: How English teachers negotiate theory and practice between preservice and inservice spaces* (pp.121-144). New York: Peter Lang.

DeVoss, D.N., Cushman, E., & Grabill, J.T. (2005). Infrastructure and composing: The when of new-media writing. *College Composition and Communication, 57* (1), 14–44.

Dewey, J. (1915, May 5). *The New Republic,3,* 40–42.

Dewey, J. (1987). Democracy and educational administration. In J.A. Boydson (Ed.), *John Dewey: Later works, 1925-1953.* Carbondale & Edwardsville: Southern Illinois University Press. (Original work published 1937.)

Duncan-Andrade, J. (2004). Toward teacher development for the urban in urban teaching. *Teaching Education, 15(*4), 339–350.

Edwards, R. (2000). The subject of citizens: Developing social justice. Studies in the Education of Adults, p. 1.

Epstein, K. (2005). The whitening of the American teaching force: A problem of recruitment or a problem of racism? *Social Justice, 32*(3), 89–102.

Fish, S. (1999). *The trouble with principle.* Cambridge: Harvard University Press.

Flores-Gonzalez, N. (2002). *School kids, street kids: Identity and high school completion among Latinos.* New York: Teachers College Press.

Foucault, M. (1980). *Power-knowledge: Selected interviews and other writings, 1972–1977.* New York: Pantheon Books.

Fraser, N. (1997). *Justice interruptus: Critical reflections on the "postsocialist" condition.* London: Routledge.

Fraser, N. (2003). Social justice in the age of identity politics: Redistribution: recognition, and participation. In N. Fraser & A. Honneth (Eds.), *Redistribution, or recognition? A political-philosophical exchange.* London: Verso.

Fraser, N.. (2005). Reframing justice in a globalizing world. *New Left Review,* 36. Retrieved December 24, 2008, from http://www.newleftreview.net/?page=article&view=2589

Fraser, N. (2006). Retrieved November 11, 2006, from http:///www.newschool.edu/GF/polsci/faculty/fraser

Freire, P. (1970). *Pedagogy of the oppressed.* New York: Continuum Publishing.

Futrell, M. (2000). The challenge of the 21st century: Developing a highly qualified cadre of teachers to teach our nation's diverse students. *Journal of Negro Education, 68*(3), 318–334.

Gerwitz, S. (2002). *The managerial school.* London: Routledge.

Gillborn, D. (2006). Public interest and the interests of white people are not the same: Assessment, educational policy, and racism. In G. Ladson-Billings & W.F. Tate (Eds.), *Educational research in the public interest: Social justice, action, and policy* (pp. 173–195). New York: Teachers College Press.

Giroux, H. (2008). Obama's betrayal of public education? Arne Duncan and the corporate model of schooling. *Truthout.* Retrieved March 2, 2009, from http://www.truthout.org/121708R

Giroux, H., & McLaren, P. (1986). Politics of teacher education. *Harvard Educational Review, 56* (3), 213–238.

Harvey, D. (2005). *A brief history of neoliberalism.* Oxford: Oxford University Press.

Hursh, D. (2009). Beyond the justice of the market: Combating neoliberal educational discourse and promoting deliberative democracy and economic equality. In W. Ayers, T. Quinn, & D. Stovall (Eds.), *Handbook of social justice in education* (pp. 152–170). New York: Routledge.

Kailin, J. (1999). How White teachers perceive the problem of racism in the schools: A case study in "liberal Lakeview." *Teachers College Record, 100,* 724–750.

Kozol, J. (1991). *Savage inequalities.* New York: Crown Publishing.

Kozol, J. (2005). *The shame of the nation: The restoration of apartheid schooling in America.* New York: Three Rivers Press.

Kirkland, D. E. (2009). The skin we ink: Tattoos, literacy, and a new English education. *English Education, 41*(4), 375–395.

Kirkland, D. E., & Filipiak, D. (2008). Quiet tensions in meaning: A conversation with a "social justice" teacher. In s. Miller, L. B. Beliveau, D. E. Kirkland, P. Rice, & T. DeStiger (Eds.), *Narratives of social justice teaching: How English teachers negotiate theory and practice between preservice and inservice spaces* (pp. 45–64). New York: Peter Lang.

Ladson-Billings, G. (1994). *The dreamkeepers: Successful teachers of African-American children.* San Francisco: Jossey-Bass.

Ladosn-Billings, G. (2000). Preparing teachers for diversity: Historical perspectives, current trends, and future directions. In L. Darling-Hammond & G. Sykes (Eds.), *Teaching as the learning profession: Handbook of policy and practice* (pp. 86–87). San Francisco: Jossey-Bass.

Ladson-Billings, G., & Tate, W.F. (2006*). Educational research in the public interest: Social justice, action, and policy.* New York: Teachers College Press.

Leathwood, C. (2005). Assessment policy and practice in higher education: Purpose, standards and equity. *Assessment & Evaluation in Higher Education, 30(*3), 307–324.

Levinson, B. A., Foley, D. E., & Holland, D., (Eds.). (1996). *The cultural production of the educated person.* Albany: State University of New York.

Lingard, B. (2005). Socially just pedagogies in changing times. *International Studies in Sociology of Education, 15*(2), 165-186.

Lingard, B., & Mills, M. (2007). Pedagogies making a difference: Issues of social justice and inclusion. *International Journal of Inclusive Education, 11*(3), 233–244.

Linn, R.L. (2000). Assessment and accountability. *Educational Researcher, 29*(2), 16.

Macedo, D., & Bartolomé, L. (1999). *Dancing with bigotry: Beyond the politics of tolerance.* New York: St. Martin's Press.

Mathison, S. (2009). Public good and private interest in educational evaluation. In W. Ayers, T. Quinn, & D. Stovall (Eds.), *Handbook of social justice in education*(pp. 5–14). New York: Routledge.

McDonald, M. (2008). The pedagogy of assignments in social justice teacher education. *Equity & Excellence in Education, 41*(2), 151–167.

McDonald, M., & Zeichner, K. M. (2009). Social justice teacher education. In W. Ayers, T. Quinn, & D. Stovall (Eds.), *Handbook of social justice in education* (pp. 595–610). New York: Routledge.

McLaren, P. (2000). *Che Guevara, Paulo Freire, and the politics of hope: Reclaiming critical pedagogy.* Lanham, MD: Rowman & Littlefield.

McLaren, P., & Fischman, G. (1998). Reclaiming hope: Teacher education and social justice in the age of globalization. *Teacher Education Quarterly,* ^, 125–153.

Miller, s., & Norris, L. (2007). *Unpacking the loaded teacher matrix: Negotiating space and time between university and secondary English classrooms.* New York: Peter Lang.

Moffett, J. (1994). *The universal schoolhouse.* Portland: Calendar Islands Publishers.

Morrell, E. (2005). Critical English education. *English Education, 37*(4), 312–322.

Nieto, S. (2000). Placing equity front and center: Some thoughts on transforming teacher education for a new century. *Journal of Teacher Education, 51*(3), 180–187.

Nieto, S., & Bode, P. (2008). *Affirming diversity.* Boston: Pearson Press.

Nozick, R. (1974). *Anarchy, state, and utopia.* New York: Basic Books.

Nussbaum, M. (2006). *Frontiers of justice.* Cambridge: Belknap Press.

Olson, L. (1999). Shining a spotlight on results. *Educational Week, 17*, 8–10.

Olssen, M., Codd, J., & O'Neill, A.M. (2004*). Educational policy: Globalization, citizenship, and democracy.* Thousand Oaks: Sage.

Popkewitz, T.S. (2000). The denial of change in educational change: Systems in the construction of national policy and evaluation. *Educational Researcher, 29*(1), 17–29.

Popkewitz. T.S. (2006). Hopes of progress and fears of the dangerous: Research, cultural theses, and planning different human kinds. In G. Ladson-Billings & W.F. Tate (Eds.), *Educational research in the public interest: Social justice, action, and policy* (pp. 119–140). New York: Teachers College Press.

Rawls, J. (1971). *A theory of justice.* Oxford: Clarendon.

Reed, J., & Black, D. (2006). Toward a pedagogy of transformative teacher education: World educational links. *Multicultural Education, 14*(2), 34–39.

Scheurich, J.J., & Laible, J. (1995). The buck stops here in our preparation programs: Educational leadership for all children (no exceptions allowed*). Educational Administration Quarterly, 31* (2), 313–322.

Seddon, T. (2003). Framing justice: Challenges for research. *Journal of Education Policy, 18*(3), 229.

Skrla, L., Scheurich, J., Johnson Jr., J., & Koschoreck, J. (2001). Accountability for equity: Can state policy leverage social justice? *International Journal of Leadership in Education, 4*(3), 237–260.

Spring, J. (2001). *The American school 1642–2000.* Boston: McGraw-Hill.

Spring, J. (2005). *Political agenda for education: From the religious right to the green party* (3rd ed.). Mahwah: Lawrence Erlbaum Associates..

St. John, E. (2007). Finding social justice in education policy: Rethinking theory and approaches in policy research. *New Directions for Institutional Research, 133,* 67–80.

Tarrou, A., & Holmesland, I. (2002). Building equality and social justice through education. *European Education, 34*(2), 13.

Taylor, S. (2004). Researching educational policy and change in "new times": Using critical discourse analysis. *Journal of Education Policy, 19*(4), 433–451.

Tierney, W. (2006). Hate speech and academic freedom in the academy. *Educational Researcher, 35*(3), 33–37.

Ukpokodu, O. (2007). Preparing socially conscious teachers: A Social Justice-Oriented Teacher Education. *Multicultural Education, 15*(1), 8–15.

Valencia, R.R. (1997). *The evolution of deficit thinking: Educational thought and practice.* London: Falmer.

Valenzuela, A. (1999). *Subtractive schooling: U.S.–Mexican youth and the politics of caring.* Albany: State University of New York Press.

Walker, M. (2006). Towards a capability-based theory of social justice for education policy-making. *Journal of Education Policy, 21*(2), 163–185.

Wiedeman, C. (2002). Teacher preparation, social justice, equity: A review of the literature. *Equity & Excellence in Education, 35*(3), 200–211.

Young, I. (1990). *Justice and the politics of difference.* Princeton: Princeton University Press.

Zimpher, N. (1989). The RATE project: A profile of teacher education students. *Journal of Teacher Education, 40*(3), 27–30.

Zinn, H. (1980). *A people's history of the United States.* New York: HarperCollins.

Conceiving Social Justice

One of the great merits of qualitative research is its design, as it has far-enacting transferability and perspicacity with policy makers. Unfortunately, those of us committed to a career path in qualitative studies in education who also identify as critical pedagogues or teach critical theory and/or critical pedagogy often find our research critiqued by policy makers as lacking in valid or sustainable contributions to the data that can later become policy. A possible reason for this sidelining from the common presumption amongst qualitative researchers is that the quantitative field recognizes our formidable threat to reveal the particular nuances about the specific differences in how student learning outcomes are determined. We can further assume that this presumption also recognizes that teachers have great influence on students' ideas and ideologies, that teacher authority is never neutral, that it has the ability to instill critique and agency in students, and that it is "always broadly political and interventionist in terms of the knowledge-effects it produces, the classroom experiences it organizes, and the future it presupposes in the countless ways it addresses the world" (Giroux, 2008–09, p. 61). The meritocracy-based education system that envelops our country, and which is fed by data-driven outcomes and "evidence-based best practice" (Mathison, 2009, p. 10) as a way to "measure" student success, poses an inhospitable challenge to the qualitative field. With that said, this section contains three chapters with carefully crafted road maps of social justice based research which guide critical English educator researchers and policy makers toward a critical turning point in amassing a body of research that conceptualizes how social justice theory can move us toward policy.

Denzin and Lincoln (1994) in their groundbreaking *Handbook of Qualitative Research* note that over the years, qualitative research has become more political and activist oriented and calls into question former models of classic norms of representation. In fact, the alleged crimes of qualitative research are in what it presupposes: (1) that "the task of education is for students to become critical agents who actively question and negotiate the relationships between theory and practice, schooling and everyday life, and the larger society and the domain of common sense" (Giroux, 2008–09, pp. 61–62); (2) that those who teach critical pedagogy open up a space where students come to terms with their own power as critical agents (Derrida, 2001); and (3) that critical pedagogy represents a commitment to the "future and it remains the task of educators to make sure that the future points the way to a more socially just world" (Giroux, 2008–09, p. 62). In other words, if we can verify through research that socially produced injustice exists, then we threaten the very core of what has sustained our education system since its inception—perhaps giving even more causality to why qualitative research is often dismissed as fallible.

This brings us to a "crisis of representation" about how qualitative and quantitative studies in social justice can qualify as valid research that informs policy. As we know, for any qualitative research approach in education to be considered valid, certain norms are expected to be in place. The process of determining and setting up a study is anything but simple, for it is in the very setup that it can be attacked for lack of veracity. For instance, if research examines power dynamics in schools, then the frame for the research must carefully reflect and establish that the research is grounded within studies of dynamics of power and related theoretical studies in social spaces. The researcher is expected to carefully and masterfully articulate the purpose of the research, design research questions and subquestions, set delimiters, identify the type of qualitative research, reflect on prior research, establish a theoretical framework in order to determine possible contributions to the current research (noting its uniqueness), consider the characteristics of a pool of participants and the rationale for it, determine the kinds of instruments that will be used to collect the data, determine the type and layers of analysis for the data, consider the mode of expression for the data, and discuss the data and then consider its implications and transferability (Merriam, 2001). There are also ethical considerations that factor into the design of the study if it is to be considered valid and reliable. To ensure the research(er) is trustworthy, s/he lays out the mechanisms that guarantee internal validity through triangulation, member checks, long-term observation, peer examination, collaborative modes of research, and by revealing his/her positionality (Merriam, 2001). To determine its external validity, the researcher must discuss the study's generalizability and transferability to other research contexts through rich, thick description, typicality, or multisite design. Lastly, the researcher must also consider the ethics involved in the study. Stake (1994) reminds us that, "Qualitative researchers are guests in private spaces of the world. Their manners should be good and their code of ethics strict" (p. 234). Researchers should therefore consider whether they are honoring or breaking cultural barriers, reflect on how a story may make a participant vulnerable, or consider if transgressions might have occurred that could impact the outcome of the research. Researchers should be careful to not re-create hierarchies of power, especially if there is an intent to unpack from within the context of the study. *Social justice research as praxis therefore benefits others as it is carefully considered, revisited, and negotiated with its interactants, during its entire tenure.* A mentor of mine in graduate school made me mindful of the kinds of observations I was conducting of my participants in schools—each of whom had experienced various levels of oppression. She said, "Don't do to your participants what the world has already done to them—forefront the ethic of reciprocity," and that mindfulness is an ethic that those of us conducting social justice research can also heed.

Conceptualizing Social Justice: An Emerging Theoretical Framework

The authors in this section support the view that social justice research in English education should be grounded within a theoretical framework that has a historical understanding of the origin of a social injustice. Further, through the expressed narrative of participants, possible moments for change may be revealed as well as how agency and/or emancipation may or may not have been enacted. However, although by no means essentialized, emerging social justice research in English education might be grounded in other hybrid interplays of research theories. These authors take unique approaches that might lead to intersections which together conceive a framework for social justice here as well as in future collaborative work related to social justice.

All three scholars in this section recognize the foundational link between grounded theory and the practice in schools through the interplay of critical theory, critical pedagogy, and social justice. Their unique hybrid of research frames calls for not only understanding how the misuse of power can lead to oppression, but it also seeks to understand how participant agency does or does not operate in the context of the research while it seeks to understand accountability or lack thereof for transgressions.

By identifying the particular moments wherein or whereby participants could enact or might possibly have enacted agency, the research itself is personified as an "actant" (Latour, 1996)—an "accomplishment of human social practice"

(Brandt & Clinton, 2002, p. 344), in the lives of both the researcher and the researched. Such findings presume then that social justice–based research be predicated on the lived-through experience of praxis and reflexivity—"the researcher's engagement, through written text, in a dialectical process among the researcher, the informants, the data, the researcher's ideological assumptions, and the relevant socio-cultural forces" (Smithmeir, 1996, p. 7). Reflection and action are thereby intimately connected. In research which is emancipatory in design, in which power is shared, reflexivity is central, and produces action which can bring us closer to understanding how to fortify social justice research, methods and theory.

These essays reveal that agency is intimately bound to the design, even to a point that it takes on the personified particulars of an individual with agency. This can best be understood through the work of Latour and Brandt and Clinton, who recognize that a person with agency typically has the self-awareness that s/he can interact with the self or others to change an element of a situation in order to create an emancipatory outcome. Latour (1996) suggests that interactions occur within frames, and within frames certain objects stabilize the actors so that while something may happen within the frame locally, it can be relocated or redistributed globally. Brandt and Clinton (2002) further expand on this understanding of the personification of research through their question, "Can we not approach literacy as a technology—and even as an agent?" (p. 343). They purport that literacy is not a situated social practice; rather it has the ability to "travel, integrate, and endure" (p. 337). They suggest that literacy is not just a thing to be done but is a mediator or participant who can connect actors locally and globally. By applying this concept to our research then, if we view research as an agent of literacy that not only acts locally to make meaning of how social justice operates in schools but also has the capacity to impact the globalization of social justice research, it has global transferability and generalizability.

In this section the contributors work in tandem inlaying a conceptual language for conceiving a theory for social justice research in English education. Their essays on the literature that currently frames our understanding of social justice leave readers with common understandings of the following topics: (1) the literature related to social justice research emerges out of prejudice and oppression and seeks to return human dignity to every person; (2) the research related to social justice research critiques an existing power structure and its embeddedness in some institutional capacity; and (3) provides emancipatory language that seeks to instill agency in the individual or in the collective. These authors have left us with questions such as these as we read around conceptualizing social justice research: *As we conduct research in social justice, do we need codified criteria as benchmarks to help us conceive of or recognize that we are undertaking social justice in context? How do participants' stories inform and reinform our understandings of social justice research. What does social justice mean to the lives of participants and how do their stories impact researcher positionality?* We invite you to see these and other questions as you read and hope that you will join in the dialogue.

Bibliography

Brandt, D., & Clinton, K. (2002). Limits of the local: Expanding perspectives on literacy as a social practice. *Journal of Literacy Research, 34* (3), 337–356.

Denzin, N.K., & Lincoln, Y.S. (1994). *Handbook of qualitative research.* Thousand Oaks, CA: Sage.

Derrida, J. (2001). The future of the profession or the unconditional university. In P. Kamuf (Trans.) and L. Simmons and H. Worth (Eds.), *Derrida downunder* (pp. 11–34). Palmerston North: Dunmore.

Giroux, H. (2008-09). Academic unfreedom in America. Rethinking the university as a democratic public sphere. *Works and Days, 51–54* (26/27), 45–71.

Latour, B. (1996). On interobjectivity (G. Bowker, Trans.). *Mind, Culture, and Activity: An International Journal, 3,* 228–245.

Mathison, S. (2009). Public good and private interest in educational evaluation. In W. Ayers, T. Quinn, & D. Stovall (Eds.), *Handbook of social justice in education* (pp. 5–14). New York: Routledge.

Merriam, S. (2001). *Qualitative research and case study applications in education.* San Francisco: Jossey-Bass.

Miller, s. (2008). Fourthspace—Revisiting social justice in teacher education. In sj Miller, L. Beliveau, T. DeStigter, D. Kirkland, & P. Rice, *Narratives of social justice teaching: How English teachers negotiate theory and practice between preservice and inservice spaces* (pp. 1–21). New York: Peter Lang.

Mortensen, P., & Kirsch, G.E. (1996). *Ethics and representation in qualitative studies of literacy.* Urbana, IL: NCTE.

Smithmeir, A. (1996, June). *The "double bind" of re-representation in qualitative research methods.* Paper presented at the Qualitative Research in Education Conference, St. Paul, MN.

Stake, R.E. (1994). Case studies. In N.K. Denzin and Y.S. Lincoln (Eds.), *Handbook of qualitative research* (pp. 220–235). Thousand Oaks, CA: Sage.

ONE

Theoretical Roots of Social Justice: A Literature Review

sj Miller

Theoretical Roots of Social Justice Theory in Schools

As mentioned in the *Introduction* to this collection, Wiedeman (2002) traces the origins of social justice teaching as an outgrowth of the several movements of anti-oppression work: multicultural education, critical theory, anti-racist education, and critical race theory which were all direct responses to the dominant Anglo-American Protestant tradition. Each of these fields has a history related to injustices stemming from the infallible Constitution and its interpretation, and have emerged by recognizing injustices during different times within our ever-changing democracy. Below are summaries of the reviews of the literature about social justice which set a common stage for articulating a social justice pedagogy. The chapter concludes with a discussion of how social justice theory intersects with preservice teacher preparation and how we can prepare them when teaching for social justice about possible controversy in their schools and classrooms.

Multicultural Education

Multicultural education from the 1960s through the 1980s can be traced to trailblazers like James Banks, Geneva Gay, Carl Grant, and Sonia Nieto, although the movement is linked to the Civil Rights Era (Spring, 2001). The multicultural movement challenged but did not critique hierarchies of social, cultural, historical, and economic power though it became a site for mobilizing around common goals in schools for social equity for students of color and impoverished children (Gay, 1995). The movement was largely about sensitivity training for teachers and students, and tends to promote a color-blind approach to teaching—by normalizing multiculturalism in classrooms, lunchrooms, hallways, and curriculum. However, this movement failed to look at gender issues, how to reduce prejudice, or look at students with disabilities. A controversial outgrowth of this movement was an ethnocentric education that could restore cultural understandings about groups that were disenfranchised. Thus ensued educational cultural wars. Critical multicultural pedagogy has been connected with this time period.

Critical Pedagogy

Critical pedagogy during the 1990s can be traced to trailblazers like Peter McLaren, Henry Giroux, Ira Shor, Michael Apple, and Stanley Aronowitz. This theoretical movement unpacks how dominant culture sustains and strengthens itself by reinforcing a social, cultural, economic, and political dependence of traditionally marginalized groups and how that plays out in the schooling process—especially with students of color. This movement calls for a radical overhaul of the dominant ideological structures that maintain and sustain privilege while others are oppressed. This movement articulates that teachers become active agents in shifting the power structures of dominant culture by resisting oppressive pressures to create schooled identities and to manufacture students who would be prepared to serve society (Apple, 2002). While some teacher compliance in schools can help students acquire skills to have functional literacy, meta-compliance can render students unprepared to handle the realities and demands of society. Often equated with this movement is the echo for revolutionary and transformative pedagogy.

Anti-racist Education

An anti-racist education locates the roots of power, race, and ethnicity within the context of colonialism (McLaren & Mayo, 1999) and challenges essentialist perspectives of identity. A key feature to anti-racist education is placing an emphasis on collaborative decision making. Although no one particular pedagogy is connected to anti-racist education, research suggests that an anti-racist pedagogy should entail "exploratory learning that is collaborative in nature and which is informed by the local community," where the "teacher acts as facilitator who listens, negotiates, and compromises with her students; the styles of teaching and learning are flexible and responsive to students and communities" (Wiedeman, 2002, p. 204). Students would develop requisite skills to critique and challenge oppressive social and educational structures.

Critical Race Theory

Critical race theory (CRT) has also contributed to the movement we now understand as social justice. CRT can be traced to the mid-1970s and to the research of Derrick Bell, Allen Freeman, William Tate, Gloria Ladson-Billings, and Danny Solorzano. CRT is an outgrowth of critical legal studies (CLS) which was a leftist legal movement that challenged traditional legal scholarship (Ladson-Billings, 2000). CRT begins from the premise that racism is deeply ingrained in American society and because of this, it is normalized. CRT exposes the counter-narratives and myths of subordinated and marginalized groups to share different perspectives of oppression. CRT offers research that is interdisciplinary, and is both a methodology as well as a pedagogy.

Democracy Conflated with Justice: Capability Theories

We must also connect the roots of social justice by furthering the discussion of the social contract and the capability approach. John Rawls (1993), whom many consider as the preeminent theorist on justice, was said to name general principles because of the continuum of beliefs and moral doctrines that clouded moral clarity. These general principles were said to be contained separately from the historical and sociocultural backgrounds that can interfere with seeing clearly. While Rawls does not provide any particular principles per se, Fish (1999) provides examples such as "features relating to social position, native endowment, and historical accident, as well as the contents of persons' determinate conceptions of good" (p. 10). Rawls' goal was to separate the chatter from what interferes with seeing reality objectively. This principled stance, while quite ideal, has implications for understanding the social injustices that have stratified individuals and groups and can help us formulate our own principles related to social justice.

Rawls' separation delineating moral doctrines from general principles begets a question for us: Should justice be extracted from the codification of social justice? Would that be wise, or even possible for us? Although each term has characteristics that make them distinct unto themselves, the two are likely to remain intertwined as we move into reification. Since social justice is subjective, the reification of social justice must take into account multiple points of view as they intersect with current rulings of justice and injustice. In fact, if social justice were to don central human capabilities as described by Nussbaum (2006), we must also consider what happens when social justice is achieved, and how justice would treat "inequalities over the threshold" (p. 75):

> A society that does not guarantee these [capabilities] to all of its citizens, at some appropriate threshold level, falls short of being a fully just society, whatever its level of opulence. And although in practical terms priorities may have to be set

temporarily, the capabilities are understood as both mutually supportive and all of central relevance to social justice. Thus, a society that neglects one of them to promote the others has shortchanged its citizens, and there is failure of justice in the shortchanging. (p. 75)

Nussbaum provides timely reminders that every person has a right to a life treated with dignity which begins from the premise of justice for all. Once however, the political process enters ("a constitution [with] various allocations of powers, a certain type of economic system," p. 82), it can affect the circumstances and outcomes over time and in new contexts. We must ask ourselves then, is each person (student) afforded equal capabilities? We know the answer to be false, but we can consider these philosophies as we move forward in establishing a case for social justice policy in schools. We would be remiss in our efforts to move policy forward if we do not bear in mind that *not* all students have the same essential moral, physical, and intellectual capabilities due to the historical inheritance of oppression and class status. Perhaps the more salient question is, how can we conceive of a social justice theory that accounts for inequitable histories and which can specify them, and can not only bring students up to their capability thresholds to meet minimums but can also prepare them to sustain and take on challenges beyond school.

Understanding Social Justice Controversy

McLaren's work, though quite controversial, offers us a concrete and utopic vision and analysis for how to approach social justice by connecting critical pedagogy with the struggle for socialism. I pay particular attention to him because of the attacks he has faced from the Right so that we can learn how to position our research strategically. He positions himself as a classical Marxist, and Marxist humanist, or as one who sees social violence as a direct consequence and symptom of class divisions (personal communication, May 14, 2008). Like many of his predecessors and revolutionaries whom he studied, and the modernist writers and artists, liberation theologians, the Frankfurt School theorists, existential phenomenologists, surrealists, symbolic interactionists, Freudian and Jungian psychologists, Freirean educators, Zen Buddhists, performance theorists, ethnographers, ethnomethodologists, Gnostics, theosophists, Hegelians, historical materialists, comparative symbologists, and members of the Situationist International, McLaren's work leaves little wonderment about his ultimate vision—a quest for world peace (McLaren, 2008). He suggests that "academics must take a principled and nonnegotiable stance against exploitation and oppression of all living creatures, one that strives for social justice and dignity for all human beings. And if this means inflicting a blow on history, then we are obliged to participate with all the force of Thor's Mjolnir" (p. 472). He asserts that revolutionary critical pedagogy [author added—term coined by Paula Allman] operates from an understanding that the basis of education is political and that spaces need to be created where students can imagine a different world outside of capitalism's law of value (i.e., social form of labor), where alternatives to capitalism and capitalist institutions can be discussed and debated, and where dialogue can occur about why so many revolutions in past history turned into their opposite. (p. 477)

This view seems somewhat improbable considering that education has historical roots in Anglo-Saxon beliefs and class divisions. McLaren's hope is that peace is predicated on a socialist future, as an alternative to a postcapitalist country that is deeply divided by class antagonisms. Yet, it is quite hard to imagine a world that is separate from hegemony or even think that we may become a more classless society. The opposition wants him silenced because his politics undermine their superiority.

Peter McLaren's work has potential to help students adopt a pedagogy of revolution through a Freirean-based dialogic. But therein surfaces an important moral dilemma that begets a paradox: *Do we, as English educators, have an obligation to impose our own morality in our classrooms, i.e., such as with an agenda for social justice, when to impose or teach an agenda that privileges us as moral authority, especially when we oppose others who impose their own moral authority?* So are we ready for McLaren's revolutionary critical pedagogy when social justice has yet to become a mainstay in our field? Have we even built a strong enough agenda for social justice so that it can hold up his suggestions? There are indeed barriers to making this happen. Once we've resolved some of our own questions and have a strong national policy in education about social justice, perhaps we can consider how to build classless classrooms and a classless educational system, but we still have a long way to go and miles to go before we sleep.

Thinking Ahead: Preservice Teachers Enacting Social Justice

In addition to the barriers to enacting a social justice policy already identified in the *Introduction,* we must also look at the practical issues of the embodiment of teaching with a social agenda as it could effect policy development. One key struggle in working within a framework for social justice is that as teacher-researchers, we are ethically committed to be open to the expressions of all students, lest we be hypocritical. However, this openness can produce a moral anxiety when teachers are expected to make moral decisions about students' opinions. A question for us as we move into policy development is, how can social justice policy identify and clarify the distinction between social justice and social injustice? The distinction is significant to supporting teachers who identify social injustice in their classrooms. For instance, such a policy could help a teacher if s/he is faced with a student who writes a bigoted paper even when it meets the criteria for a strong essay. Or, it could help support a teacher to make meaning of a student who wants to argue a pro-Taliban stance whereby killing is articulated as socially just because it is done for the greater good. Or, it could help a teacher determine how to respond to a student who argues that honor killings for religious reasons should be condoned (as with some Palestinians and extreme Afghani sects or in Bangladesh, Great Britain, Brazil, Ecuador, Egypt, India, Israel, Italy, Jordan, Pakistan, Morocco, Sweden, Turkey, and Uganda where reports to the United Nations Commission on Human Rights continue to reveal honor killings of women). Such a policy could take the onus off of teachers and absolve them from imposing their own morality on students, it could resolve the difference between what is socially just and unjust, and it defers to a policy that is the ultimate adjudicator of the moral rights of students in schools.

Considering that the U.S. lacks a national policy relating to social justice in schools, teachers are vulnerable to making moralistic and ethical decisions until a judicial ruling is provided. Such difficulties need to be carefully explained and worked through with our preservice students, whose inchoate teacher identities are not only vulnerable to being co-constructed but who may lack the experience of working within a larger matrix of issues that impact the school and its students. Even now, many of these loaded questions are handled by individual teachers who have limited rights in schools and are left to fall back on either the First Amendment, district policies, or the moral beliefs of the school and its constituents.

As preservice students come to understand what social justice means to them, it is imperative that we have conversations about the politicized nature of social justice and that we draw from examples of the trailblazers who have paved the way. As with any particular pedagogy, our preservice teachers benefit when we are able to explain the theories that transmit and constitute a definition. When preservice teachers are provided contexts to embody those pedagogies, they are more likely to understand the impact on students. Cochran-Smith (2004) polemicizes this in her book *Walking the Road* when she states, "for teacher education to move toward a social justice agenda it must be conceptualized as both 'a learning problem and a political problem' " (p. 2). When we adopt any pedagogy, we are aligning with a value system and have a pedagogical responsibility to explain this to our inchoate student teachers. We dishonor our work to social justice if we fail to articulate the possible consequences that teaching for social justice might bring—(even if that means taking hits in our teaching evaluations)—regardless of our own code of ethics. Our classrooms can become a critical dialogical space wherein students begin to develop a sense of the continuum of teaching for social justice as they are invited to explore a pedagogy that aligns with their principles.

We can have discussions with our preservice teachers by inviting them to explore their own principles. We can pose real-world questions and provide scenarios to help them consider their principles. We might ask: Do you as inservice English teachers have an obligation to impose your own morality in your classrooms when students use vitriolic discourse in papers or openly use hate speech? We can then invite that student to have a simulated discussion and attempt to create a context to try to understand where s/he is coming from without making their morality seem prescriptive. We might encourage the preservice teacher to pose critical questions that may bring the classroom student to a different level of consciousness, or even encourage the student to consider offering countering points of view through more extensive research. To the extent possible, we should provide authentic contexts to scaffold in learning about teaching for social justice and support students in developing their own principles.

Note

I thank Laura Bolf-Beliveau for her feedback about the organizational structure of this chapter.

Bibliography

Apple, M. (2002). *Official knowledge*. New York: Routledge.

Cochran-Smith, M. (2004). *Walking the road: Race, diversity and social justice in teacher education*. New York: Teachers College Press.

Fish, S. (1999). *The trouble with principle*. Cambridge, MA: Harvard University Press.

Gay, G. (1995). Mirror images on common images: Parallels between multicultural education and critical pedagogy. In C. Sleeter & P. McLaren (Eds.), *Multicultural education, critical pedagogy, and the politics, of difference* (pp. 155–189). New York: State University of New York Press.

Giroux, H., & McLaren, P. (1986). Politics of teacher education. *Harvard Educational Review, 56* (3), 213–238.

Ladson-Billings, G. (2000). Racialized discourses and ethnic epistemologies. In N. Denzin & Y. Lincoln (Eds.), *The handbook of qualitative research 2nd ed.*, (pp. 257–278). Thousand Oaks, CA: Sage.

McLaren, P. (2000). *Che Guevara, Paulo Freire, and the politics of hope: Reclaiming critical pedagogy*. Lanham,MD: Rowman & Littlefield.

McLaren, P. (2008). This fist called my heart: Public pedagogy in the belly of the beast. *Antipode 40* (3), 427–481.

McLaren, P., & Fischman, G. (1998). Reclaiming hope: Teacher education and social justice in the age of globalization. *Teacher Education Quarterly, 25*, 125–153.

McLaren, P., & Mayo, P. (1999). Value commitment, social change, and personal narrative. *International Journal of Educational Reform, 8* (4), 397–408.

Nussbaum, M. (2006). *Frontiers of justice*. Cambridge, MA: Belknap.

Rawls, J. (1971). *A theory of justice*. Oxford, UK: Clarendon.

Rawls, J. (1993). *Political liberalism*. New York: Columbia University Press.

Reed, J., & Black, D. (2006, Winter). Toward a pedagogy of transformative teacher education: World educational links. *Multicultural Education, 14*(2), 34–39.

Spring, J. (2001). *The American school 1642–2000*. Boston: McGraw-Hill.

Wiedeman, C. (2002, September). Teacher preparation, social justice, equity: A review of the literature. *Equity & Excellence in Education, 35*(3), 200–211.

Two

Practice What You Preach: A Personal and Pedagogical Social Justice Policy

Tara Star Johnson

In February of 2009, I had an epiphany while I was preparing a talk about the last Harry Potter book (Rowling, 2007) for the English department's Books & Coffee series at Purdue, an institutional tradition dating back to the sixties in which a faculty member discusses a book of choice with a diverse audience of university and community members. I focused my presentation on heteronormative affirmations and disruptions within and around the book, with special attention to Rowling's outing of Dumbledore, Harry's revered mentor and Headmaster, during a Q & A session on one of her book tour stops at Carnegie Hall. I speculated why Rowling chose to wait until the series was over to make this pronouncement about one of the principle characters in the series. Like many fans, I was surprised at the revelation; my own heteronormative assumptions had obfuscated my initial reading.

I had been thinking how I might have reacted to the news that Dumbledore was gay as a young reader. I was a pious child; I remember standing out on the back porch of our antebellum farmhouse, looking up at the sky and praying for Jesus to come, and feeling like it was some failure or lack of faith on my part that didn't engender an immediate parting of the clouds. So one might imagine my devastation upon finding out that Mr. Murray, my seventh-grade science teacher whom I respected and admired, was an atheist, which he revealed to me in a private conversation at the end of class one day. It rocked my world because I had been taught that anyone who didn't believe in God was bad, was destined for hell—and so I was forced to reconcile this new knowledge about Mr. Murray, whom I knew to be a good person, with old beliefs. I mark that moment as pivotal to my subsequent critical examinations of the assumptions that governed my youth.

I've come to realize over the past fifteen years of teaching at the high school and university levels that *relationship* is essential to building bridges with others who have different experiences and beliefs to a place of understanding if not advocacy when it comes to matters of social justice. My epiphany: I think Rowling shares this insight. Waiting until readers had learned to revere Dumbledore before outing him, much as Mr. Murray did for me, is an effective means for disrupting young readers' complacent heteronormativity. Had Mr. Murray announced his religious orientation on the first day of class, I likely would have closed myself off from anything he had to teach me. I am mindful of this inclination toward resistance in my teaching of students with backgrounds similar to mine—I respect that it's no easy matter to acknowledge the privileges and prejudices to which people are sometimes unwittingly attached. Becoming aware that issues of social justice are something everyone should be concerned about is a process, and I have found it effective to begin by meeting students where they are and building a relationship with them through sharing stories from my own life as well as literary characters' or friends' experiences that illustrate the kinds of injustices faced by people who don't fit the white, middle-class, male, heterosexual norm.

However, I am cognizant of the paradoxical privilege I possess on two levels: First, my students are essentially a captive audience, and no matter how vociferously I articulate my desire for a safe classroom environment in which all perspectives can be heard, students with views that are antithetical to mine either learn to couch them carefully or are silenced. Second, as a white woman whose classes are populated by people who for the most part look like me, I have an institutionalized advantage over my colleagues of color whose bodies speak before they say a word—and their embodiment has implications for the kinds of relationships that they can have with students.

These two unearned privileges require an added responsibility on my part to practice what I preach—to enact a critical theoretical stance at home as well as in the classroom. It can be more difficult, though—my audience doesn't have to listen, and my relationships are more complex than that of teacher-student. Take my father, for example. He is one of the most fair-minded and moral people I know, but as a socially and fiscally conservative Baptist who believes that Fox News *is* fair and balanced, he has some concerns about the transformative effect my liberal graduate training has had upon me. I do think he appreciates the intellectual stimulation of our dialogues, which had primarily been unidirectional until I reached my thirties: his voice instructional, mine deferential. However, one afternoon during a visit home I thought I may have pushed him too far. He was lamenting the fact that most of his friends and fellow farmers in his white, rural community would prefer their daughters date a white atheist over a Christian of color. I pondered this a moment before I said, "I see what you're saying, Dad, but what would you do if I brought home a Christian woman?" His eyes widened and he shifted uncomfortably in his chair, saying little after that. I felt a pang of compunction for upsetting him with a question that, coupled with other conversations in which I had challenged his homophobic views, may not have been hypothetical in his mind. But I deliberately didn't set him straight.

Much like teachers who often aren't aware of the impact a casual comment in the classroom can have—like Mr. Murray's revelation—I didn't expect to change my dad's mind. But I may have opened it a little. Sometime later one of my sisters told Dad about some embarrassing artifacts her husband had discovered in the process of going through his closeted uncle's personal effects upon his death. Expecting words of condemnation matching her sentiments for his secret lifestyle, she was surprised and humbled when Dad said, "There's probably a lot of people out there like that, more than we might think, who feel isolated and do what they do to ease the loneliness. So maybe we shouldn't judge them for that."

The degree to which I could affect the mind-set of a set-in-his-ways seventy-year-old had everything to do with our relationship—the love and respect my father and I hold for each other, regardless of our different worldviews. But I have been at a complete loss several times in my life when I have been confronted with racism from people with whom I have no personal connection. One such incident occurred when I was collecting boxes to move to my first academic position at Georgia Southern University after completing graduate school at the University of Georgia. I went to a new construction site where I'd seen ample cardboard and encountered a fiftyish white man, presumably an electrician, finishing up some wiring in one of the houses. As Southerners are wont to do, he cheerfully engaged me in conversation and soon had me nodding in sympathy to his tales of woe involving not one but two ex-wives who had fleeced him of his life savings. "I tell you what," he concluded. "Next time I'm gonna marry me a nigger, 'cuz she won't do me wrong." I didn't know what was worse—that he believed an African American woman would know her place and thus feel honored that a white man would deign to marry her, or that he felt comfortable expressing this sentiment using the language he did to a complete stranger. Speechless, I beat a hasty retreat.

A more recent and profoundly disturbing speechless moment occurred for me while I was collecting data for my current research project investigating the effectiveness of a professional development program entitled The S.M.A.R.T. Solution (Sexual Misconduct Awareness and Response Training) for educators and school personnel. The program was piloted in a county in the Southeast which has been beleaguered by lawsuits stemming from several incidents of misconduct. This site is of particular interest to me as a researcher because it involves situations in which race was a factor: Within the space of eighteen months, three cases of white female teachers having sex with seven black male students in the county were exposed—and that's just what made the papers. As I was preparing for my visit, I came across interesting tidbits of information that gave me a sense of how deeply racially divided the community was. Initially I Googled the cases of misconduct, which led to my discovering a vitriolic debate over whether the teachers received relatively light sentences because they were white and their victims, black. A chief spokesperson for the African American community was the pastor at a local African American church who has also relentlessly pursued justice in opposition to the other element that makes the county infamous: Its KKK museum and Confederate memorabilia shop, located prominently in one of the town squares across from the historic county courthouse. Although the Reverend was not part of the S.M.A.R.T. program, he graciously granted me an interview and thus has become a key informant for my understanding of both the cases of misconduct and the historical context of the community (thus my use of "Reverend" as a sort of pseudonym). He assured me I would be safe at the shop, so I went to see it for myself.

A fiftyish woman behind the counter was the only other person in the place—save her protector "George," a mannequin clad in Klan regalia who ominously stood watch in the hallway between the store and museum. Mindful of my researcher role, I wanted to talk with her but was concerned she'd clam up at the sound of my Yankee accent. I need not have worried. As I think was the case with the electrician, she assumed that our mutual whiteness meant solidarity. The unmitigated contempt for African Americans that issued from this woman's mouth as dispassionately as if she were describing the weather is something that will be permanently inscribed on my memory. She must have seen me eyeing the mannequin nervously—I was remembering an earlier conversation with a S.M.A.R.T. participant who told me robed Klansmen still roam the county freely without sanction—because she said, "Yeah, a coupla niggers came in once and asked me if I was alone in here. I said, 'No, George is in the back.'" Then she glared at me defensively. "I wasn't lyin'!"

I was mostly interested in what she thought of a flag juxtaposing an image of President Obama with the Confederate flag, which was displayed prominently in one of the shop windows and on a flagpole in front of the building (the Reverend had organized demonstrations protesting its in-your-face location on the sidewalk, a publicly owned space, to no avail). Her brow furrowed for a moment at my query. Then her face cleared. "Well you know, he hates America. He's a Muslim." And on she went, concluding her diatribe with a shake of her head. "Such a disgrace. Having a nigger president."

It was a surreal moment, my mind a jumble of thoughts, wondering whether I should tell her how offensive she was to me—as a mother to a biracial child, as an American, as a human being. Wishing I had my tape recorder on (I'd debated beforehand and decided it wouldn't be ethical and maybe not safe, unsure of what I would find) because *this was good data* and I wanted more than my memory to recount it. Thinking how completely wrong the pundits are to say we're living in a post-racial society. Musing whether she'd come by this hate through learning or experience and feeling a sense of horror and helplessness to do anything to diffuse it. Ultimately I ventured feebly that I didn't understand where she was coming from because I'd grown up in an all-white community ("Boy, you were lucky") and wondered why she thought it was so bad ("They cause enough trouble around here as it is. Now it's gonna get worse") before succumbing to speechlessness once again. I left, sick inside, and still not knowing what that flag meant to her.

The flag resurfaced about a month later—this time for my daughter's father, who is a political science and African American studies professor. One of his students, a white female, gave him a full-sized one: "Here. This is for you." He didn't know what to make of it—clever insult or clueless gift?—and he neither asked for nor received an explanation. This flag is a little different from the ones I saw at the shop, though: HOPE is inscribed at the bottom. I've shared the flag

Figure 2.1: Obama juxtaposed with the Confederate flag. From Google pics
(http://images.huffingtonpost.com/gen/110400/thumbs/s-OBAMA-
CONFEDERATE-FLAG-large.jpg

saga with my students, and they've done some smart theory work around what these flags might mean in different contexts. I have the HOPE flag hidden away in my office, though, much like I turn the spine of Kennedy's (2002) book *Nigger* toward the wall until I have to use it for a lesson. Regardless of their intent, just looking at them fills me with an inchoate sadness.

I felt like a failure following both of my speechless moments with the electrician and the proprietress. I wanted to respond with something so clever and profound that they'd realize the error of their ways, or at the very least be mortified—but I ended up the one feeling ashamed, because silence suggests complicity, right? Even though I know that silence can mean resistance—a refusal to participate in a particular discourse (e.g., Gallas, 1998)—I still want and need to work on handling these kinds of situations that sadly aren't so singular more adroitly than I've done. However, even if I did have the snappy-comeback skill I am so envious of in people who are more socially adept than I, it wouldn't effect the kind of change I'd like to see, which requires relationship. More simply put, according to bell hooks (2000), it requires love. I cannot alter the hearts and minds of random racists who cross my path, but I can at least use their stories as stepping stones for discussion with people who are within my sphere of influence.

One of the S.M.A.R.T. program participants I interviewed, Nailah (a pseudonym), embodies hooks' (2000) scholarship on love. She is the Reverend's cousin, although she wasn't quick to admit it, raising a skeptical eyebrow when I mentioned at her table following the S.M.A.R.T. workshop that I'd talked with him the night before and found him to be personable and delightful. His particular brand of confrontational radicalism isn't productive, according to her; she wins the respect and admiration of her middle school students, many of them the offspring of Klansmen who might rather she be dead than teaching their children, through loving them. And it must be working, because she was recently a runner-up for her state's Teacher of the Year award. For Nailah, whether or not race was a factor in the misconduct cases was irrelevant: What mattered was that the victims were children, who should have been protected regardless of their race, and their attacker a teacher, who consequently put the status of her profession as well as the reputation of her school in jeopardy.

Essentially a generational difference exists between the Reverend, who bemoaned his perception that young African Americans are growing up without a sense of their history, and Nailah, who is finding a way to work within and against the institutional racism that remains as a legacy of the more brutal and visceral atrocities and injustices the Reverend has witnessed and experienced in his lifetime. Racism, both latent and blatant, continues to thrive in their community, and so I think there is a place for both of their philosophies of activism to function in tandem. I applaud the Reverend's bravery in openly defying oppressive power structures and tirelessly hounding politicians and courts to do something about the KKK museum at great personal risk (he's lost count of the death threats he's received). His approach reminds me of the righteous rage Cornel West spoke of when CNN's T. J. Holmes interviewed him about his memoir *Brother West: Living and Loving Out Loud*. Like West, the Reverend wears the mantle of the angry black man purposefully and effectively. But I also admire Nailah's method of converting one mind at a time through love and relationship; I think a heart as hardened as the proprietress's would eventually soften in her company. They practice what they preach—the Reverend, quite literally—and thus serve as models, along with J. K. Rowling and my science teacher Mr. Murray, for how to enact a personal and pedagogical policy of social justice.

As I think is the case with many teachers, I have found it difficult, and debatably undesirable, to separate the personal from the pedagogical. My teaching identity is inextricably intertwined with my identities as woman, mother, sister, friend, and so forth. One of my brilliant student teachers this semester, Brooke Allen, wrote about this very issue in her journal—of how impossible it was to leave school at school. She observed that her students, whose life stories fill me with the same inchoate sadness I mentioned earlier, experience the same thing in reverse: They can't leave home at home. I have been fortunate in that, for the most part, my plural identities are consonant; the few instances when disjunctures have forced me to privilege or sacrifice one identity over another have given me empathy for colleagues for whom the perpetual navigation of competing and conflicting identities has fractured their lives.

The same interconnectedness has become true for me as a researcher. Public and private spaces are blurred through my storytelling, whether I'm sharing my own experiences as I've done in this chapter or representing the stories of my research participants in a research report. I didn't set out to be someone who studied issues of social justice; initially in my graduate training I was skeptical of the save-the-world mentality I associated with a critical theoretical perspective. But I felt a frustration with the solipsism and insularity I perceived in much of academia and kept returning to the fundamental questions of *does this matter?* and *can it be changed?* Here is where I think a social justice perspective differs from other research paradigms. As colleagues of mine and I have noted in our analysis of the pedagogical paradigms that have shaped the discipline of English education (Murphy et al., 2004), a teacher with a liberatory worldview may adopt transmissionist or constructivist methods, but the underlying motive is, as Miller and Kirkland so eloquently put forth in the first chapter of this volume, "reclaiming justice in education . . . and promoting social justice as a schooling practice" (p. 2). The same holds true for education research: A variety of epistemologies and methodologies may be employed to inform and conduct a project, but when the purpose is always already to improve the human condition, and that purpose is evident not only in a researcher's work but in her or his life and teaching, then I think it's safe to say said researcher is operating within a social justice paradigm.

Bibliography

Gallas, K. (1998). *"Sometimes I can be anything": Power, gender, and identity in a primary classroom.* New York: Teachers College Press.

hooks, b. (2000). *All about love: New visions.* New York: HarperCollins.

Kennedy, R. (2002). *Nigger: The strange career of a troublesome word.* New York: Pantheon.

Murphy, S. L., Johnson, T. S., Hundley, M., Sanford, A., Bickmore, S., & Zoss, M. (2004). Pedagogical paradigms in English education. Available from The BRIDGE, www.teachersbridge.org

Rowling, J. K. (2007). *Harry Potter and the deathly hallows.* New York: Arthur Levine.

West, C. (2009). *Brother West: Living and loving out loud.* New York: Smiley.

THREE

Freire, Vygotsky, and Social Justice Theories in English Education

Mariana Souto-Manning & Peter Smagorinsky

The educational theories developed by Brazilian teacher and visionary administrator Paulo Freire have influenced and inspired social justice educators for many decades. Freire sought to uncover effects of external social realities and structures on people's lives and help them develop tools for countering inequitable conditions. Educators have also found the research of Belarusian psychologist Lev Vygotsky to be provocative, although more for his insights on the ways in which social mediation channels human development toward cultural ends. Vygotsky investigated how engagement with those structures and social practices helped to shape one's "higher mental functions": processes that meld practical and formal learning to produce abstractions that serve as frameworks for thinking in both established and new situations.

To get a sense of how often the work of these two scholars has been referenced in academic papers, we ran citation searches through Google Scholar. Freire recorded 52,150 references, and Vygotsky 19,198. Undoubtedly, they are among the most frequently cited thinkers in all of academia. Although we were not able to refine this search to link their writing to publications centering on issues of social justice in English education, we can make an educated guess that these two, particularly Freire, are often invoked to justify educational approaches centered on issues of equity, inclusiveness, and liberatory structures.

Although each derived his ideas from the views of Karl Marx, they incorporated Marxist principles into different social, cultural, and disciplinary frameworks emerging from the societies in which they grew up and the educational problems they faced. Freire and Vygotsky foregrounded different aspects of the dialectic relation that people have with their particular circumstances. Freire was concerned with how people interpret their environments, read their worlds, and can act to change them. Freire's work was focused on using Marx's capitalist critiques to help lower-class Brazilians develop critical meta-awareness of their worlds and seek to change economic structures in order to encourage the leveling of social classes. His pedagogy aimed to teach those oppressed by inequitable educational opportunities and income distribution to question their locations in society and ultimately seek to alter personal agency and economic structures in order to live more fulfilling lives.

Vygotsky's position as a Soviet psychologist focused his research on studying, understanding, and explaining the process of how people internalize ways of thinking. He was primarily interested in how people's consciousness is shaped through engagement with social mediation. As a member of the burgeoning communist Soviet empire, he had little need to critique capitalism given that it had been legislated out of existence in his society, and so had little reason to be concerned with matters of economic disparity and injustice.

The positions of Freire and Vygotsky produced different career trajectories and emphases. Freire was raised in a middle-class family in Brazil that, like many others, was devastated during the Great Depression. His experiences with poverty influenced his teaching career by impressing on him the importance of providing the poor with literacy practices and social tools to construct new futures for themselves. He was thus an educational philosopher whose ideas emerged from his practical experiences with the Brazilian oppressed. His liberatory pedagogy was seen as a threat to the military government as evidenced by the events which immediately followed the military coup of 1964: Freire's programs were dismantled. He was jailed and then exiled for over 15 years. During his expulsion, Freire continued his work in Chile, the U.S., and Africa, bringing global recognition to his ideas. Upon his return to Brazil, he worked in the area of adult literacy and later as Secretary of Education for São Paulo. He moved to administrative positions that enabled him to affect pedagogical policy, including his engagement with the practical problem of alleviating poverty and oppression through liberatory pedagogy.

Vygotsky came of age during the Bolshevik Revolution that produced the formation of the Soviet Union. As a Jew in an anti-Semitic culture, that took an official stance of atheism, he rose through the Soviet psychological ranks on the basis of sheer intellectual brilliance. He further had the courage and chutzpah, even in his twenties, to challenge the reigning titans of his day, including Ivan Petrovich Pavlov, a Nobel laureate 57 years his senior. He began his career as a teacher and then became a clinical psychologist; it is somewhat ironic that he developed and articulated a sociocultural theory of human development in the relatively isolated context of laboratory studies. In his brief life and career—he died at age 37 from tuberculosis, which had debilitated him for much of his adult life—he worked more as an experimenter and theorist, rather than immersing himself in the gritty realities of daily life. Although he was never exiled, he likely would have been, given his interest in individual internalization of cultural frameworks for thinking in a Soviet society driven by a brutally enforced Marxism that did not allow the individual an agentive role in constructing the setting of his or her life.

Both Freire and Vygotsky, then, began as teachers and adopted a generally Marxist perspective that emphasized the role of social mediation in teaching and learning. Freire employed this focus to advocate for changes in consciousness that produced intellectual and social tools to promote changes in individual beliefs, practices, and projected life trajectories. His career project thus concerned using a Marxist framework to help people acquire and develop tools and strategies to change their circumstances. He affirmed that the literacy process involved not only reading words but worlds and their intricacies within the context of socioculturally and historically shaped structures. Literacy was conceptualized by Freire as a vital instrument to change one's location in society, as a way to reclaim control of one's life, to engage in transformation and promote social justice. In Freire's (1970a) notion of conscientização, or critical consciousness, people look at their history and the social construction of their realities, seeking to problematize and separate personal beliefs from institutional discourses. Through dialogue, histories are considered, present realities and conditions are deconstructed, and futures are collectively envisioned.

Vygotsky was less of an activist and more of a descriptive psychologist. He aimed to account for how people learn, rather than to change the circumstances and thus the quality of their lives, although he did suggest ways in which concepts could be taught more effectively in the context of school (1926/1992). Both found roles for the individual within a Marxist perspective, an orientation that likely would have ultimately sent Vygotsky to the Gulag, had he survived his illness (Zinchenko, 2007). Although some have conflated Freire's social activism with Vygotsky's cultural psychology (e.g., Fiore & Elsasser, 2001; Trueba & McLaren, 2000), we see their work as being different in key ways, deriving at least in part from the different cultural milieus in which each one's life and career took place.

Although in many ways an orthodox Marxist—not, however, enough to suit the state, which banned his work shortly after his death because of his focus on individuals in relation to society, rather than on the collective itself (Daniels, 2007)—Vygotsky did not write about capitalist exploitation. If anything, he contributed in part to the Soviet effort to impose homogeneity according to Soviet notions of equality. Luria's (1976) study of illiterate peasants in remote villages of Uzbekistan and Kirghizia, which Vygotsky helped to plan, produced the insight that Muslims were backward people because they conceptualized social groupings differently than did Western subjects in Moscow. The Soviet national goals included taking the many and varied countries that were being assimilated into their emerging Russian-based culture and "elevating" them to the height of Soviet beliefs, whether they wanted to cogitate so or not. Vygotsky and Luria did not seek to empower these remote peasants to rebel against Soviet intervention into their lives and construct liberated social futures for themselves; such social action was for those who sought to labor in Siberia.

Vygotsky postulated that people's frameworks for thinking are internalized through social practice; that is, the setting of their learning provides them with tools, signs, and practices that suggest a societal destination (what Wertsch, 2000, calls a teleological end) and the means for achieving it. Freire, in contrast, encouraged learners "to bring their culture and personal knowledge into the classroom, help them understand the connections between their own lives and society" (Fiore & Elsasser, 2001, p. 71), empowering each person to engage in challenging their realities and collectively negotiating context-specific ways for taking action to change their conditions (Rymes, Souto-Manning, & Brown, 2005).

Lev Vygotsky recognized the reciprocal relationship between people and their cultures in that he saw people having agency to affect their environments, even as they inevitably internalized their structures, goals, and practices. He foregrounded, however, the process of internalization. Freire, in contrast, foregrounded the other end of this process, externalization, in which people acquire tools in order to work on and alter their environments to create new settings, social destinations, personal and group trajectories, and means for producing them.

These contrasting, but complementary, emphases are indicative of another key difference between the two through their focus on different life phases in human development. Vygotsky was a developmental psychologist, adopting a "genetic" method—a term referring not to genes and thus biological development, but rather to the social process of internalization through which people learn how to think—to understand how children develop higher mental functions, the culturally specific ways of thinking that enable them to function within a society. His emphasis was evident in his belief that psychologists should study training sessions rather than the performances that follow them, in that the training sessions provide an opportunity to study how one learns to perform a task, which he found theoretically much more compelling than studying the operations involved in an already-learned process (Vygotsky, 1934/1987). His clinical research focused on young children. When adults were involved in dyads—such as those through which he postulated the zone of proximal development and its illumination of performance through more expert assistance—their presence was designed to illustrate how children internalize existing means of mentation from their elders (or, less often, their more experienced peers).

Freire, in contrast, specialized in adult literacy and liberatory education. He was interested in teaching adults to critique their sociohistorical locations and take new action to change them. His notion of conscientização, or critical meta-awareness, focused on helping adults to develop a complex understanding of the world and its social and political contradictions so as to provide them with tools with which to act against oppressive circumstances. Freire was less interested in the processes through which young children internalize the values of their societal surroundings. Nevertheless, his approach (culture circles) offers fertile ground for social justice in early educational settings (Souto-Manning, 2009, 2010). All in all, Freire sought to foster critical consciousness so that oppression became exposed and adults developed strategies for diminishing it.

Together, their substantial differences aside, the work of Vygotsky and Freire account for the cyclical processes of social mediation through engagement with life's settings, the internalization of a worldview based on the use of cultural mediational tools such as speech, and individual and group efforts to re-create that setting through a raised consciousness of life's possibilities even if such a vision runs counter to the prevailing dominant culture. Even with this complementarity, we must emphasize that Freire's critical pedagogy was not available to Vygotsky in the context of the Leninist and Stalinist Soviet Union, in which dissent was met with swift and brutal reprisal.

A Freirean and Vygotskian Framework for Social Justice in English Education

In spite of this seemingly prohibitive limitation in Vygotsky's work, his mediational framework enables some possibilities for being joined with Freire's Marxist capitalist critique to inform the work of English educators who take a social justice perspective. Given that Freire's career was dedicated to liberatory pedagogy and social justice education, applying his ideas to English education—given literature's concern with the human condition—is relatively straightforward and requires little interpretation. Vygotsky, as a clinical psychologist whose emphasis focused on socioculturally mediated human development, and whose research was conducted with young children working in dyads on problems outside the English curriculum, requires greater extrapolation, especially to issues of social justice that were not a part of his research program. Two fruitful areas in which their work does overlap concern the ways in which social institutions provide mediational means that establish the basic framework for human development, and the ways in which higher mental functions enable the self-regulation and agency to act on one's environment.

To Freire, societal inequities follow from the ways in which competitive capitalism establishes class distinctions that are detrimental to the life trajectories of those at the lower tiers of education and income distribution. Vygotsky's research outlines the ways in which societies establish institutions and their attendant semiotic sign systems that people internalize to form the basis of how they conceptualize life in society (see his discussion of inner speech, 1934/1987). Freire theorized that when people internalize a conception of society, they tend to reinforce its explicit and implicit hierarchical relationships through their activity within its routines and practices. Freire's educational vision centered on disrupting debilitating internalizations of socioculturally and historically constructed structures among oppressed people that perpetuate their circumstances over a series of generations. Vygotsky's value to this project comes in his empirical documentation of how social values are reflected in individuals' word use, particularly the ways in which one's attribution of meaning to words evolves over time to indicate concept development. When these concepts reinforce social hierarchies, Freire believed, it is the province of education to facilitate the process whereby learners negotiate ways to employ tools to critique, problematize, and change social structures to provide more equitable access to a society's benefits.

Paulo Freire's critical activist interpretation of the principle of internalization produces the following assumptions regarding the externalization of understanding available in school through collaborative, speech-mediated, experience-informed action to change societal structures—i.e., through praxis (Souto-Manning, 2010):

- When students arrive in the school or classroom, they already have knowledge of their own language and everyday worlds.

- Students are the subject of their own learning. In this kind of educational setting, each student investigates and engages in inquiry employing problem posing, critical dialogue, and problem solving.

- Conflict is the basis for learning. When old knowledge and new knowledge conflict, participants ask questions and engage in dialogue, critically constructing their own bodies of knowledge.

- Learning takes place collectively rather than in isolation.

- Culturally relevant pedagogy (Ladson-Billings, 1996) is not spontaneous; it requires continual inquiry and research. There is much planning, yet the teacher/facilitator must know how to critically take advantage of teachable moments and engage students/participants from multiple backgrounds and communities in meaningful learning experiences (Freire, 1970b).

Freire pointed toward the need to create positive learning environments in which individuals can recognize their oppression(s) and take active roles, collectively constructing their futures as they consider the histories of their collective and unique contexts. His liberatory pedagogy (1970a) promotes active involvement and meta-awareness of the transformative process. Individuals must actively and collectively engage in their own struggle for social justice. According to Fiore and Elsasser (2001):

> Often, Freire says, students unaware of the connections between their own lives and society personalize their problems. To encourage students to understand the impact of society in their lives, Freire proposes students and teachers talk about generative themes drawn from the students' everyday world. Investigating issues such as work or family life from an individual and a socio-historical perspective, students bring their own knowledge into the classroom and broaden their sense of social context. (p. 70)

Smagorinsky (2007) provides examples of how the social setting of activity invokes norms that may or may not be appropriate for all involved. U.S. schools tend to validate and perpetuate the values of middle-class Whites, especially in terms of what counts as a sense of propriety in terms of the volume, diction, occasions, and other aspects of speech. Students who are relatively loud and speak out of turn are typically viewed as disruptive and often subjected to disciplinary action. In Georgia's Houston County in 2007–2008, for example, where the student population was 54% White and 35% Black, 61% of suspended students were Black and 31% were White. When asked about possible racial bias in discipline, James Kinchen, Houston's Director of School Operations, responded, "Discriminating based on race, no, that doesn't happen in Houston County" (Hubbard, 2009, n.p.). And perhaps it doesn't, at least not intentionally. One way to interpret this phenomenon is to consider the possibility that Black students are punished for acting in ways that they find appropriate, yet that their teachers find disruptive.

From a Vygotskian perspective, Black and White students have internalized different conceptions of what constitutes appropriate behavior in formal social settings such as church and school. If Black students are enculturated to the "call and response" style of an African American church—see, e.g., a sermon by Rev. Jeremy James at http://www.youtube.com/watch?v=MR0WM2xL4rg&feature=related—and view such behavior as appropriate in any formal social setting, including school, then they might be viewed as disruptive and become subject to disciplinary action, including suspension, in school.

From a Freirean perspective, the fact of disproportionate suspension rates would provide the opportunity for critical social awareness designed to produce a just outcome and more equitable approach to discipline in school, considering the sociohistorical issues shaping such oppression while seeking to challenge and redefine what is "acceptable" in schools and society. This kind of critique has occurred in English classes, as when Fecho's (2001) students engaged in inquiry in order to address their feelings of threat in his high school English class. His inquiry method is one among many ways of critiquing social inequities within the confines of the English curriculum; others include Hillocks, McCabe, and McCampbell's (1971) organization of literature according to themes and other concepts such as social responsibility and discrimination (e.g. Smagorinsky, 2008; Beach & Myers, 2001). Fundamental to each of these approaches is the opportunity to use texts more central to students' lives as vehicles for raising questions about what sort of society we inhabit and how, through social action, teachers and students can envision what needs to happen in order for it to serve all of its members equitably.

This critique could come from another overlap between Freire and Vygotsky, that being their mutual interest in the ways in which one develops the faculties necessary to reach a state of conscientização. Among Vygotsky's postulations in his formulation of the notion of higher mental functions, or scientific concepts, is that the ability to conceptualize a problem provides one with the tools for regulating one's own thinking about it, consequently leading to action. This being the case, education can strive to help young people develop something approaching conscientização, a state that may be available to students of different ages, experiences, levels of maturity, and other developmental factors (Souto-Manning, 2009, 2010). What they need, then, is a curriculum that continually spirals among themes related to social justice: discrimination, social responsibility, mental health, gender roles, the banality of evil, censorship, cultural conflict, immigration, and so on (see, e.g., the units of instruction outlined at http://www.coe.uga.edu/~smago/VirtualLibrary/Unit_Outlines.htm). This routine and systematic engagement with themes related to oppression and inequity could help students to develop a concept of social justice that could provide the basis for the sort of praxis that Freire found central to a critical consciousness.

Conclusion

In this chapter we have argued that, their substantial differences in emphasis aside, the work of Freire and Vygostsky may be bridged to suggest related possibilities for social justice education. Synthesizing their work can be productive, if labor intensive. Reading Vygotsky is a tall order. In his "Translator's Foreword and Acknowledgements" to *The Collected Works, Volume 3*, Van der Veer (1997) noted,

> I have not attempted to improve Vygotsky's style of writing although it was at times difficult to refrain from doing so. It is clear that Vygotsky . . . never rewrote a text for the sake of improving its style and readability. Hence the redundancy, the difficulty to follow the thread of his argument, the awkward sentences, etc. (p. v).

Given the many perils of translating Vygotsky and the subsequent challenges of reading a translation (which itself might be problematic), undertaking the sort of extensive reading of Vygotsky that produces an understanding of his cultural project is beyond the patience of many policy makers and teacher candidates. And yet accepting summaries of his work written by others can lead to gross distortions of his views (Smagorinsky, 2009). Furthermore, Vygotsky's work emphasized attending to contexts, making it difficult for the sort of generalized plans favored by policy makers. If Vygotsky's work suggests anything to policy makers, it may be that teaching and learning involve situated practice, and so site-based management makes better sense than top-down administration of large educational bureaucracies.

Freire's work has more immediate possibilities for policy. He intentionally wrote more accessibly and practically, with some of his later work being published in dialogue format (e.g., Freire & Macedo, 1995; Freire, 1997). As an educational administrator, he understood and was concerned with the work of making policy, of linking theory and practice. Freire believed that:

> We must not negate practice for the sake of theory. To do so, would reduce theory to pure verbalism or intellectualism. By the same token, to negate theory for the sake of practice, as in the use of dialogue as conversation, is to run the risk of losing oneself in the disconnectedness of practice. It is for this reason that I never advocate either a theoretic elitism or a practice ungrounded in theory, but the unity between theory and practice. (Freire & Macedo, 1995, p. 382)

Given that he was an activist for social justice, Freire wrote in order to affect social change. Such a career lends itself far more easily to adoption into policy than do the reports of experimental psychological research in which Vygotsky specialized.

The points of connection that we have identified between Freire and Vygotsky can help English educators consider how a school curriculum can be structured, and how teachers can encourage a critical perspective on social inequity that can provide students with tools for acting on the injustices that they perceive in their worlds. What remains to be seen is the extent to which teachers adopting this perspective must engage with, and possibly be exiled from, academic institutions as they urge their students to critique and overturn the very structures through which they challenge inequity and oppression.

Bibliography

Beach, R., & Myers, J. (2001). *Inquiry-based English instruction: Engaging students in life and literature*. New York: Teachers College Press.

Daniels, H. (2007). Pedagogy. In H. Daniels, M. Cole, & J. V. Wertsch (Eds.), *The Cambridge companion to Vygotsky* (pp. 307–331). New York: Cambridge University Press.

Fecho, B. (2001). "Why are you doing this?" Acknowledging and transcending threat in critical inquiry classrooms. *Research in the Teaching of English, 36*, 9–37.

Fiore, K., & Elsasser, N. (2001). "Strangers no more": A liberatory literacy curriculum. In K. Halasek K., & Highberg N. P. (Eds.). (2004). *Landmark essays on basic writing* (pp. 69–82). Mahwah, NJ: Hermagoras.

Freire, P. (1970a). *Pedagogy of the oppressed*. New York: Continuum.

Freire, P. (1970b). Cultural action for freedom. *Harvard Educational Review*, Monograph Series No. 1.

Freire, P. (Ed.). (1997). *Mentoring the mentor: A critical dialogue with Paulo Freire*. New York: Peter Lang.

Freire, P., & Macedo, D. (1995). A dialogue: Culture, language, and race. *Harvard Educational Review, 65* (3), 377–402.

Hillocks, G., McCabe, B. J., & McCampbell, J. F. (1971). *The dynamics of English instruction, grades 7-12*. New York: Random House. Retrieved July 24, 2009 from http://www. coe.uga.edu/~smago/Books/Dynamics/Dynamics_home.htm.

Hubbard, J. (2009, June 14). *Suspension rates for black students out of line, says NAACP*. Retrieved June 22, 2009, from http://www.macon.com/198/story/747540.html

Kincheloe, J. (2005). *Critical pedagogy*. New York: Peter Lang.

Ladson-Billings, G. (1996). Multicultural issues in the classroom: Race, class, and gender. In R. W. Evans & W. Saxe (Eds.), *Handbook on teaching social issues* (pp. 101–110). Washington, DC: National Council for the Social Studies.

Luria, A. R. (1976). *Cognitive development its cultural and social foundations* (M. Lopez-Morillas & L. Solotaroff, Trans.). Cambridge, MA: Harvard University Press. Available in part at http://marxists.anu.edu.au/archive/luria/works/1976/problem.htm

Rymes, B., Souto-Manning, M., & Brown, C. (2005). Being "critical" as taking a stand: One of the central dilemmas of CDA. *Journal of Critical Discourse Studies, 2*(2), 195–198.

Smagorinsky, P. (2007). Vygotsky and the social dynamics of classrooms. *English Journal, 97*(2), 61–66.

Smagorinsky, P. (2008). *Teaching English by design: How to create and carry out instructional units*. Portsmouth, NH: Heinemann.

Smagorinsky, P. H. (2009). The culture of Vygotsky. *Reading Research Quarterly, 44*, 85–95.

Souto-Manning, M. (2009). Negotiating culturally responsive pedagogy through multicultural children's literature: Towards critical democratic literacy practices in a first grade classroom. *Journal of Early Childhood Literacy, 9*(1), 53-77.

Souto-Manning, M. (2010). *Freire, teaching, and learning: Critical pedagogy across contexts*. New York: Peter Lang.

Trueba, E. T., & McLaren, P. (2000). Critical ethnography for the study of immigrants. In E. T. Trueba & L. I. Bartolomé (Eds.), *Immigrant voices: In search of educational equity* (pp. 37–74). Oxford: Rowman & Littlefield.

Van der Veer, R. (1997). Translator's foreword and acknowledgements. In L. S. Vygotsky, *Collected works* (Vol. 3: *Problems of the theory and history of psychology*) (pp. v–vi) (R. W. Rieber & J. Wollock, Eds.; R. Van der Veer, Trans.). New York: Plenum.

Vygotsky, L. S. (1934/1987). Thinking and speech. In L. S. Vygotsky, *Collected works* (Vol. 1) pp. 39–285) (R. Rieber & A. Carton, Eds.; N. Minick, Trans.). New York: Plenum. Available in   part at http://www.marxists.org/archive/vygotsky/works/words/index.htm

Vygotsky, L. S. (1926/1992). *Educational psychology* (R. Silverman, Trans.). Boca Raton, FL: St. Lucie Press. Available in part at http://www.marxists.org/archive/vygotsky/works/1926/educational-psychology/index.htm

Wertsch, J. V. (1985). *Vygotsky and the social formation of mind*. Cambridge, MA: Harvard University Press.

Wertsch, J. V. (1991). *Voices of the mind: A sociocultural approach to mediated action*. Cambridge: Harvard University Press.

Wertsch, J. V. (2000). Vygotsky's two minds on the nature of meaning. In C. D. Lee & P. Smagorinsky (Eds.), *Vygotskian perspectives on literacy research: Constructing meaning through collaborative inquiry* (pp. 19–30). New York: Cambridge University Press.

Zinchenko, V. (2007). Thought and word: The approaches of L. S. Vygotsky and G. G. Shpet. In H. Daniels, M. Cole, & J. V. Wertsch (Eds.), *The Cambridge companion to Vygotsky* (pp. 212–245). New York: Cambridge University Press.

Closing Comments
Conceiving Social Justice

The authors in this section have provided critical approaches to understanding the significance of fortifying a meta-framework for researching social justice in English education. Through their essays, they share the immense importance of a research framework for social justice that presupposes: (1) reflection—identifying historical causality of oppression; (2) change—revealing its oppressive mark or impact on an individual, group, or context; and (3) participation—generating potential outcomes for change, i.e., agency/empowerment and even emancipation. Readers have learned how researcher stance on social justice affects an ever-evolving continuum of how we read the spaces where we engage in social justice research. In fact, Tara teaches us the importance of remembering how our own understanding of social justice can both be challenged and simultaneously in flux as we encounter new contexts. Her understanding of social justice reveals that the participants with whom we are fortunate to work can, by example, teach us much about how to "enact a personal and pedagogical policy of social justice."

Mariana and Peter's illuminating work about the inimitable contributions of Freire and Vygotsky provides a foundational context that supports the grounding of social justice research. They unpack that both Freire and Vygotsky "have influenced and inspired social justice educators for many decades" (and are among "the most frequently cited thinkers in all of academia." Some of the most significant contributions of these scholars to pedagogical applications in teacher education include: the role of social mediation in teaching and learning, "the internalization of a worldview based on the use of cultural mediational tools such as speech, and individual and group efforts to re-create that setting through a raised consciousness of life's possibilities even if such a vision runs counter to the prevailing dominant culture." Freire's and Vygotsky's research has influenced and changed the fabric of teaching possibilities and has greatly enhanced a greater consciousness in students from all backgrounds. Mariana tells us that Freire and Vygotsky have opened up avenues to more equitable pedagogical approaches and that Freire has taught us that "education can strive to help young people develop something approaching conscientização, a state that may be available to students of different ages, experiences, levels of maturity, and other developmental factors" (Souto-Manning, 2009, 2010). Peter tells us that the work of Freire and Vygotsky has led teachers to employ more equitable pedagogical approaches in the classroom context for all students, and he wonders where we'd be today if Freire and Vygotsky had not paved the way.

sj has extended the foundational gleanings of Mariana and Peter's work on Freire and Vygotsky and added to the historical overview of how research related to prejudice and oppression has amassed into different yet related genres related to social justice. This body of literature can provide critique and expansion as the field of social justice in English education continues to emerge. sj also links the discussion of social justice to the field of capability theories and provokes questions that can impact research inquiry about researcher positionality as moral authority. sj invites self-reflection relating to social justice in both the researcher stance and in classroom contexts with preservice teachers about how to be mindful so as to not position the self as moral authority which can undermine the foundational ideas upon which social justice is predicated.

Tara's stories reveal how participants play an active part in our social justice research as they become "informants" who share their lived experiences. The Reverend's "tip" to Tara that local KKK members frequent the neighborhood shop led her to experience firsthand particular "real-time" contexts that will undoubtedly leave an indelible mark and influence her pursuit of unpacking prejudice and oppression through the eyes of those with whom she conducts research. Her position as researcher is greatly informed by the patching of the social milieu in which she sews together the space, time, and experiences of those who guide her to conceptualizing a larger narrative.

Together, these essays help us come to a more solid grounding of the historical roots of social justice research. We unpack that its historical context is deeply embedded within diverse social struggles and that its legacy has impacted generations by sometimes privileging and at other times, disadvantaging others. Regardless of outcome, for both the privileged and the disadvantaged, there is much to learn from within the master narratives of how individuals play out their life stories and about why and how people seek out change. Their lived experience, we see, is a tri-fold relationship that illuminates their lived histories relating to social justice: reflection, change, and participation. As we move through other sections in the book, this tri-fold relationship will keep us grounded in the historicality of social justice as other contributors continue to unpack different contexts and nuances wherein they recognize through their own experiences, that *change matters*.

Bibliography

Souto-Manning, M. (2009). Negotiating culturally responsive pedagogy through multicultural children's literature: Towards critical democratic literacy practices in a first grade classroom. *Journal of Early Childhood Literacy, 9* (1), 53–77.

Souto-Manning, M. (2010). *Freire, teaching, and learning: Critical pedagogy across contexts*. New York: Peter Lang.

Multi Social Justice Methods in English Education

Popular understandings of methodology are located in the conduct of research. However, in its relationship to social justice, methodology has dual functions: (1) as marker for teacher preparation, and (2) as classroom method or practice. We see an emerging trend in social justice research that blurs the boundary between methodology and method, and note that methods can grow from methodologies and methodologies can grow from methods. Based on our understanding of English education to date, Social Justice Theory (re)conceptualizes a critical review of language and literature that supports social justice methods both in the classroom and through research methodologies. It includes creating new and drawing from current methodologies that speak to the languages and literatures that are juxtaposed with the counter-narratives of participants. Sometimes the distinction between methods and methodologies may be vast and at other times they may be one and the same because our methods can become our methodologies.

Thus social justice as critical methodology within English education offers a framework to measure, qualify, quantify, and assess the nature of power and its presence in society. As new phenomena arise, researchers and practitioners are challenged to construct new methodologies that reveal hidden knowledges and realities, authenticate critical findings, and hold long-standing efficacy.

Social justice research methodologies have grown out of transdisciplinary bodies which "cut across all perspectives and modes of thought" (Soja, 1996,

p. 3). These methodologies are concerned with just outcomes and challenge the notion that the past is spatially and temporally fragmented and binds atomistic research. This could include but is not limited to fields that tend toward nonbinary thinking such as feminist, queer, critical hip-hop, sociocultural, equity, liberatory, transformative, identity, critical geographies, new literacy, and hybrid/spatiality and temporal studies. Many of these areas speak of power in teaching and in the preparation of teachers, particularly those relationships that help foster and maintain uneven social and educational outcomes. It also recognizes that space and time are fluid and constantly changing—which helps scholars situate and understand social justice over space and time. To this end, English educators who embrace social justice as methodology in their work transcend binary constructs and share the belief that a politics of "difference and identity built on the opening of new spaces" relocates us to a place where counter-hegemonic principles can lead to a liberal democracy (Soja, 1996, p. 111). Such a politics lifts us out of binary identifiers and relocates us to a space where ideas can "coexist concurrently and in contradiction" (deLauretis, 1987, p. 26).

So social justice as classroom methodology considers how constructed spaces can reflect social justice in pedagogy. Classroom design, in this way, reflects a commitment to social justice. This might include letting the flow of dialogue determine how activities position and/or self-position desks and tables. It might also include a critical reflection of the texts (in all of its various definitions) we use, and how they support classroom discussion and activity. If we use artifacts such as posters, leaflets, newspaper clippings, etc., it considers their sociopolitical messages and how they might impact students' identities. Along this continuum, our teachings might foster inquiry and critique and include (in classroom space and online) activities that promote self-reflection such as through journals, both planned and extemporaneous discussions, research projects, hands-on activities, media analyses, community-based learning, student teaching, lesson and unit plan designs, interviews, and social action projects, etc. Many teachers who engage through self-reflection (Loughran, 2007; Zeichner, 2007; Zeichner & Liston, 1996) and inquiry recognize that future teachings emerge experientially and it is important that we in education remain committed to critical reflection about what is and isn't working in classrooms so that we can best meet our students as they intersect with the world around them.

The essayists in this section address emerging multi methods and methodologies supported by research in English education and which have the collective power to move us in the direction of policy. Together, these innovative approaches to framing social justice research provide inspiring and visionary conductors of how to move social justice research closer to policy. Their intended audience is both the policy maker and the English educator. We are excited about these possibilities and their unforeseen outcomes. The contributors seek to answer their own questions in hopes of providing a repertoire of possibilities for advancing these methodologies. Their thoughts on social justice methodologies may leave readers with common understandings around the following topics: (1) research that challenges and intercepts prejudice and oppression; (2) human dignity; and (3) the threefold Theory of Social Justice—reflection, change, and participation. They also leave us with questions such as: *How can we amass the unique studies, methodologies, data analyses, and representations for data that address social justice issues? What makes a methodology appropriate in framing social justice and what does that look like? How can a practice-based framework for social justice have efficacy over space and time, moving from the university classroom into the K–12 classroom? How can social justice pedagogy inform its policy? And, What do policy makers need to know that we know about the importance of a policy about social justice in K–12 schools?*

Of course, all of these questions will not be answered in this section. We include them here as a way of forecasting the direction of the texts and so that you can keep them in mind in order to help you better connect the parts as you read.

Bibliography

deLauretis, T (1987). *Technologies of gender: Essays on theory, film, and fiction*. Bloomington, IN: Indiana University Press.

Loughran, J.J. (2007). Researching teacher education practices: Responding to the challenges, demands and expectations of self-study. *Journal of Teacher Education, 58* (1), 12 - 20.

Soja, E. W. (1996). *Thirdspace: Journeys to Los Angeles and other real-and-imagined places*. Malden, MA: Blackwell.

Zeichner, K. (2007). Accumulating knowledge across self-studies in teacher education. *Journal of Teacher Education, 58*, 36–46.

Zeichner, K., & Liston, D. (1996). *Reflective teaching: An introduction*. Mahwah, NJ: Lawrence Erlbaum.

FOUR

Scaffolding and Embedding Social Justice into English Education

sj Miller

Social Justice Pedagogy

Why does pedagogy matter? Pedagogy is the amalgam of how particular theories drive behavior in teaching. As we begin to help our students articulate their pedagogies, it is important to help them become clear about their belief systems and their principles because it will drive their pedagogies. A poorly articulated pedagogy is like driving a car with a blindfold. The more clear students are about their belief systems, the more informed they can be in articulating and revising their pedagogies (see Appendix B for sample assignment). Jane Danielewicz in her book *Teaching Selves: Identity, Pedagogy and Teacher Education* and Janet Alusp in *Teacher Identity Discourses: Negotiating Personal and Professional Spaces* offer wonderful detailed examples for structuring activities, combining theories, and situating contexts to help students develop an emergent pedagogy.

In order to truly begin to make meaning of and embody a social justice pedagogy, preservice and student teachers need varied and authentic learning contexts with culturally, linguistically, economically, and otherwise diverse classrooms. As our students engage in such contexts in (un)familiar settings, it is important that we affirm and help stabilize their emotional, cognitive, and corporeal responses to their own classrooms because

> Teaching is more than an intellectual act, it involves how teachers move, laugh, dramatize, perform, smile, point, sigh, joke, gesticulate, write, and move around the room as

necessary, and we want them thinking through each of these transitions and we want our teachers to be aware of their feelings, thoughts, and emotions as they respond in kind and thoughtful ways to students. (Miller & Norris 2007, pp. 15–16).

This means that we have to set up our methods classrooms so that we can address the experiences of students in the field. This could be done through inquiry projects, student interviews, research, "talking," and/or community involvement.

As we also consider how to support students develop a social justice–minded pedagogy, we can draw from DeStigter's suggestion in the *Introduction* (See Miller, 2008) that social justice be the eye of teacher's principled habits. Social justice then, as the foci of principled habits, could be understood as a pedagogy which presupposes that all students are worthy of human dignity, that all are worthy of the same tenets in an education, that the contract they enter into in schools must honor their sociocultural advantages and disadvantages, that it must seek to offer the same educational, sociocultural, and psycho-emotional opportunities to each student in order to help them meet and obtain a (determined) basic threshold that is mutually beneficial to each party who enters into the school space. Social justice pedagogy then would strive for equity for all students, support the affective, corporeal, and emotional growth of individuals in relation to a descriptive and fluid definition of social justice, become an embodied identity that has efficacy in multiple contexts, and recognize that students bring inequitable histories, and in spite of that strives to bring each student up to their capability threshold. Social justice as pedagogy embraces the paradox of its conflicting principles, that there is a simultaneous need to make a firm decision about how to promote justice while at the same time to critically interrogate (i.e., doubt or even refuse) those decisions—or at least leave open the possibility that we might be wrong. Social justice must also recognize that social justice to one person may not be social justice to another. Such honesty about a social justice–based pedagogy can drive the method and the content of how we teach about it.

Social Justice as Institutionalized Identity

Research on the constitution of a preservice teacher identity helps strengthen an argument about the validity of social justice as policy. A matrix of preservice English teacher research by Alsup (2006), Britzman (1991), Danielewicz (2001), Miller (2006), and Vinz (1996) each illuminate that belief systems impact identity. These studies articulate that belief impacts behavior and that behavior shapes identity formation. Such studies provide a foundation for reconceptualizing how we might consider employing methodology and pedagogy which facilitate the co-construction of a social justice English teacher identity in our methods courses.

An identity is something one comes to embody and own as s/he self-defines different aspects of the self and comes into different contexts in space and time (Gee, 1996). An identity is illuminated based on the relationship the individual has within and to the various contexts or social spaces. For instance, if a person is standing in front of a group of students who are sitting on desks, an identity that person embodies during that space and time might be, "teacher." If that same person after school goes to coach soccer players, that person's identity becomes "coach." Does that mean that the person is no longer a teacher? No, what it implies is that we don an identity in a given moment and as we switch contexts, we simply wear the identities that we have come to embody over time.

Teachers' beliefs inform their curricular decisions, relationships with students, and educational philosophies (Brown, 2006, p. 259) and teachers' expectations and perceptions of youth affect students' achievement (Brown, 2006, p. 260). In looking at cultivating a social justice identity that we can attach to a research agenda, we can define it as—an identity that develops in relation to understanding how hegemonic hierarchies oppress people and teaches empowerment for all. Therefore, in our methods courses, we can create authentic experiences in various social spaces for supporting the exploration of a developing social justice teacher identity. Social spaces are central to understanding an identity in terms of "race, ethnicity, social class or gender … [because] those identifications shape engagements in spatial tactics of power and in everyday social, cultural and literate practices" (McCarthey & Moje, 2002, pp. 234–235). Because social spaces are impacted by political (power) and social ideologies (Foucault, 1980, 1986; Lefebvre, 1991) they are never neutral. Foucault (1986) and Bourdieu (1980) suggest that the effects of power construct identities, and that the embodiment of identities is vulnerable as a result of power. Because social spaces are defined in relationship to society, such as a school, café, or bar, identities are highlighted by those social spaces and by the way their identities have been defined in relationship to society. Selves therefore are illuminated by their identities within specific social spaces and yet can be excluded when their identities are not defined by their relationship to that space. Identity can therefore either be stabilized or affirmed in a given social space, or destabilized when a social space excludes or is unwelcoming of a particular identity, or even restabilized once the individual has had time to regroup. As individuals change and merge with other social spaces, their identities can become hybrids layered with a multitude of subjectivities. Preservice teacher identity co-construction is thereby sociospatial (Leander, 2002) and teacher identities are discoursed.

When we consider how to scaffold a social justice identity, we should consider how to support the emotional, corporeal, and cognitive development of students in different social spaces (see Appendix A). While Lazarus (1999) contributes to our understanding that emotions "refer to a complex organized system consisting of thoughts, beliefs, motives, meanings, subjective bodily experiences, and physiological states" (p. 100), other research on teachers' emotions has focused on the role emotion plays in teaching as focused through social relationships within the school context (Hargreaves, 1998, 2000, 2001). However, Jaggar's (1989) and Zembylas' (2003) research on teachers' emotions has greater efficacy here. Jaggar's (1989) feminist perspective on outlaw emotions suggests that emotion is linked to power and states:

> [Outlaw emotions] may provide the first indications that something is wrong with the way alleged facts have been construed, with accepted understandings of how things are. . . . Only when we reflect on our initial puzzling, irritability, revulsion, anger, or fear may we bring to consciousness our "gut level" awareness that we are in a situation of coercion, cruelty, injustice or danger. (p. 161)

Jaggar sustains this by suggesting that naming our emotions can lead to change by provoking initiatives to alter unjust contexts. Zembylas (2003) brings these issues to a head when he suggests that sociopolitical issues and cultural aspects undergird the emotions of the teacher. In fact, Zembylas (2003) suggests that "teachers' emotions can become sites of resistance and self- (trans)formation" (p. 106).

The corporeal responses of teachers can be understood as how teachers' emotions affect their physical responses to situations. The theory of emotional contagion "suggests that all participants in communicative exchange are susceptible to each other's emotions and the contagion effect" (Hatfield, Cacioppo, & Rapson, 1994; Mottet & Beebe, 2000). As such, emotions tend to influence behavior, or bodily responses (Cacioppo & Gardner, 1999; Russell & Mehrabian, 1978). Mehrabian (1971) found that students' nonverbal responses reflected a teacher's positive perceptions of teaching effectiveness and satisfaction and reflected how students felt about the course and the instructor. Thus, the emotional health of the teacher has great causality on the responses of the students so it becomes critical that we open up spaces to discuss the relationality of emotion to a student's response especially when we are discussing the loaded complexities of social justice teaching.

Strategies for Scaffolding Social Justice Identity

We are now ready to explore how preservice teachers can embody a social justice identity through two combined models which set the stage for scaffolding social justice identity into methods. Such a model is conceptualized developmental in its breadth. The first model, which is referred to as the meta-framework, comes from Nieto and Bode (2008), who provide a framework for supporting individuals through developmental stages in becoming multiculturally sensitive: (1)

tolerance, (2) acceptance, (3) respect, and, (4) affirmation, solidarity, and critique. Instead of naming the first stage as "tolerance," which means to "put up" with something even though one's principles may malign with it, it will be called "critical reflection." The second model comes from a nonempirical model as described in *Narratives of Social Justice Teaching* (Miller, 2008), where the once called 5 "re-s," but now referred to as the 6 "re-s," are introduced as what happens during the "critical pause time" when the preservice teacher can quickly reflect, reconsider, refuse, reconceptualize, rejuvenate, and reengage in a manner of seconds.

This process can support preservice and student teachers develop these skills whereby they move from a potentially destabilizing moment into a restabilizing stance and articulate a response to the best of their ability. Such movement, albeit unseen to the audience, is a strategy to preserve and enhance social justice and other kinds of teaching in the classroom. The 6 "re-s" can exist with any of the four meta-framework stages. Building upon the amalgam of these two models, these proposed strategies can be appropriated into methods as we work toward scaffolding a social justice identity. It is highly likely that students come to us at varying levels in this developmental model and on a continuum of understanding but we can ask them to revisit each stage based on their current awareness of themselves. This model is nonlinear as people are likely to move back and forth quickly between stages. Therefore some activities can include various levels at once. Instructors would need to assess when students are ready to be pushed on to different levels. It is up to the instructor and student to select activities based on the student's need, and even where to begin the work. In fact, the developmental identity model for social justice can be individualized based on a student's awareness around social justice.

As we work within this model, the curriculum we teach and how we construct our lessons will support and facilitate the cognitive, emotional, and corporeal growth of our students. The 6 "re-s" (Appendix A), reflect, reconsider, refuse, reconceptualize, rejuvenate, and reengage, can be applied to the lessons and become practice for the possible social justice and injustice issues faced by students in the field. *Reflection* can support a teacher to make a transition when something isn't going well or even when extensions can be made to other topics. *Reconsider* references that something might need to be changed to make a situation flow more effectively. *Refuse* allows for a student to negotiate against ideas, to not actively participate, to disagree or even refuse and reject altogether. *Reconceptualize* enables students to understand that there is more than one way to do or respond to something. *Rejuvenate* becomes a sense of "My principles about social justice matter in the context of this classroom and I will not abandon them." In other words, the practice students have in methods classes should work toward stabilizing students' belief systems especially if they are not supported by the school environment. *Reengage* helps students stay present and involved in their teaching for social justice even when they may feel that the school system seems to be unsupportive of equity for all. Although the structure provided is a sample for how to scaffold social justice identity, it will have efficacy in the context of students' teaching lives. Helping them embody the model is what is significant at this juncture, so when faced with "live" scenarios, students have the framework from which to draw. A possible outcome of this research for social justice as policy is that a social justice teacher identity can become a seamless link that travels with a person both in and out of school contexts.

By applying these stages to our methods courses, and even scaffolding them by different semesters of years in a program, we can begin to cultivate more social justice–minded educators who are prepared to teach within any governing democracy. As we affirm their stances and beliefs we may develop their confidence and stabilize or restabilize their abilities to stay true to the road for social equity. While we cannot be assured of this or even that they might even abandon it altogether, we can continually revisit what we are doing to enact and activate social justice in methods and continue to apply the 6 "re-s" to our own thinking and teaching. At the root of our (in)actions and reflections lie our individual and collective principles which do have a causal effect on the lifespan of what can happen to social justice now and in the future.

Bibliography

Alsup, J. (2006). *Teacher identity discourses: Negotiating personal and professional spaces*. Mahwah, NJ: Lawrence Erlbaum.

Britzman, D. (1991). *Practice makes practice*. Albany, NY: State University of New York Press.

Bourdieu, P. (1980). *The logic of practice*. Stanford, CA: Stanford University Press.

Brown, E. (2006). The place of race in teacher identity: Self-narratives and curricular intervention as the practice of freedom. *Teacher Education & Practice, 19*(2), 257–279.

Cacioppo, J.T., & Gardner, W.L. (1999). Emotion. *Annual Review of Psychology, 50*, 193–214.

Danielewicz, J. (2001). *Teaching selves: Identity, pedagogy and teacher education*. Albany, NY: State University of New York Press.

Foucault, M. (1980). *Power-knowledge: Selected interviews and other writings, 1972–1977*. New York: Pantheon.

Foucault, M. (1986). Of other spaces. (J. Miskowiec, Trans.). *Diacritics, 16*(1), 22–27.

Gee, J.P. (1996). *Social linguistics and literacies: Ideology in discourses* (2nd ed.). New York: Falmer.

Hargreaves, A. (1998). The emotional practice of teaching. *Teaching and Teacher Education, 14*(8), 835–854.

Hargreaves, A. (2000). Mixed emotions: Teachers' perceptions of the interactions with students. *Teaching and Teacher Education, 16*(8), 811–826.

Hargreaves, A. (2001). The emotional geographies of teaching. *Teachers' College Record, 103*(6), 1056–1080.

Hatfield, E., Cacioppo, J.T., & Rapson, R.L. (1994). *Emotional contagion.* New York: Cambridge University Press.

Jaggar, A. (1989) "Love and Knowledge: Emotion in Feminist Epistemology." *Inquiry, 32*(2), 151-176.

Lazarus, R.S., (1999). *Stress and emotion: A new synthesis.* New York: Springer.

Leander, K. (2002). Locating Latanya: The situated production of identity artifacts in classroom interaction. *Research in the Teaching of English, 37*, 198–250.

Lefebvre, H. (1991). *The production of space.* Oxford: Blackwell.

McCarthey, S., & Moje, E. (2002). Identity matters. *Reading Research Quarterly, 37*(2), 228–238.

Mehrabian, A. (1971). *Silent messages.* Belmont: Wadsworth.

Miller, s. (2006). Foregrounding preservice teacher identity in teacher education. *Teacher Education & Practice, 19* (2), 164–185.

Miller, s. (2008). Fourthspace—Revisiting social justice in teacher education. In sj. Miller, L. Beliveau, T. DeStigter, D. Kirkland, & P. Rice, *Narratives of social justice teaching: How English teachers negotiate theory and practice between preservice and inservice spaces* (pp. 1–21). New York: Peter Lang.

Miller, s., & Norris, L. (2007). *Unpacking the loaded teacher matrix: Negotiating space and time between university and secondary English classrooms.* New York: Peter Lang.

Mottet, T., & Beebe, S. A. (2000, November). *Emotional contagion in the classroom: An examination of how teacher and student emotions are related.* Paper Presented at the Annual meeting of the National Communication Association, Seattle.

Nieto, S., & Bode, P. (2008). *Affirming diversity.* Boston: Pearson.

Russell, J.A., & Mehrabian, A. (1978). Approach-avoidance and affiliation as functions of the emotion-eliciting quality of an environment. *Environment and Behavior, 10*(3), 355–387.

Vinz, R. (1996). *Composing a teaching life.* Portsmouth: Boynton/Cook.

Zembylas, M. (2003). Caring for teacher emotion: Reflections on teacher self-development. *Studies in Philosophy and Education, 22*(2), 103–125.

FIVE

Finding Fragments and Locating Friction: Understanding Social Justice in the Postmodern World

Laura Bolf-Beliveau & Ralph Beliveau

Fragments of Power/Power in Fragments

As Miller and Kirkland say in their *Introduction*, social justice must be linked to English education, English education policy, and even education policy. By studying how habitus (per)forms research, this chapter focuses on ways in which students/researchers can (re)inform their practices to (re)consider human experience. Our method suggests that textual analysis, a mainstay of English education, can be reconstructed in a postmodern way to meet Miller and Kirkland's reflection, change, and participation. We also believe that social justice varies for individuals, and often begins with a sense of difference, what some (Bolf-Beliveau, 2007) call a disrupting force.

So as we consider studying social justice and priming it for action in research and our classrooms, difference offers an opportunity to go beyond color blindness, reductive identification, the melting pot, etc. Studying difference provides opportunities to see how habitus denies a fuller understanding of self/other. Audre Lorde (1983) believes "difference must not merely be tolerated, but seen as a fund of necessary polarities between which our creativity can spark like a dialectic" (p. 99). Through such dialectic, researchers and classroom practitioners can study the relationship between social justice and difference, see cultural frictions as something intellectually and spiritually pleasurable, and locate the power of difference.

Using this method of textual analysis, steeped in the traditions of post-modern rhetoric, we suggest that students (preservice teachers) and researchers (English educators) reexamine traditional analysis and move from the past to the future. We propose fluidity among/between various spaces for methodological change. Fragmentation is the key. Subverting the author/critic stance allows students/researchers not to be bound by traditional historical contexts. Rather, they create their own texts out of fragments of culture across time/space. This chapter provides readers with an application of the theory by connecting two fragments—the film *Half Nelson* and Barack Obama's March 18, 2008, speech on race.

Given the fluidity of difference and social justice, the method by which students and researchers study the field can create contexts that suggest or encourage individuals to subvert the traditional sense of texts, often described as apparently finished, bounded, self-contained (McGee, 1990, p. 280). McGee (1990) argues that the apparently finished text "is in fact a dense reconstruction of all the bits of other discourses from which it was made" (p. 279). In addition to looking back to sources, the apparently finished text anticipates its role in the world, projecting itself into a particular context. Both of these directions—the sources and the anticipation of power—typically urge a taken-as-given route to interpretation.

Often it is the habitus of students/researchers to work from the assumption that these two senses are the entirety of the meaning of the "completed" text, even though the need for such interpretation already insinuates that apparent completion is replaced by a fragmented text and bounded interpretation. The process of accessing meaning thus fails due to the same alienating excesses described in Paulo Freire's "banking model" (2002, p. 72). Interpretation arrives through the agency of the already empowered teacher, within an already recognized hierarchy. The window for social justice opens when the completed text is replaced by the sense of the text as fragmented. This fragmentation opens an opportunity for criticism and interpretation that allows students/researchers to create their own texts. Herein lies the empowerment—the ability of the individual students/researchers to articulate meaning connected to their own social, cultural, economic, etc., contexts.

Borrowing from McGee's (1998) performative criticism, also termed critical rhetoric, students/researchers are able to reflect, anticipate action, and play "in the presence of power" (p. 161). McGee (1998) believes, "Understanding power is thus always a question of interpreting fragments of it...Rhetoric has always been a study of influential fragments mobilized as a response to exigent situations" (p. 161). McGee's framework allows for fragments to be identified and connected for a richer understanding of the postmodern. Whereas traditional textual analysis sees the text as "intact" and presumes that the author has already constructed the meaning of the text, that approach is disempowering for students/researchers and runs contrary to social justice.

Our proposed framework suggests a method by which students/researchers look forward. We suggest empowering them with a method by which they look among apparently finished texts, seeing them as fragments and, "rewinding and fast-forwarding the stories over and over again, looking for the subtle themes, subtexts, and threads." (Corbin, 1998, p. vi). Corbin (1998) suggests that McGee's work "collapses the distinctions between language and action, or language and the material world, with instantiation of concepts and the dialogic process with which we recognize abstractions" (p. viii). McGee's (1998) "Fragments of Winter: Racial Discontents in American, 1992" presents a postmodern reading of King's *I Have a Dream* speech and Spike Lee's *Do the Right Thing*.

The method suggested here will pay close attention to the tension between the texts. Through this friction, a desirable state can emerge. Connecting fragments and finding friction should allow for an ethically pleasing state. There should not be a desire to efface difference but to find common substance in difference. This "in-between state" becomes the place where social justice can be discussed. As mentioned, performative criticism could, in its present design, work well as a methodological inquiry. Alternatively, the research practice involved could be described as a pedagogical approach, where students are guided to discover in their own connections between different fragments. Students/researchers could be empowered to see how fragments from their own experiences of friction lead them to grasp the advantages of seeing difference as a call to social justice.

Friction Mirrors Difference

Using McGee's own fragmented text, we decided to treat two recent cultural artifacts, Ryan Fleck's film *Half Nelson* (2006) and Barack Obama's speech (2008) on race, as fragments dependent upon each other for a sense of completion. They were chosen because we each found them incomplete. *Half Nelson* asks questions that are left unanswered. Obama's speech answers questions that are not fully formed. Here we perform an act of critical interpretation that seeks to frame the questions and answers as crucial to social justice.

The exigent circumstances of *Half Nelson* lie in the relationship between the protagonist Dan Dunne, an inner-city history teacher from a white, liberal background, and one of his students, an African American 13-year-old girl named Drey. In the film, the disrupting force of difference is experienced in the relationship between these two. Early in the film, Drey finds her teacher high in the girls' locker room. She takes care of him, and their relationship becomes complex as he teaches her, coaches her, and grows protective over her. Drey's home life is lonely; her divorced mother works double shifts, her father wants little to do with her, and her brother is in prison for selling drugs for a neighborhood dealer named Frank.

It is peculiar to consider the terms of a relationship between a young sensitive white man in a position of power and a young African American girl at the start of realizing her own social and sexual identity who, it becomes clear, both looks up to her teacher as an important part of her life and is in need of someone to step into the role of the absent father. One of the things that makes this film compelling, however, is how it uses this tension to remind us of the problems of power and justice that are inscribed in race, class, and gender terms. The relationship between these characters is fraught with potential disaster. Dunne is clearly capable of bad behavior, and Drey is clearly looking and asking all the people around her how she can become a person.

Drey struggles with the pull between the neighborhood and the financial security offered by Frank and dealing drugs, and the possibilities of future promised through education and Dunne. We can clearly see Drey acting out both scenarios as she confronts the boy who stole her bike as Frank cheers her on. Yet she also tries out the path of education as she and her classmates strive to understand dialectics through a variety of research projects highlighting historical events.

These two forces converge as Drey thinks about the future. She asks Dunne if he knew her brother and then says, "Think I could end up like him?" Unsure of what to say, Dunne's answer is, "Do you?" This response compels Dunne to confront Frank, the man for whom Drey's brother went to prison. Dunne seems convinced that Frank will cause Drey's downfall. Dunne finds Frank and says, "Okay, look, I hate to be this guy right now, right? But I need you to stay away from Drey." Frank protests, "Look, man, Drey is my family. She's my friend, man."

Frustrated, Dunne keeps pleading his case: "I'm telling you to do something good. Are you capable of that?" Frank responds, "So now we back to the point of what is white is right, right?" But he does not stop there; Frank has sold drugs to Dunne and sarcastically says, "It's good for Drey to have somebody like you looking out for her, Mr. Model A1 fucking citizen." Dunne's response is, "I don't know. I don't know. Because I'm supposed to do something, right? But what am I supposed to do?"

Both Dunne and Drey are frustrated in their search for identity. They are too constrained by the historically typical models (Frank, Drey's mother, Dunne's hypocritical liberal parents). So how can we move forward to forge new identities yet acknowledge a crucial understanding of history without being imprisoned by it?

This friction mirrors questions of difference in our postmodern context. We are tangibly aware of how easily things can go wrong, yet we are compelled to act because the need for just treatment in schools, in prisons, and in neighborhoods still suffering from a troubled history have not really arrived on an adequate set of ways of responding. This friction is the central problem framed in *Half Nelson*. A response is needed, but the correct response has not yet been realized.

From Fragments the Union Grows Stronger

Instead of being trapped by the past, we turn to Obama's speech as answer to the question of finding identity without being constrained by the past or ignoring it completely. The question of exigent circumstances that led to Obama's March 2008 speech on race included his presidential run as well as the proliferation of videos of the Reverend Jeremiah Wright from YouTube to conservative media to mainstream media. There was a need to frame racial relations within a new understanding of history.

Obama began his speech with this line from the Constitution, "We the people, in order to form a more perfect union." Although 220 years have passed since those words were written, Obama noted, the document remained "unfinished." Obama's goal in the speech was to reframe history, which at that moment suffered from enormous amounts of distortion that happened both in Wright's speeches as well as the way they were framed in popular media.

Wright's distortions were born out of an over identification with the frustrations and failures in the history of the civil rights movement. Obama was not suggesting that they be ignored; he was suggesting that they be embraced but seen as a trap if they constrained an understanding of where race relations needed to go. Past injuries were justifiably painful in the experience of the generation of civil rights activists (like Wright), but if the pain resulted in resentment, it also resulted in immobility. When Obama said of Wright, "I can no more disown him than I can disown the black community. I can no more disown him than I can my white grandmother," he was ultimately answering a question of identity and noted, "These people are a part of me. And they are a part of America, this country that I love."

To illustrate his point, Obama recalled a story of a young white girl, Ashley, and an "elderly black man." Ashley was an Obama community organizer working in a mostly African American neighborhood in Florence, South Carolina. At a roundtable event, Ashley told of her mother's battle with cancer and the family's descent into bankruptcy. Only a child at the time, Ashley convinced her mother that she loved to eat "mustard and relish sandwiches," one of the cheapest meals. She did this until her mother's health improved and she could go back to work.

After finishing her story of how her mother's plight encouraged her to work for Obama's campaign, she asked everyone around the table "why they were there." An elderly black man replied, "I am here because of Ashley." In his speech on race, Obama said, "'I'm here because of Ashley.' By itself, that single moment of recognition between that young white girl and that old black man is not enough. It is not enough to give health care to the sick, or jobs to the jobless, or education to our children." Obama's comment is reminiscent of Dunne's question in *Half Nelson*, "Because I am supposed to do something, right? But what am I supposed to do?"

Obama (March 18, 2008) answers the question in the last paragraph of the speech. Perhaps "I am here for Ashley" is not enough,

> But it is where we start. It is where our union grows stronger. And as so many generations have come to realize over the course of the two hundred and twenty-one years since a band of patriots signed that document in Philadelphia, that is where the perfection begins.

Obama's speech answers the question by suggesting a starting point that does not merely end with the sentiment, "I've done enough."

This fragment of Obama's speech completes the ending of *Half Nelson* where Dunne's course of self-destruction meets with Drey's hopeful course of action. Friendship will heal. Drey finds a hung-over Dunne, whose party friends have left him, and insists that she is still his friend. Her actions—getting Dunne out of his self-destructive course, taking him home and cleaning him up, being there for him as a friend when everyone else is gone—these are the actions borne out of hope, concern, and perhaps even love. At the end of the film, Dunne may not have found the answer for what he is supposed to do, but it is a starting point, and it may be where the perfection begins.

Endings Are New Beginnings

So the question, "What do I do?" is answered: Don't lose hope and embrace the contradictions of the past as well as the contradictions of the future. Our histories need to be understood, but they must not become a constraint, or we lose the hope of self-actualization that is the root of social justice in all students and teachers. Our future needs to be framed as a hope for the perfectability of our relations among one other.

This postmodern form of textual analysis could disrupt the classroom and (re)inform habitus, afflicting the comfortable teacher and comforting the afflicted student. To gain the most out of these changes, classroom participants should begin this process by considering these questions:

- How could English educators reflect on current curricula and then adapt it to identify and interpret fragments? Using this postmodern textual analysis, how could English educators also reflect on their roles as both teacher and learner?

- What tools do teachers need to help students explore the benefits of friction? What changes in current practice could help students/researchers find friction and understand difference as they link fragments?

- In what ways can we encourage participation to help communicate to students that this process could articulate their own theory and practice? How can we learn to be patient with fragment connections that make sense to them but not us?

- Finally, could this method feed the desire to embrace friction, to seek it out? The best sign of success, we believe, is when students find connections between fragments but still understand they are not complete. How can all classroom participants embrace the dialectical sense of difference?

There might be pain and frustration along the way, and we acknowledge our potential to stumble into nostalgia, or to be constrained by ignorance. But the hope for justice is a belief that these, too, shall pass, that our concern for each other, our ability to care for a mutual outcome, can break the walls of future action erected by our failures and our fears. On this path, the pedagogy and practice of care and hope replace both the cynical idea that things will never change as well as the frustrations of not really being sure who we are or what we ought to do. Our identities, our understandings of history, and our hope for the future are all flawed, but it is in the potential for correcting those flaws that we strive for social justice.

Bibliography

Bolf-Beliveau, L. (2007). *English/language arts teachers' emotional responses to difference: A feminist poststructural analysis*. Ph.D. Dissertation, The University of Oklahoma. Retrieved January 15, 2009, from Dissertations & Theses @ University of Oklahoma database. (Publication No. AAT 3284123).

Corbin, C. (Ed.). (1998). *Rhetoric in Postmodern America: Conversations with Michael Calvin McGee*. New York: Guilford.

Fleck, R. (Director). (2006). *Half Nelson*. [Motion Picture]. U.S.: Sony Pictures.

Freire, P. (2002). *Pedagogy of the Oppressed: 30th Anniversary Edition*. New York: Continuum.

Lorde, A. (1983). The master's tools will never dismantle the master's house. In C. Moraga & G. Anzaldúa (Eds.), *This bridge called my back: Writings by radical women of color* (pp. 98–101). New York: Kitchen Table, Women of Color Press.

McGee, M.C. (1990). Text, context, and the fragmentation of contemporary culture. *Western Journal of Speech Communication, 54*, 274–289.

McGee, M.C. (1998). Fragments of winter: Racial discontents in America, 1992. In C. C. Corbin (Ed.), *Rhetoric in Postmodern America: Conversations with Michael Calvin McGee* (pp. 159–188). New York: Guildford.

Obama, Barack. (2008, March 18). Transcript: Barack Obama's speech on race. *The New York Times*. Retrieved from http://www.nytimes.com.

Six

Youth Writing Across Media: A Note About the What and the How

Korina M. Jocson

Many qualitative researchers whose frameworks draw from feminist, post-modern, and critical theories have raised questions about various forms of domination. They, in turn, have demanded the use of critical research for establishing a more democratic social order. According to Kincheloe and McLaren (1998), a critical researcher is someone who announces partisanship in the struggle for a better world, someone who enters an investigation with her/his subjective and self-conscious criticism of power relations. He/She is someone who lays these views out on the table, with social justice in mind through social inquiry, critique, and action. While these are made explicit, the term "critical" alone does not fully capture what informs my research and my role as a researcher. "Multicultural" is another ideological term that needs to be considered. From it springs forth experience with various populations and cultures that are key in alleviating human struggle. This experience is important if one is to engage in work that renders social justice as an objective. In light of such work, this chapter first delves into the critical and the multicultural, and later illustrates the connections of this particular lens to a study on youth writing across media.

Critical and Multicultural

In today's historical bloc of increased/ing diversity, many researchers are drawn to how the concept of "Self-Other" unfolds in research. For example, Fine (1998) explores the notion behind "working the hyphen" where the hyphen "both separates and merges personal identities with our inventions of 'Others'"; that is, it un-packs what is in "between." It reveals self while defining the other, and vice versa, a negotiation that at the very least confronts dominant ideologies, practices, and perspectives in research. As a Filipina American studying youth across racial and ethnic groups, I build on the complexities of this hyphen in order to break free from objective accounts of the "Other." This "Othering" is what Rosaldo (1989) has long since critiqued in colonial studies—a positivist, "third world" phenom-enon during the earlier moments of qualitative research. The integral multicultur-alist stance to which I subscribe draws on this critique and further challenges uni-versal forms of knowledge that presently shape how researchers see themselves in local communities whenever they observe, analyze, and document the "Other." As a critical researcher, it is important to weigh in on the influences of what I call "multicultural hybridities" from varied experiences that contour subjectivities and positionalities. Often, these are molded within existing relations of power through markers of difference such as race, ethnicity, class, gender, sexuality, and language, among others. By multicultural, I mean the multiplicity of cultures emerging from heterogeneity or the blending (often blurring) of varied experiences in different contexts, a dramatic change that alters "the way we think about ourselves" (Takaki, 1993, p. 2). The familiar becomes unfamiliar in new cultural terrains, allowing us a chance for reflection and action. In other words, the many cultural interactions I have had from varied experiences in different contexts influence how I formulate the questions I ask, methods I use, and interpretations I make. As Denzin and Lincoln (1998) point out, it is from this notion of blurring and concern for repre-sentation that define the movement toward future moments in qualitative research. Thus, the term "critical" forms the basis of my approach, while "multicultural" guides my ability to be self-reflexive. These are two paradigmatic sites significant to the methodological designs of my research. Together, critical multiculturalism has become the lens through which I seek an understanding of youth's experiences with writing as well as other literacies.

Specifically, I draw from one study conducted at a racially diverse compre-hensive high school in northern California. There, I worked directly with teachers, students, and student-teacher-poets from a local university to examine the pres-ence of June Jordan's Poetry for the People program in English classes. Details of the program, pedagogy, curriculum, and teachers' and students' experiences have been described elsewhere (Jocson, 2008). Likewise, in another study conducted at a different high school with similar characteristics, I examined the literacy learn-ing processes of students as related to new media technologies in both English and social studies. In brief, I was active in the development of the studies both as a researcher and as a co-teacher in the classroom. Critical ethnography al-lowed me to reveal my value orientation as a critical researcher and, more impor-tant, guided me to recognize the epistemological shifts surrounding power/truth, facts/values, and symbolic representation during the investigation (Carspecken, 1996). I utilized various methods to collect data, including field notes, student and teacher interviews, student and teacher survey-evaluations, and videotaped class-room episodes. I also gathered curricular texts and materials, printed and digital artifacts, student-produced audio and video projects, student official records, and school- and district-wide data. Consistent with critical multiculturalism, it was important to pay attention to the ways culture and power relations were being disrupted in students' writing and other types of production. Central in my in-vestigation were the complex social, cultural, historical, and political contexts in which they were situated. It was important to aim for a constant examination and analysis of data that shaped the interpretation of findings. Patterns surfaced to distinguish the epistemological shifts in researching youth and, ultimately, youth's representation in research. I recognized, for example, the value of consulting youth themselves and following their lead to arrive at specific interpretations. Shadowing participants in their natural environments was as essential as it was in-sightful. Additionally, the inclusion of participants' voices drawn from interview transcripts or excerpts from whole works produced in and outside of class was a conscious decision during the write up.

Data Analysis and Considerations in Youth Poetry

Researchers on literacy development have positioned multiliteracies at the center of pedagogy in order to further shape the ways in which students learn. To de-velop categories for analyzing a complex mosaic of data sources in my research, I used Street's (1984) ideological model of viewing literacy as being inextricably linked to power and cultural structures in society. The view embraces a variety of cultural practices associated with reading and writing in different contexts. I employed Street's concept of *literacy practice* to analyze students' engagement with poetry in relation to their everyday interactions and relationships. Whether in school or elsewhere, the dominant culture with its rules and norms served as the backdrop for these interactions and relationships. To clarify, literacy practice as used here means any goal-oriented or valued activity recurring in one's natural environment (Scribner & Cole, 1981), including, but are not limited to, writing, reading, or performing poetry. Building on this definition, I extended Street's concept to include multiple literacies, taking into account literate practices that involve cultural media forms such as television, film, music, and others. While this is so, inherent in such literacy practices are also issues of control, power, and access that allow youth with ease to consume but not produce media. In these new media times, it is important to recognize the dialectical relationship between consumption and production and what it means for youth who actively engage various media forms. Arguably, dissemination through do-it-yourself technologies is another consideration as more digital media tools become available and accessible to users, including children and youth. Many young people are not only consuming cultural media, but also producing and distributing their own. Thus, it is crucial to understand reading and writing as broadly construed. In trying to understand students' poems, I examined students' literate activities associated with mediums beyond conventional meanings of reading and writing such as performing onstage, watching movies, listening to music, or producing their own media. Embedded in the poems were literal and figurative meanings reifying students' experiences situated within the dominant culture and, as will be pointed out, choosing to use specific cultural tools to challenge or disrupt it.

The framework shown in Figure 10.1 identifies the three domains of poetry used for analyzing student poetry. Process, product, and practice propelled me to probe deeper into how poetry manifested in the everyday lives of students while keeping in mind their common experiences in Poetry for the People. Briefly, for *process*, I drew on Vygotsky's (1978) theories of learning to delineate processes that arise from an individual's zone of proximal development. I also borrowed Bakhtin's (1935/1981) notion of dialogic encounters to address the social aspects of learning and interaction. For *product*, I turned to Wenger's (1998) definition of reification to argue that poetry gives form to one's experience. For *practice*, I used Street's (1984) understanding of literacy as a social practice that is linked to cultural and power structures in society. Through the process, product, and practice

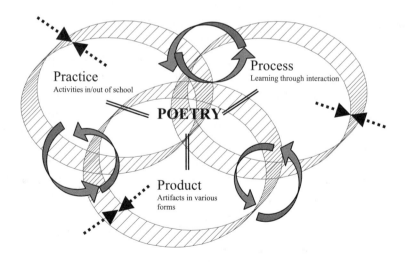

Figure 10.1: Organizing framework for examining poetry.

(PPP) framework, what seemed disparate and disconnected at first turned out to be patterns in students' personal narratives, poems, and other literacy artifacts. These patterns were indicative of the institutional, cultural, and social structures that shaped students' experiences in school and in other contexts (represented by perforated arrows in Figure 10.1). Below is a look at one student's experience with and beyond poetry.

Writing Poetry and Writing Across Media

African American Naier was a sixteen-year-old sophomore in high school when he participated in June Jordan's Poetry for the People program in his English class. His interest in writing extended to his senior year during which he produced mixed-media poetry based on the poems he had written for Poetry for the People. At the time of the study, Naier listened to various types of music from contemporary jazz to neo-soul, R&B, and rap that he considered poetry too. Artists he followed at the time included Najee, Jill Scott, Alicia Keys, Musiq Soulchild, Nas, Missy Elliott, Cee-Lo, Talib Kweli, Mos Def, and Goapele. One of these artists was integral to the production of a mixed-media poem. To make sense of his surroundings, Naier found it essential to reflect and write about forms of oppression and other social ills that he witnessed daily. He noted the importance of poetry in his life:

> If you drive down [name of] Street, in a sense you kind of feel like it's a burnt out city…as if you were living in some other country and where…they don't have any money and the buildings are all desecrated and burnt down or smoked out…You see that, when you're sitting on the bus. And you know seeing it. And then I just rap about it. I rhyme about it. I write poetry about it, because I want it to change.

These extemporaneous markings from bus rides and other social encounters shaped his writing, subsequently producing a poem entitled "Wastes Away" to represent a critical response to his slain brother's lifestyle (see lines 1–26 in Appendix 10.1). The poem paints a picture of what he hopes to change. This personal response is what Kelley (1994) articulates as working-class black youth participating in forms of politics and acts of resistance, or as race rebels in postindustrial working-class communities. The writing—whether through poetry or other cultural productions—serves as a symbolic representation of lived experiences. This is important to highlight given the pathological nature of cultural explanations that feeds already existing misrepresentations of youth, particularly youth of color from poor and working-class backgrounds. Through a critical multicultural lens, I was able to deconstruct with Naier not only the role of poetry in his life, but the layers of meaning reflective of his and his brother's social realities that are present in the poem. I asked open-ended questions that were guided by my own subjectivity and cultural experience in similar environments he talks about. As he responded, I opted for more questions and let the conversation serve as a conduit for speaking his "truth."

Wastes Away #2

1   as he twists and turns through life
his soul turns from divine to unkind from time
will he forever be punished for past sins of his lifetime
as he dies, i see the whites of his eyes turn red from greed
5   he feels the need to lie, cheat, and steal
all to make that bill he thinks he needs so badly
but doesn't he see that while he's a G
that his gun is destroying reality for you and me
doesn't he realize that he's erased the tracks
10   made by the broken backs of his ancestors
but as proceeds his family bleeds
the pain which he causes
and as time pauses he falls into a cycle of ill-begotten dreams
that shatter like glass that last for a lifetime
15   he says that he loves his life
but is cold enough to take another
he wants his family to love each other
but cannot love his baby's mother
he is running for cover
20   as the cold hard wind of reality hits his face
and the sun rises up from the shadows
and shines the last hint of darkness away
he stays away from the light
afraid that his mask will decay
25   and dare I say
he wastes away
awww
look what happened to you
got shot like a fool
30   on life support
six inches from that basket called a casket
I heard shots fired, screeching of raw tires
I saw your body there
motionless and expired
35   why did you have to leave, why did you have to die
I never knew you, but i can't

'cause some dumb niggas screwed you
as I lay a rose on your casket I pray to god
that one day I will meet you some day
40 hopefully
one day
you never saw the bite of the snake
until the venom killed you
and I prayed to god every day that he's with you
45 I miss you
I wish you could teach me all the things
like how to get that and hit that
and deal with the girls who never used to call back
I wish I could rewind back
50 tell you to solve your problems with liquor
they only make your problems come quicker
and make you sicker
because when death was knocking at your front door
you were too drunk to listen
55 you died by the gun, that's the way you went out
pouring liquor blazing the trigger with glory without a doubt
but whose glory
my story
ain't goin out like that
60 awww
black brotha
stripped from my mother
too soon and broomed
with brothers to an early tomb
65 society's poster child
for destruction and gloom created for doom
black brotha
descended from slaves
locked in iron chains
70 behind steel bar cages
that lasted ages then to now
black brotha
spits bars in Cadillac cars
behind school parking lots
75 showing
WHY HE DON'T GET SERVED

During his senior year in high school, Naier participated in an after-school Digital Visual (DV) Poetry program. As a part of his literacy practice, he revisited the original poem "Wastes Away" in order to produce a video poem that ultimately combined two other poems entitled "Fool" (lines 28–59) and "Black Brotha" (lines 61–76). The three poems are distinguished by the sound unit "awww" (in lines 27 and 60). As revealed in an interview, Naier brought together the essence of three poems to create a larger revelatory piece that would complement other materials in his college application portfolio. This new version called "Wastes Away #2" raises concerns about cultural and power structures that constrain and, in the case of his brother, victimize black youth in society. As a researcher aware of the re-productive consequences of such structures, I keyed in on what Naier had to say and how he represented his concerns in the video poem. I wanted to understand his subjectivities that provided the circumstances and events that unfolded in his life to shape his decisions. Beyond race, class, and gender, there were sets of social conditions that only he could illuminate for the researcher (and for the researcher to document with keen awareness its potential to offer insights into particular issues some black youth face in American society). "Wastes Away #2" begins with a statement that reads "dedicated to my / big brother / Andre / I miss you kid," a clear indication of Naier's inspiration and purpose for the production. It is then followed by his narrating voice.

To understand the poem is to understand the actual production. Briefly, for three months as a participant of DV Poetry, Naier collected various Internet images using Google and other search engines, sketched a storyboard, laid down an audio track (his own voice), inserted instrumental rap music ("Nas Is Like" by artist Nas), and with the assistance of program instructors meshed these poetic compositions together to create a five-minute video using an editing software called Adobe Premiere. After the credits roll and the background music stops at the end of the video, the phrase "to be continued" appears on the left-bottom screen connoting that, as long as the issues Naier tackles in his poetry exist, his interest in writing (and in this case other types of productions) will also continue.

Content analysis of Naier's video poem "Wastes Away #2" yields a number of visual representations. Among them are slaves and torturous acts to depict slavery; dollar bills to stand for capitalism; liquor and guns to associate with drugs and crime; children and families to denote unity; open paths, meadows; and the cosmos to allude to the future or uncertainty. The sounds (voice and music) and images (words and photographs) on the edited timeline afford layered meanings that otherwise might be circumvented by a lone written text (i.e., a printed poem). Editing effects such as zoom, dissolve, fade, and motion (31 in total), as well as the placement of words on the screen (24 in total) and the use of red-color fonts (2 in total) for emphasis also give additional texture to the production. Indeed, features of multimodality contribute to the production's design and make possible hybrid discourses within a text. The making of Naier's five-minute video consisted of more than lacing of words, images, voice, music, and transitional effects on a time line. It involved structuring ideas and meanings to be represented multimodally with new media writing tools. At the very least, it involved manipulating 26 different photographic images and corresponding them with multiple poetic verses. It points to the significance of multimodality in youth's literacy practices. It also raises questions about what it takes to examine threaded written and visual literacies in multimedia composition. Indeed, the difficulty in analyzing multimedia's constructed meanings has been discussed by others (see, for example, Burn & Parker, 2003; Hull & Nelson, 2005). Focusing on the intertextualities within Naier's video poem as a result of dialogic encounters with prior texts further sheds light on the topic.

To probe deeper into Naier's production, I discuss elsewhere (Jocson, forthcoming) specific aspects in "Wastes Away #2," including multiple layers of emulation that further exemplify the nature of dialogism (Bakhtin, 1981, 1986; Kristeva, 1980). For instance, Naier's use of Nas' instrumental song, on the one hand, reflects his affinity to rap music and rap artists as part of his literacy practice; on the other, it represents an emulation of style and form to produce another text. Nas' song "Nas Is Like" from the album *I Am*, released in 1999, addresses similar social conditions as in Naier's poem. The first verse of the song contains references to freedom, pain, struggle, drugs, guns, and survival. According to Naier, it was a conscious choice to use only the instrumental version of the song in order to lay a new voiceover (his own) and create a multimedia text from the perspective of another young black male (his). Lacing his words with carefully selected images from the Internet was part of the creativity that Naier had hoped would convey part of a larger message about present-day social inequities. For the researcher, the careful attention to Naier's production—the what and the how—was deliberate. It was important to listen to explanations he offered about lacing three original poems together with image and sound. It was important to analyze the video poem as situated within cultural and power structures, to recognize that cultural productions are constructed in dialectic ways. Naier consumed media to produce his own media and along the way raised similar issues relevant to black youth, also present in rapper Nas' song. What this suggests is Naier's disruption of perceived norms about young black males and their experiences in American society, a point of clarification on his end, perhaps a node of inquiry yet to be rendered by others.

Conclusion

A brief account of research on youth poetry highlighted the importance of process, product, and practice. Critical multiculturalism served as a lens. It was important to delineate the relationship between the critical and the multicultural to make explicit the purpose of research as well as the role of the researcher. The case of a student writing poetry and writing across media illustrated the ways in which the researcher's value orientations shaped the questions asked, the methods used, and the interpretations made. However, such orientations alone do not generate the knowledge necessary to help us as educators and researchers to think in transformative ways about youth. The patterns that surfaced from poems, videos, interviews, and other data led to epistemological shifts that provide alternative explanations about youth, youth culture, and youth cultural practices. That is, youth are active consumers as well as knowledge producers who with support from others are able to participate in the democratic order and confront social inequities in their lives. These epistemological shifts in qualitative research would serve us well in order to achieve the following:

- Increase the possibilities for better serving youth, particularly youth of color from poor and working-class backgrounds, as they negotiate their personal, social, and academic lives in and out of school.

- Support future investigations employing various methods and approaches in an attempt to understand the growing cultural phenomenon of youth poetry and other related artistic forms across contexts.

The work will require asking harder questions and employing more sophisticated tools of analysis. Hopefully, past and present efforts will propel us forward into new directions in literacy and youth studies. The call to do socially just work is without human struggle in tow.

Bibliography

Bakhtin, M.M. (1935/1981). *The dialogic imagination.* Austin, TX: University of Texas Press.

Bakhtin, M.M. (1986). *Speech genres and other late essays.* Austin, TX: University of Texas Press.

Burn, A., & Parker, D. (2003). *Analyzing media texts.* London: Contiuum.

Carspecken, P.F. (1996). *Critical ethnography in educational research: A theoretical and practical guide.* New York: Routledge.

Denzin, N.K., & Lincoln, Y. (1998). Introduction: Entering the field of qualitative research. In N.K. Denzin & Y. Lincoln (Eds.), *The landscape of qualitative research: Theories and issues* (pp. 1-34). Thousand Oaks, CA: Sage.

Fine, M. (1998). Working the hyphens: Reinventing self and other in qualitative research. In N.K. Denzin & Y. Lincoln (Eds.), *The landscape of qualitative research: Theories and issues* (pp. 130-155). Thousand Oaks, CA: Sage.

Hull, G., & Nelson, M. (2005). Locating the semiotic power of multimodality. *Written Communication, 22*(2), 1-38.

Jocson, K.M. (2008). *Youth poets: Empowering literacies in and out of schools.* New York: Peter Lang.

Jocson, K.M. (2010). Unpacking symbolic creativities: Writing in school and across contexts. *Review of Education, Pedagogy and Cultural Studies, 32* (2), 206–236.

Kelley, R. (1994). *Race rebels: Culture, politics, and the Black working class.* New York: The Free Press.

Kincheloe, J., & McLaren, P. (1998). Rethinking critical theory and qualitative research. In N.K. Denzin & Y. Lincoln (Eds.), *The landscape of qualitative research: Theories and issues* (pp. 130-155). Thousand Oaks, CA: Sage.

Kristeva, J. (1980). *Desire in language: A semiotic approach to literature and art.* New York: Columbia University Press.

Rosaldo, R. (1989). *The culture and truth: The remaking of social analysis.* Boston: Beacon.

Scribner, S., & Cole, M. (1981). *The psychology of literacy.* Cambridge, MA: Harvard University Press.

Street, B. (1984). *Literacy in theory and practice.* Cambridge, UK: Cambridge University Press.

Street, B. (Ed.) (1993). *Cross-cultural approaches to literacy.* Cambridge, UK: Cambridge University Press.

Takaki, R. (1993). *A different mirror: A history of multicultural America.* Boston: Back Bay.

Vygotsky, L. (1978). *Mind and society: The development of higher psychological processes.* Cambridge: Harvard University Press.

Wenger, E. (1998). *Communities of practice: Learning, meaning, and identity.* Cambridge, UK: Cambridge University Press.

SEVEN

Literacies and Identities for All

Margaret Hagood

Allie Feng: I like to read English and Chinese stuff, but Chinese stuff takes a lot longer. So I sometimes give up after a while. But in English I like to read mystery stuff. I really, really love it. In Chinese stuff, I usually read about sixth grade, seventh grade because I can actually understand it. I'd love to read something harder, but I just can't do it.

Margaret: Do you like to read mysteries in Chinese?

Allie Feng: Uh, no. In Chinese, I like to read about normal people's lives. I don't know. It's like I'm kind of living it, and I didn't really get a chance to do that since I moved here [to the United States]. But yeah—

Margaret: Do you have access to any of that at school?

Allie Feng: (Bewildered expression on her face.) The Chinese stuff? Uh, no!

Margaret: Where do you get it?

Allie Feng: China. You can't really even get it here because it's really overpriced.

Allie Feng (pseudonym) was a seventeen-year-old high school senior who moved with her parents for a two-year period to the U.S. when she was eight. Nine years later, the family still lives in the U.S., and they have decided to become American citizens. As Allie demonstrates in this brief excerpt taken from a larger study of literacy, learning, and identities using new literacies' tools of digital storytelling, her literacy interests are closely tied to American and Chinese identities she espouses within different communities (Skinner & Hagood, 2008).

In this essay, I briefly examine how literacy and identities are central to an emphasis on social justice in education. I outline several principles of social justice and describe how research and instruction about these relationships hold potential for furthering the work of social justice in educational settings.

Situating Literacy in Social Justice

In *Social Justice in Education: An Introduction*, Barry Bull (2008) outlines principles of social justice via four educational purposes. These include (1) personal liberty: developing students' concepts of what to pursue and what's worth pursuing; (2) democracy: engaging students in the evolutionary process of overlapping consensus; (3) equality of opportunity: cultivating students' attention to fair allocations of prospects; and (4) economic growth: building students' understanding of the role of economy in relation to pursuits.

The field of literacy education is ripe for bringing these four principles of social justice to fruition. Three shifts in literacy education that have occurred over the last thirty years align with principles of social justice and signal implications for research and practice so as to acknowledge and develop literacies and identities for all.

Shifts in the Foci of Literacy Studies

The first shift in literacy education that speaks to principles of social justice is the social turn (Street, 1984). This movement of research and ultimately of practice reallocated attention from an autonomous, purely cognitive view of reading and writing as an acquisition of universal, individually learned skills to an interactive view of reading and writing that is situated in and deeply influenced by social practice. From a sociocultural perspective, reading and writing develop in context—in community—and different communities read and write in different ways. Communities of practice privilege some forms of literacy over others. In Allie Feng's world, for example, she negotiated several competing communities of practice while navigating literacy learning in English and Chinese. She discussed how her language and text use changed by context and how her pleasures for reading and writing shifted, dependent upon her identities.

The social turn also opened the field of literacy studies to consider variables not considered up to that point. Context, experience, and background became foci for learning about communities and individuals' valued literacies. Moreover, by studying community literacy practices, it became apparent that literacy encompasses more than the ability to read, write, and make meaning with print-based texts.

A second delineation of the social turn highlights the connections between literacy and identity. The social aspect of literacy calls attention to users' interactions and text engagements and the concomitant identities that produce and are produced by text users. A multitude of studies have examined literacy and identity and participation. Most of these studies illustrate the complex negotiations that take place between literacy and identity (e.g., Black, 2006; Blackburn, 2002; Lewis & Fabos, 2005). Often text users construct their own uses of texts that reflect identities and subjectivities that they desire others to associate with them. For Allie Feng, as with most people, literacy and identity are closely linked. The kinds of identities she desires to know about and enact for herself drive the kinds of texts she chooses to read. As a result of her family's move to the U.S., she missed out on experiences of middle childhood identities in China. Now she spends time learning about those identities when reading books in Chinese. Conversely, her fluidity in English allows her to explore identities associated with adult motives and ideas found in mysteries that she so enjoys.

Thus, these two shifts in literacy studies—the social turn and a focus on identity—allow for a more equitable view of literacy. Deepening our understandings of how different groups' literacy practices in community and the various identities they construct of literacies, including various modalities such as oral language, storytelling, designing, writing, drawing, etc., supports personal liberties of different ways to develop knowledge and views of selfhood. A focus on identity also deepens understanding of democracy to build consensus among a group of readers with whom we share these identities and literacy interests.

A third shift in literacy education that opens possibilities for bringing social justice principles to fruition is the focus on new literacies (including media and technologies) associated with the technological boom that has impacted the ways that we use literacies and interact with one another (Lankshear & Knobel, 2006). The shift from Web 1.0 to 2.0 tools illustrates how literacies, identities, and learning are morphing and changing. These shifts have resulted in "participatory cultures" (Jenkins, 2006), which "shift the focus of literacy from one of individual expression to community involvement" (p. 4) and involve four forms: affiliations (such as social networking sites), expressions (such as creations of mash ups or fan fiction writing), collaborative problem solving (teamwork for the development of new knowledge), and circulation (ways to shape the flow of knowledge through media). Thus, working with new literacies, users collaborate, design, network with and mentor one another, deepening their understandings and uses of literacies in communal ways.

Reflecting on a digital story she constructed about her literacies and identities, Allie Feng noted:

I wrote the stuff first (on my computer). And it was like all ideas just pouring out. And after I wrote it up I tried to find pictures to put with the words. And then I worked with a friend to scan the pictures because some of them were really old, and I didn't have them in a digital format... Then I put them in story [Photo Story] and found music that fit for the background.

Although Allie completed this digital story as an independent project, she collaborated with a friend and used several kinds of texts (words, pictures, music) to give depth to her story. These new literacies practices came easily to her, having grown up using such technologies in her day-to-day life.

These three shifts have moved away from an individualistic, private view of the world as information processing (relative to behaviorism and cognitive revolution), embracing instead the influences of community and context in developing literacies. These shifts highlight the need to develop both technical and social skills to be able to engage in a 21st-century world.

Advancing Social Justice through Research and Practice

It is important to understand how connections between literacy and identity impact each other. Brandt and Clinton (2002) remind us that "understanding what literacy is doing with people in a setting is as important as understanding what people are doing with literacy in a setting" (p. 337). That literacies and identities impact and are impacted by users is key for helping develop more socially just approaches that validate personal liberty, democracy, equal opportunity, and economic growth. Instructional practices and research are central components in making a more just society, and teachers and researchers must be front and center in building a democratic education for students. This work can be developed through attention to three areas of developing literacies, identities, and participation for all.

First, multimodal texts must be assumed into the larger educational curriculum, not just included as an add-on course or activity to the language arts program (Knobel & Lankshear, 2007). Changes in developing literacies should result in a paradigm shift that reshapes how we approach teaching existing subject matter (Jenkins, 2006). Literacy instruction must inherently include both the tools and the shift in mind-set of how texts are used. Instruction must be built on a multiplicitous view of literacy that targets the acquisition of print skills and that attends to other affordances, such as visual and iconic texts, along with study of the related social and collaborative practices. Doing so provides equal opportunities for learners to demonstrate their literacy competencies and to develop new ones. Research must examine how students view literacies in a context where multimodalities are viewed as literacy and how personal liberties and identities are related to such views.

Second, instructional practices must provide opportunities for students to develop and hone literacies that are important for productive citizenry and potential jobs. Thus, it is imperative for students to have access to and instruction with new literacies and technologies in schools. A focus on explicit instruction is key to begin to address gaps in uses of multimodal texts. Educators cannot assume that students have access to or are adept with multimodal texts, and the need for explicit instruction is paramount for equal opportunities for students to develop these competencies. Others have discussed the import of explicit instruction in models of literacy that account for 21st-century texts. The New London Group (1996) called for the development of a metalanguage to assist learners in reflecting upon uses of texts, and Jenkins (2006) reported that overt instruction is a central component for success with media education.

The explosion of texts fundamentally changes not only users' capabilities but their possibilities for text uses. To prepare learners for productive citizenry and lives and to be a part of economic growth, learners need explicit instruction and time to explore tools of multimodal texts. Examples include how to construct a digital movie, to engage in social networking online, to conduct research on the Internet, to type on a keyboard, to scan images to upload, to name a few. Beyond addressing the technicalities of textual tools, explicit instruction should address engagement with multimodal literacy practices. This focus needs to connect users to the multimodality of contemporary life.

Researchers must work collaboratively with teachers to study how students work together and collaborate as they develop these skills. They must use methodologies that will highlight relationships and identities formed in these collaborative practices.

Instruction needs to include technical skills of tools of texts, adapted traditional skills such as researching and synthesizing information, social skills necessary for collaboration and networking, critical literacy skills necessary to make informed decisions about meaning and uses of texts, as well as honed skills for ethical practice (Bruce, 2002; O'Brien, Stewart, & Beach, 2009). Such instruction needs to assist users in developing critical consumer stances and in formulating critical perspectives of text design.

Third, instructional time must include projects for students to study the relationships between their own text use and their identities. Students must develop their own understandings of identities that are central to their lives and how these identities work in relation to others' identities in the community. Students must also be able to connect identities to media uses and have opportunities and supervision to develop critical awareness of the ethical choices and responsibilities that should shape their literacy practices. Much has been written of late describing the various kinds of identity research that has been conducted and how various perspectives illustrate different uses of identities (e.g., Hagood, 2008; Lewis &

Del Valle, 2009). Delving deeply into identities aids in the developing knowledge of the workings of democracy within classroom settings. Working with students to identify appropriate audience engagement (including voice and content) using various identities in online contexts is one such example.

Issues of social justice are paramount for meaningfully engaging literacies in schools and communities.

> An attention to social justice must foster students' ability and willingness to participate in public decision making processes so that they acknowledge and respect the other political commitments of their society and so that they make constructive contributions to, learn from, and act on the results of those processes in both their own and others' communities. (Bull, 2008, p. 33)

The work of literacy educators and researchers must include opportunities to learn about these texts, to explore identities they create and are created for/about them from texts, and to participate in instructional practices that deepen their understanding of connections between themselves and others. Then we will be able to align the work in literacy education with the aims of personal liberty, democracy, equal opportunity, and economic growth as principles of social justice.

Bibliography

Black, R. W. (2006). Language, culture, and identity in online fanfiction. *E-Learning, 3,* 170–184.

Blackburn, M. (2002). Disrupting the (hetero)normative: Exploring literacy performances and identity work with queer youth. *Journal of Adolescent & Adult Literacy, 46,* 312–325.

Brandt, D., & Clinton, K. (2002). Limits of the local: Expanding perspectives of literacy as a social practice. *Journal of Literacy Research, 34,* 337–356.

Bruce, B. (2002). Diversity and critical social engagement: How changing technologies enable new modes of literacy in changing circumstances. In D. Alvermann (Ed.), *Adolescents and literacies in a digital world* (pp. 1–18). New York: Peter Lang.

Bull, B. L. (2008). *Social justice in education: An introduction.* New York: Palgrave Macmillan.

Hagood, M. C. (2008). Intersections of popular culture, identities, and new literacies research. In J. Coiro, D. Leu, M. Knobel, & C. Lankshear (Eds.), *Handbook of research on new literacies* (pp. 531–551). New York: Peter Lang.

Jenkins, H. (2006). *Confronting the challenges of participatory culture: Media education for the 21st century.* Chicago: The MacArthur Foundation.

Knobel, M., & Lankshear, C. (2007). Sampling "the new" in new literacies. In M. Knobel & C. Lankshear (Eds.), *A new literacies sampler* (pp. 1–24). New York: Peter Lang.

Lankshear, C., & Knobel, M. (2006). *New literacies: Everyday practices and classroom learning* (2nd ed.). New York: Peter Lang.

Lewis, C., & Del Valle, A. (2009). Literacy and identity: Implications for research and practice. In L. Christenbury, R. Bomer, & P. Smagorinsky (Eds.), *Handbook of adolescent literacy research* (pp. 307–322). New York: Guilford.

Lewis, C., & Fabos, B. (2005). Instant messaging, literacies, and social identities. *Reading Research Quarterly, 40*, 470–501.

New London Group. (1996). A pedagogy of multiliteracies: Designing social futures, *Harvard Educational Review, 66*(1), 60–92.

O'Brien, D., Stewart, R., & Beach, R. (2009). Proficient reading in school: Traditional paradigms and new textual landscapes. In L. Christenbury, R. Bomer, & P. Smagorinsky (Eds.), *Handbook of adolescent literacy research* (pp. 80–97). New York: Guilford.

Skinner, E., & Hagood, M.C. (2008). Developing literate identities with English language learners through digital storytelling. *The Reading Matrix: An International Online Journal 8 (2)*. Available at http://www.readingmatrix.com/articles/skinner_hagood/article. pdf

Street, B. V. (1984). *Literacy in theory and practice.* Cambridge, UK: Cambridge University Press.

EIGHT

Beyond Member Checks: Moving Toward Transformative Data Analysis

Janet Alsup

In a Conference on English Education (CEE; June 2009) Position Statement, social justice–inspired research is defined as

> grounded within a theoretical framework that has a historical understanding of the origin of the determined oppression in said story and how, through its narrative, the possible moments for change are revealed, and how agency and/or emancipation merge. (June 2009)

Educational social justice–inspired research identifies the history of oppression in an educational setting, reveals its continuing effects, and explores how the participants in the study and/or the researcher might change the situation and liberate the oppressed from their plight. The social justice researcher not only plans a research study but conducts it, and presents findings; he or she also must consider how said findings actually make an educational setting more fair and just.

In this chapter, I provide a working definition of the elements of social justice–inspired data analysis, particularly in educational research. Through this definition, I address questions of bias, generalizability, patterns and anomalies, positionality of the researcher, and the fraught nature of social justice as a concept that affects data analysis. I conclude by raising questions for continued contemplation by the social justice–inspired researcher.

Beyond Member Checks and Researcher Confessionals

When I was a graduate student working on my PhD in the late 90s, member checks, along with transparency regarding researcher biases, seemed the answer to conducting ethical educational research that had the potential to change participants' lives. So-called member checks involve sharing your data and its analysis with your participants during and perhaps after the research process so they can provide input and respond to how you understand their actions, words, or relationships. This member checking was revolutionary to those who were used to working in the domain of "scientific" research, whereby any such sharing would taint the data and keep it from being purely "objective."

However, sometimes member checking turns into sharing a study with a participant after it is completely finished, with the participant having no real influence on it; other times it means sharing selected, uncontroversial portions just so that the researcher could say he or she did so. Often the researcher listens to the participant's commentary and simply disregards it as uninformed and incorrect. Clearly, simply performing a member check does not automatically result in socially transformative research or research that is sensitive to the point of view of participants. However, member checking can lead to transformative results when the researcher pursues truly open communication with participants resulting in reciprocal benefits for both parties, such as increased knowledge for the researcher and heightened self-awareness for the participants.

The same can be said for researchers stating their biases in a study's context or describing how their gender, culture, history, and socioeconomic origin might affect their understanding of the data. Such researcher transparency may lead to more thoughtful and useful research; alternately, it may result in additional confusion and misunderstanding. In a chapter I wrote for a collection entitled *Ethnography Unbound: From Theory Shock to Critical Praxis* (Brown & Dobrin, 2004), I problematized the notion of including personal information in a final research report or write-up. While revealing one's personal story and background a researcher can provide context and help the reader understand the final analysis of the data and the subsequent findings, it can also open the researcher up to accusations of unfairness and suggestions that his or her findings are not valid. Whether stated or not, personal agendas should not be allowed to taint a researcher's open-minded analysis.

When Does Data Analysis Promote Social Justice?

While research meant to eliminate inequity and transform education, it is often qualitative in design in order to focus on individuals rather than anonymous groups, and not all studies with qualitative components are guided by social justice concerns. In the section that follows I outline some suggestions for conducting socially transformative data analysis—beyond the member check and researcher confessional—to promote transformative findings with the power to decrease instances of oppression and enhance equal opportunities for all students in our schools, regardless of ethnicity, race, age, gender, sexual orientation, ability, or social class.

Suggestion #1: Employ Narrative Research Techniques

In their text *Narrative Inquiry: Experience and Story in Qualitative Research* (2000), Clandinin and Connelly were among the first to define "narrative research" and provide actual guidelines for conducting it. However, since the 1980s narratives have been commonly used in the field of education to organize data and to share classroom experiences. Educators and educational researchers have explored how teacher narratives or educational histories can help new teachers broaden their professional identities and overcome the temptation to simply teach as they were taught (Knowles & Holt-Reynolds, 1991; Lortie, 1975; Lyons & La Boskey, 2002). Asking research participants to tell stories, either about their lives as a whole or particular incidents, results in rich, discursive data that can be mined for clues as to how the participant understands his or her world and place within it. These stories can then be analyzed through various forms of critical discourse analysis (Fairclough, 1989), such as socially or politically informed content analysis, or more linguistic, structural, or even grammatical analyses depending on the researcher's questions. The resultant patterns can shed light on why a participant is responding or behaving in a certain way within a social system. With such understandings, a researcher can suggest changes in a context or culture that can empower, lift up, or assist the participants.

Narrative methods are consistent with social justice–inspired research because they necessitate a close researcher–researched relationship. This attentive, receptive researcher stance increases the potential that institutionalized oppression and inequality might be revealed, oppressions and inequalities that perhaps the researcher had not previously considered. Furthermore, since oppression is sometimes internalized (Freire, 1970), not even the participant may consciously identify it, and he or she might make personally transformative discoveries in the process of storytelling.

Suggestion #2: Engage in Participatory or "Action" Research

There has been much written about the power of the educational practitioner asking questions and seeking new knowledge in his or her own classroom. Theorists such as Hubbard and Power (2003) and Lankshear and Knobel (2004) have written handbooks for the teacher–researcher seeking to discover new knowledge and investigate problems in his or her teaching. Teacher research, sometimes called action research, is in essence the teacher or practitioner asking burning questions of his or her own context and seeking answers in the form of data, such as student work, interviews, close classroom observations, and assessment results. The teacher is a researcher, looking at classroom challenges from a more critical perspective and exploring new directions for improved classroom practice.

Cochran-Smith and Lytle (2009) explicitly link teacher research to social justice perspectives. They write:

> We regard "inquiry as stance" as a grounded theory of action that positions the role of practitioners and practitioner knowledge as central to the goal of transforming teaching, learning, leading, and schooling. We see inquiry as stance as a positive thesis that goes beyond mere critique of the current educational regime and contributes to efforts to re-envision the work of practitioners in global societies. (p. 119)

More specifically relevant to this chapter is the idea that the teachers are analyzing the data from their own classrooms with the full knowledge of the context of the situation in which the data were collected. Since they are the practitioners, the researchers, and in some cases also the participants in the research project, they can bring all their knowledge to bear as they interpret the classroom data collected and use it to make their schools better places for all students to learn.

However, as Zeichner (2009) states, just conducting teacher inquiry or research does not automatically mean it will promote a more just classroom environment in which students and teachers are treated respectfully and resources are distributed equally. Zeichner asserts:

> As an action research community, we need to have a greater public social conscience and become more explicitly connected to the struggle to bring about a world in which everybody's children have access to decent and rewarding lives. We all ought to ask ourselves every day, "What am I doing in my involvement with action research to help move us closer to this kind of world?" (p. 84)

The teacher–researcher must view his or her meaning making as part of a larger attempt to improve the conditions of schooling for all children and all teachers.

Suggestions #3: Use Grounded Theory

Grounded theory as a foundation for data analysis was first popularized by Glaser and Strauss in 1967, and it usually refers to a type of qualitative data analysis whereby the researcher reviews data, "codes" it for emerging themes and patterns, and, finally, develops findings as well as a theory for explaining such findings. Important to grounded theory data analysis is beginning the process with an open mind and maintaining this openness as much as possible at least during the initial coding. Coming to a data set with a set of codes developed prior to data collection precludes the use of a true grounded theory approach to analysis. The ending result of a study using a grounded theory approach to data analysis becomes not only a discreet list of findings but also a theory to explain *why* these findings exist.

Such inductive theory creation seems particularly relevant to social justice–oriented educational research. When we are hoping to discover events, realties, perceptions, and relationships that can both explain and reveal instances of injustice in schools, sometimes these revelations will be unexpected or will be so woven into the fabric of the school days that at first they are not seen as abnormal or unjust. Only through reassessing and critiquing institutionalized realities can the researcher truly begin to understand inherent social oppression that may otherwise go unnoticed and unquestioned—particularly if the researcher himself or herself is not a member of a historically oppressed group.

Additionally, it seems that the creation of a theory might allow research findings to have a greater effect on educators, administrators, and policy makers. When research findings go past the micro level and progress to the macro level, supporting suggestions for larger social or political change based on a scholarly theory, they potentially open the door to more systemic change in an oppressive culture.

Suggestion #4: Recognize (Not Romanticize) Anomalies

Often in qualitative research, whether it reflects socially conscious ideologies or not, researchers are urged to see patterns and repetitions, whether they are coding by hand or using any number of computerized software analysis packages. Almost as a second thought, the concept of the anomaly is noted—usually in an admonition such as, don't forget to consider anomalies! But consider them how? They often don't figure into the final findings except as a brief mention in the appendix.

Perhaps it's in the anomalies that a great deal of liberatory research results might be found, particularly when much educational research seems to be conducted in schools with students from dominate, privileged cultures and groups. One student's response, particularly if that student happens to be a member of a cultural, ethnic, racial, or gender minority, might shed light on a research question in ways that none of the other participants' results can. Now this isn't to say that one or two examples of difference can or should change the meaning of an entire data set, but the social justice researcher must ask, what can it teach me that my dominate data cannot? Perhaps new research questions or contexts can be devised by paying close attention to the anomaly. Maybe there is something missing in the original research design that somehow derailed the possibility for this minority response emerging. Perhaps a follow-up study can address this anomalous response more closely. As Creswell (2009) recommends:

Also present negative or discrepant information that runs counter to the themes. Because real life is composed of different perspectives that do not always co-alesce, discussing contrary information adds to the credibility of an account. . . . By presenting this contradictory evidence, the account becomes more realistic and hence valid. (p. 192)

Suggestion #5: Re-think Generalizability

Much is made of the ability to generalize findings to other similar participant groups, particularly in a time when legislators seek "scientifically valid" research to undergird new educational laws and policies. If the findings of a study, no matter if there are three or 300 participants, can't be generalized to larger groups of students, teachers, or parents, policy makers may ask, what's the point of it? How can it help teachers and students improve?

Generalizability has always been an issue, particularly for qualitative research-ers, who don't have the benefit of claiming something to be statistically significant. When conducting research analysis to promote social justice, generalizability must be reconsidered, perhaps even redefined. In the normal research sense, being gen-eralizable means that what is true for a small population is also true for the larger population of similar subjects. In social justice–inspired research, we must talk instead of transferability (Lincoln & Guba, 1985). Transferability often requires having enough thick description and detail so that the reader of the research can decide if the results of the study might be applicable to his or her own context. Enough context and background about the participants and the research setting must be provided, in addition to the use of validity strategies such as member checking, intercoder agreement, and triangulation, so that the reader can decide if adequate similarities exist to be able to make the transfer from one group of students to another. If not enough detail is provided, then such a decision cannot be made, and the study stands alone. While such studies might still create theories useful to understanding other settings, one-to-one transferability of findings to other populations is impossible.

The concept of social justice is fraught with controversy. Some may see the concept as fuzzy and touchy-feely, devoid of the rigor of a truly intellectual theory; others see it as a theory that is not only intellectually rigorous but also essentially humane. And still others see social justice as wrapped up with po-litical liberalism and therefore an attempt by academics to indoctrinate students, researchers, and policy makers.

While enacting social justice–inspired research, which includes data analysis consistent with the concept, might be a challenge in a world where policy mak-ers want numbers and generalizable statistics, the public wants easy answers to a troubled public education system, and university researchers seek quick publica-tion for tenure and promotion reviews, it is worthwhile for many reasons. So many of the questions that plague educators do not have simple answers and simply cannot be addressed in a contextual vacuum. It might be a matter of changing curriculum or textbooks or assessments (or even standards), but it also might be a matter of looking at hierarchies of oppression and discrimination that exist is society and are played out in the microcosm of our local school.

I propose that we pay closer attention to the analysis part of the research process. Let's move past the literature review, methodological decisions, and even data collection and consider what happens between collection and the listing of "findings" or "results." While the analysis process seems more clear-cut in statistical or experimental studies, how does the researcher's ideology affect even this process? How does it affect the types of tests run or the way data is organized for analysis? For the qualitative researcher, what happens during that quantum leap from "here's my data" to "here's what it means?" Not every qualitative or mixed method study reflects a socially conscious ideology. Let's explore these questions and start a conversation about how we make meaning in educational research and how our philosophies, ideologies, and ethical stance might affect that process in a positive way.

Bibliography

Brown, S.G., & Dobrin, S. I. (Eds.). (2004). *Ethnography unbound: From theory shock to critical praxis.* Mahwah, NJ, and Urbana, IL: Lawrence Erlbaum/NCTE.

Clandinin, D.J., & Connelly, F. M. (2000). *Narrative inquiry: Experience and story in qualitative research.* San Francisco: Jossey-Bass.

Cochran-Smith, M., & Lytle, S. (2009). *Inquiry as stance: Practitioner research for the next generation.* New York: Teachers College Press.

Conference on English Education Commission on Social Justice. (2009). CEE position statement: Beliefs about social justice in English education. Unpublished manuscript, Elmhurst College, Chicago, IL.

Creswell, J.W. (2009). *Research design: Qualitative, quantitative, and mixed method approaches,* (3rd ed.). Thousand Oaks, CA: Sage.

Fairclough, N. (1989). *Language and power.* London: Longman.

Freire, P. (1970). *Pedagogy of the oppressed.* New York: Continuum.

Glaser, B.G., & Strauss, A.L. (1967). *The discovery of grounded theory: Strategies for qualitative research.* Hawthorne, NY: Aldine de Gruyter.

Hubbard, R.S., & Power, B.M. (2003). *The art of classroom inquiry: A handbook for teacher-researchers.* Portsmouth, NH: Heinemann.

Knowles, J.G., & Holt-Reynolds, D. (1991). Shaping pedagogies through personal histories in preservice teacher education. *Teachers College Record, 93* (1), 87–113.

Lankshear, C., & Knobel, M. (2004). *A handbook for teacher research.* Maidenhead Berkshire, UK: Open University Press.

Lincoln, Y.S., & Guba, E.G. (1985). *Naturalistic inquiry.* Newbury Park: Sage.

Lortie, D.C. (1975). *Schoolteacher: A sociological study.* Chicago: University of Chicago Press.

Lyons, N., & La Boskey, V.K. (Eds.). (2002). *Narrative inquiry in practice: Advancing the knowledge of teaching*. New York: Teachers College Press.

Zeichner, K. (2009). *Teacher education and the struggle for social justice*. New York: Routledge.

Closing Comments:
Multi Social Justice Methods in
English Education

The authors in this section have provided multi social justice methodologies that support social justice in English education. Through these essays, we have been privy to methodological innovations that live within a paradigm of reflection, change, and participation, i.e., social action/agency. Emerging from these essays are ideas that are consonant with some of our initial hypotheses about how methodologies and methods emerge or rather, "speak to us" through the context of our work. In fact, by clearly observing particular phenomena in the context of our own research and how we each relate to our participants, methodologies find us. Such found methodologies provide unique glimpses into the evolving contexts of social justice in English education and help to illuminate the junctures and/or disjunctures of experiences that can prevent humans from experiencing dignity.

These essayists, through their found multi social justice methodologies, find ways to intercept and capture the moments of the actualization of social justice when it does, can, or could happen. Such pivotal moments provide critical learning opportunities in which our investigations teach us about remaining open to the layered complexities of conducting socially just work. Summarizing the essays in this section, we found similarities between their found multi social justice methodologies that lend themselves toward capturing these particular moments in time. These essayists share the belief that socially just multi social justice methodologies account for: (1) capturing a critical moment that challenges and intercepts prejudice and oppression; (2) attempting to spare humans indignity; and (3) reflecting, challenging, and (even) participating in some way in the research context.

Miller, like the other essayists in this section, described a classroom mutli-methodological model that emerged organically from classroom observation for scaffolding social justice pedagogy and identity into English education programs. Miller's research recognizes that each person is at different cognitive, corporeal, and emotional developmental levels about understanding social justice and injustice. The model highlights six different levels in each of the four levels of the framework (1) critical reflection, (2) acceptance, (3) respect, and (4) affirmation, solidarity, and critique. Educators can work with their students on 6 "re-s," reflect, reconsider, refuse, reconceptualize, rejuvenate, and reengage, by scaffolding in activities that can help foster an awareness about social justice pedagogy and identity. English educators and their students can work together and evaluate themselves as they move, shift, deny, and are challenged by the scaffolded activities. This approach can help to stabilize a teacher's identity on social justice issues so as they move from classroom to inservice, their pedagogy and identity have concrete learning experiences that they can fall back on. Significant to this multi social justice method is that English educators can conduct classroom research that emerges from within this model throughout a given semester and can encourage students to conduct research about their increasing awareness of social justice.

Bolf-Beliveau and Beliveau further noted the importance of studying how a context demands a particularized methodology as a means of understanding social justice. Unique to their research methodology is their attention to the friction between "unfinished" or "fragments" of texts. By splicing together segments of fragments, thematic ideas emerge that tell untold stories and counter-narratives. They believe that analyses of fragments fill a gap in textual readings and that such a framework "allows for fragments to be identified and connected for a richer understanding of the postmodern. Whereas traditional textual analysis sees the text as 'intact' and presumes that the author has already constructed the meaning of the text, that approach is disempowering for students/researchers and runs contrary to social justice."

Along with Miller and Bolf-Beliveau and Beliveau, Jocson's found research frame, which emerged organically from her study, described a group of youth who analyzed their world across media. Jocson's description joins a long line of scholarship that illustrates the tensions between how people construct truths for themselves and how external truths are imposed upon them. Noting that the researcher's/educator's stance must always be critical of power relations, she drew us into a context that reminds us that the research and the teaching of English and our English teachers are living, breathing entities that must be (re)interrogated at every step. Entering into a space as a critical ethnograhper, students' lived identities and the intertextualities they make to poetry became the provocative muse for the methodological framework. Listening and seeing the lived experiences of students facilitated a powerful found context of framing new English education.

Margaret Hagood discussed the ways that identities act as multimodal texts. For Hagood, it is important to understand how literacy and identity inform each other as part of a larger agenda, unifying a call for social justice in English education. Doing so might give us new ways to represent the field that might lead to reconfigurations of texts and identities along more socially just lines. She notes that situating identity work in a social justice framework brings us closer to understanding its implications for policy. The design of the study is therefore fundamental to the methodologies employed; in other words, as mentioned by Miller, methodologies that weave the meta-narratives of reflection, change, and participation help to unpack the larger story related to social injustice. Hagood, like Miller, turns to a framework whose boundaries are fourfold: personal liberty, democracy, equality of opportunity, and economic growth. In common to all essays and perhaps of greatest significance for policy makers and English educators is that "literacies and identities [which] impact and are impacted by users [are a] key for helping develop more socially just approaches that validate personal liberty, democracy, equal opportunity, and economic growth." (p. 92)

We take from these essays and those in other sections, the pulses of their "empirical" heartbeats where multi social justice methodologies emerged organically and leave us to consider the exciting opportunities that lie ahead in moving social justice into policy. These findings both encourage and invite us (and for policy initiatives) to remain open to letting contexts speak to us as they have to the researchers featured in this section. In the process, such contexts can be viewed as critical materials for policy makers and in policy design. We have much to learn from the contexts we study and are reminded by Kirkland (in the next section) whose essay suggests that learning comes from "the literacies practiced by the people," their meanings, voices, identities, and interconnectedness; or from Miller, who believes that social justice learning takes time and patience; or from Bloome, Carter, and Brown (also in the next section), who suggest that we must pay careful and close attention to the dialogical practices between teacher-student; or from Jocson, that "critical" forms the basis of a methodological approach, and other positionalities that guide researchers to be self-reflexive; and from Bolf-Beliveau and Beliveau that fragments become critical opportunities for us to continue to pay close attention. In so many ways, we are all "noisemakers" (Kirkland, in this volume) who want to carve out new spaces for learning about the junctures/disjuncutres of social justice in classrooms. As we move into the next section on how to make sense of how these multi social justice methodologies in English education can be employed through diverse approaches to inquiry that blur disciplinary lines to promote the just cause of human liberation, we hope that you, the reader, will continue to stay with us and make change happen, because change matters.

The Politics of Social Justice Representations: *Right-ing* and Re-searching

What is critical inquiry, and why is it important to the process of social justice? For all intents and purposes, critical inquiry as an orientation into research means the examination of the *stuff of things* (e.g., practices, artifacts, and words) to better understand the things themselves (culture, identity, language, etc.). It usually seeks to reveal uneven power relations in society and narratives of oppression as lived by the hidden masses. It can include a social and cultural examination of human contexts and conditions and linguistic analyses, as language provides a recognizable substance through which the human experience can be captured. In sum, critical inquiry seeks to examine and explore our humanity in order to improve it. However, any examination or exploration of a thing will be subject to the subtle and not-so-subtle drives and intentions of the examiner or explorer (Milner, 2007). It will forever beacon to the larger sociopolitical forces to which all individuals submit.

We have become all too familiar with the consequences of such submissions through the ongoing histories of the sciences of people. Examinations and explorations of the marginalized by the dominant have long lead to reproductions of the social margins (Bowels & Gintis, 1976; Giroux, 1983; Monkman, Ronald, & Theramene, 2005). We now find ourselves in a moment where certain forms of inquiry are preferred over others. Such preferences reveal the political reality that research, and the forces behind it, can lead to favored forms of knowledge that too often work to reproduce certain social conditions.

Put this way, the debate on research, like the process of conducting research itself, can never be said to be objective. Rather, it is layered between the pulses of two recognizable claims to truth—theirs and ours. In this dialectal struggle, truth claims can be enlightening and liberating for some and yet limiting and threatening for others. Arriving at truth claims—a ubiquitous goal for any researcher—can generate unstable and hard-to-predict consequences of which all researchers must be aware (Morrell, 2009). Therefore, research, whether quantitative or qualitative, can never be objective; it subjectively exists as a process of a much larger politics of truth.

Further, researchers err by following a tradition of representing their research as if God wrote their research reports. The god we have preferred, privileges the third person over the "I," the technical and mechanical over the artistic, and the discourse of impenetrability over the discourse of the people. In this scribal transaction of thought, research results and the traditions in which they are written have tended away from the registers of social and cultural penetration, opting instead for the high gates of an aloof language and a product of exclusion. The exclusive document that becomes the research report often isolates itself from the subjects it describes and examines (McLaren, 1997); it too speaks a language foreign to the rest of the world, barring the common folk from understanding or writing research for themselves (Kincheloe & McLaren, 2000).

Indeed the overeducated have explained why certain tenets of representing research are in place—the attempt at truth in reporting, rigor, exposition, objectivity, and formalism (cf. National Research Council, 2002). These foundational principles of the scientific method, some researchers argue, must lead to verifiable and replicable results that can, of course, be vetted by a jury of knowledgeable peers and withstand the tests of high scrutiny. However, the rub is that this justification, although an important element in a particular scientific game, limits who can play. Further there is a kind of social and cultural capital to writing research claims that privileges a certain space that too limits who can participate and also gives power to a narrow group of performers, who like false gods, reign over the research world.

In this way, conducting research is a political act. It raises questions as to what and who gets to research and what and who gets represented in research, and how. Hence, the politics of research make problematic the genre of researching. To the degree that they obscure participants as well as the role of the researcher, traditional approaches to research legitimate a kind of reason that has been given dominion over specific points in history. It is not unique to history, then, that the research has been the tool used to spur oppressive regimes and promote unjust policies that hurt people. These politics spread beyond the research itself and get catalyzed in the high dialect of the academy—the common tongue of the intellectual elite who wield the research report like a sword, parsing truths, concealing and revealing selected fragments of knowledge, and casting judgment against those who lack the science to defend themselves.

Indeed the human mind and the individual hunger to know, to complete the incomplete texts of our humanity, compel each of us to make sense of the world in her or his own way. Any substance within reach of our senses is up for grabs. And while each of us comes to the task of measuring the world with similar tools, there is a sixth sense that reaches beyond us, torn from our bellies and bleeding hearts, which taints the objectivity of our hands and common tastes, the certainty of sure eyes and alert ears, and the confidence of smells. As we clearly seek to touch the universe whole with far-reaching sciences to understand and improve our lives within the unknown world, we do so with tinged fingertips and impaired vision. Dimly, we begin to see it—to faintly smell, taste, and hear it. Within this range of immobile senses, we find our limits and yet never stop searching for ways to search our world. This is perhaps the most critical aspect of any form of inquiry—humility set against persistence.

In this section, contributors discuss the humility that matches their persistence. In doing so, they describe their various positions on critical educational research. These positions reveal a degree of variability that spans across multiple approaches. That is, the section is not interested in dogma. Rather, it presents variability to illustrate that even critical inquiry is neither fixed nor stable. It is ever contingent and messy, filled with unanswered questions and naked adjustments. Moreover, by discussing the complexities of the research process(es), contributors help readers see how truths, much like lies, are man-made. Isn't this what critical inquiry is about anyway: highlighting the construction of thought in order to understand the deconstruction of reality? It is no wonder then that when we researchers truly analyze data, we find ourselves wondering without really finding, questioning without always answering. Hence, the conversations in this section begin somewhere between questions and answers.

Bibliography

Bowels, S., & Gintis, H. (1976). *Schooling in capitalist America*. New York: Basic Books.

Giroux, H. A. (1983). Theories of reproduction and resistance in the new sociology of education. *Harvard Educational Review, 53*, 257-293.

Kincheloe, J. L., & McLaren, P. (2000). Rethinking critical theory and qualitative research. In N. K. Denzin & Y. S. Lincoln (Eds.), *Handbook of qualitative research* (2nd ed., pp. 279-313). Thousand Oaks, CA: Sage Publications.

McLaren, P. (1997). Decentering writeness: In search of a revolutionary multiculturalism. *Multicultural Education*, 12-15.

Milner, H. R. (2007). Race, culture, and researcher positionality: Working through dangers seen, unseen, and unforeseen. *Educational Researcher, 36*(7), 388-400.

Monkman, K., Ronald, M., & Theramene, F. D. (2005). Social and cultural capital in an urban Latino school community. *Urban Education, 40*(1), 4-33.

Morrell, E. (2009). Critical Research and the Future of Literacy Education. *Journal of Adolescent & Adult Literacy, 53*(2), 96-104.

National Research Council. (Ed.). (2002). *Scientific Research in Education*. Washington, DC: National Academy Press.

NINE

Critically Conscious Analysis: Emancipating Literacy Research

Arlette Ingram Willis

For nearly a decade, the federal government has shown unprecedented interest in literacy as evinced by increased funding of reading research within the No Child Left Behind Act of 2001 (January 8, 2002) and the American Recovery and Reinvestment Act of 2009 (February 17, 2009). These laws appear to have little in common on the surface with regard to literacy research; however, a closer look reveals that both have defined and positioned literacy research in nearly identical ways. Specifically, each emphasizes the importance of discovering approaches to help improve the academic performance of students who have traditionally been underserved in U.S. public schools (children of color, children who live in economically distressed areas or attend economically distressed schools, immigrant children, and children who do not speak English as a native language or use Standard English). Both are overwhelmingly dependent on cognitive notions of intelligence that employ standardized test scores as indicators of academic performance. Underpinning the egalitarian rhetoric is an inadequate concept of literacy founded on positivistic scientific methods and sustained by hegemonic institutional structures and academic research traditions.

Literacy research has never been acultural, neutral/impartial, or objective. It is conceived, defined, and presented from a particular viewpoint that is informed by researchers' epistemological and theoretical stances. In the U.S., this means that the majority of literacy research has been conducted to maintain the ideological domination of one group over all others (Willis et al., 2008). To emancipate literacy research, the scholarly inquiry that informs the field and policy makers cannot rely on the very tools that brought us to this moment in history. Collectively, the field must make a concentrated effort to engage a more socially just agenda that includes ideas, concepts, theories, methods, and forms of analyses. In this way, we can improve the quality of instruction and academic performance for all students. I offer brief discussions of historical and contemporary notions of critical theorizing and their connections to critically conscious literacy research. Then, I characterize how researchers have used critically conscious analysis, using exemplars from literacy research. I conclude with a summary of key features of critically conscious analysis.

Critical Consciousness

There is no definitive history of the origins of critical thought. Willis et al. (2008) place it within a larger history of ideas that are not bounded by geography or time. Researchers typically point to the theorizing of members of the Frankfurt School as a starting point for Critical Theory (CT). Members of the Frankfurt School drew from the work of Hegel, Kant, and Marx, among other theorists, or sought to develop their own theories. The scholarship of Gramsci (hegemony) and Fanon (race) expanded CT.

In the early in the 20th century, numerous African American scholars sought to interrogate how issues of race and gender intersected with issues of power. Their work was extended in the mid-20th century through efforts of Black, White, and Latin American critical theorists. In the late 20th century, critical legal scholars continued to engage criticality, and scholars of color translated their critical-raced consciousnesses into Critical Race Theory (CRT). They envisioned CRT as a means to "reexamine the terms by which race and racism have been negotiated in American consciousness, and to recover and revitalize the radical tradition of race-consciousness among African Americans and other peoples of color" (Crenshaw, Gotanda, Peller, & Thomas, 1995, p. xiv). Application of critical race consciousness has expanded to include Asian American Critical Theory, LatCrit, Critical Indigenous Studies, Critical White Studies, Red Pedagogy, Tribal Critical Studies, and critical-raced feminisms. Ladson-Billings and Tate (1995), Solórzano and Yosso (2002), and Tate (1997) helped to extend critical race consciousness to educational research.

Apple, Au, and Gandin (2009) articulate that critical research "broadly seeks to expose how relations of power and inequality (social, cultural, economic), in their myriad forms, combinations, and complexities, are manifest and are challenged in the formal and informal education of children and adults" (p. 3). Contemporary applications of criticality in literacy research draw on CT and many of the critical theories aforementioned.

Critically Conscious Literacy Research

Many literacy scholars apply Freire's (1921–1997) understanding of critical consciousness to literacy research and praxis. The central idea that grounds his work is, *conscientização*, that he defined as

> Every relationship of domination, of exploitation, of oppression, is by nature violent, whether or not the violence is expressed by drastic means. In such a relationship, dominator and dominated alike are reduced to things—the former dehumanized by an excess of power, the latter by the lack of it. (Freire, 1973, p. 10f)

He identified three stages, or levels, of critical consciousness: semi-intransitive consciousness (limited consciousness), naive transitivity (a simple trusting attitude toward reality), and critical transitivity (individual and critical awareness of problems, the ability to engage in dialogue in search of solutions). Later, Freire extended the concept to include "awareness of the historical, sociopolitical, economic, cultural, and subjective reality that shapes our lives, and our ability to transform that reality" (Freire, 1998, p. 340). His theorizing connected CT to literacy research and pedagogy and has been helpful but incomplete for addressing issues of social justice because it lacked an engagement with issues of gender, race, sexual orientation, and their intersection with power.

To be critically conscious, research must begin with the critical consciousness of the researcher who is aware of, and open to, multiple theories and methods that allow for interpretive as well as recursive data analyses. What makes critically conscious research unique is that researchers' scholarship is founded on their epistemological and conceptual "systems of knowledge" (Ladson-Billings, 2000, p. 257) informed by personal, professional, and participant experiences. They acknowledge their foundational roots and routes as they draw on extant literature by cultural/ethnic/linguistic insiders as well as the field at large. Moreover, researchers draw on how historical, cultural, social, and political contexts influence the participants' lives, and, when needed, draw on cultural brokers as they seek to interrogate the effects of intersectionality in the lives of participants. Kincheloe (1998) declares that:

> critical research assumes that the inequalities of contemporary society need to be addressed. . .for the purpose of exposing this injustice, developing practical ways to change it, and identifying sites and strategies by which transformation can be accomplished. (p. 1191)

In critically conscious research, data are gathered using traditional qualitative research techniques: extensive time in the field, focus groups, interviews, participant observation, etc. Data that appear "added" or incidental under traditional educational frameworks are essential to critically conscious analysis and interpretation.

Dyson's (2003) study unveils an insider/outsider positioning as she acknowledges that her race and age separated her from the children's experiences. Her extended engagement in this setting earned her the term "fake mama" (p. 335). She examines how a group of African American first graders conceptualize, use, and, adapt their ways of knowing and interacting in multiple worlds (home, imaginary, and school) in a culturally and linguistically diverse urban elementary school. Dyson notes how the students re-created levels of familial comfort and interpersonal relationships and used their home languages and discourses in school. Moreover, the students "drew upon familiar frames of reference and, often, old textual toys (e.g., radio songs, film dialogue, sports reports, and cartoon scenes). . . they made new kinds of practices meaningful by infusing them with cultural knowledge and comfortable peer relations" (p. 333). The focal group informally rewrote their world through narratives or games and formally as they negotiated between their fantasy world and school literacy instruction. Dyson's scholarship suggests that literacy researchers engage the linguistic landscapes of children of color by acknowledging that children develop a sense of their place within their world through culture, language, and sign/symbol systems.

Jiménez, Smith, and Martinez-León (2003) recognize the import of indigenous language in their study of language and literacy practices in central Mexico. They describe how linguistic domination arose as "the colonial experience served to create a historically conditioned context in which not only native literacies were prohibited but also Mexicans' use of the colonizers' language and literacy became defined as perennially deficient" (p. 492), or what they call "*layered colonialism*" (p. 493, emphasis in the original). The authors also examine the ideological hegemony that underlies the nation's literacy policies and school instruction. They articulate their understandings through in-depth descriptions of languages and literacies used in the community and of types of schools, teachers, and instructions. Their study was conducted in two primary and two elementary classrooms and included community literacy. They describe the language of the largest ethnic people (Nahua) in their setting, whose indigenous language is Nahatal, while noting that Spanish is the language used in schools and community. Results of their analysis within schools reveal restrictive language and literacy practices.

Importantly, the researchers reveal their country of birth, language proficiencies, and understanding of Mexican culture, in general, and within the study's specific geographic area. Although all are fluent and proficient Spanish speakers and have lived in Mexico at different periods in their lives, none of the principal researchers were Mexican nationals or native Spanish speakers; however, several of the graduate students were and their insights of cultural and linguistic knowledges added to the analysis of the data. This information articulates that although each researcher was a fluent Spanish speaker, they spoke Spanish differently, depending on the geographical location where they learned Spanish and how often they use Spanish, debunking ideas of monolithic Spanish language and discourse. Their varied Spanish cultural and linguistic backgrounds and proficiencies suggest cultural and linguistic knowledges and proficiencies are not enough to give entrée into community. Moreover, the researchers worked in collaborative and mutually informing relationships with one another and members of the community.

Literacy research that is informed by critical race consciousnesses draws on researcher, participant, and collective experiences as sources of data and to inform data analysis. Duncan (2002) conducted observations and interviews of African American male high school students, teachers, and administrators in an examination of the marginalization of African American males, using a CRT lens because it "privileges the narratives of those who have been victimized to ameliorate the conditions attendant to oppression and domination and, in particular, engages the problem from the *differend* in ways to generate new social theories in the service of liberation"(p. 141, emphasis in the original). He created counternarratives as powerful antidotes to counter imperceptive academic depictions and descriptions of the racial/ethnic epistemologies used by African American males. He recommends allowing and accepting the knowledges, languages, and voices of Black males to encourage them to navigate among and within home, community, and school contexts as well as a place to start reforming their education.

Prendergast (2002) also employs CRT in her review of the intersections of race, literacy, and federal law. She offers a legal time line to consider connections between racial polices and literacy by examining primary source documents, critiquing legal arguments, presenting biographies of the major stakeholders, and deconstructing sociohistorical contexts. She explains how the U.S. Supreme Court adopted a framework equating Whiteness and literacy as property of Whites, by examining several pivotal U.S. Supreme Court cases. Prendergast argues that historically, Whites have worked to position literacy as neutral, acultural, and racially indeterminate and depict low-literacy rates as the result of individual, familial, or racial failures.

Critically conscious literacy researchers demonstrate a commitment to social justice and draw on multiple theories and methods in response to the question(s) posed and data collected, analyzed, and interpreted. Moreover, they are linked by their commitment to equity, social justice, and valuing of multiple languages and literacies.

Critical Conscious Analysis

Critically conscious literacy researchers draw in data analysis techniques, typically used on qualitative approaches, while acknowledging the multiple forms and intersection of oppression, multiple participant identities, and domains of power used to support or sustain inequity. They engage cultural/ethnic/linguistic frames of reference; respect the voice(s) of participants as essential, and the varied contexts (historical and contemporary) where the participants are situated. Critical race and critical-raced feminism conscious literacy research is often presented as counternarratives, whether autobiographical, biographical, or composite. Solórzano and Yosso (2002) suggest that CRT data analysis be informed by theoretical sensitivity (Strauss & Corbin, 1990) and cultural intuition (Delgado Bernal, 1998). They argue that both approaches allow them to draw on their epistemological and experiential knowledges and understandings to analyze data.

Willis et al. (2008) characterize critically conscious literacy analysis as informed by the researcher's epistemological and theoretical positions and engagement with the epistemologies and theories that inform historically marginalized groups; draws from theories, concepts, methods, and analytical frameworks of historically marginalized groups; engages with cultural and linguistic brokers to broaden understandings of cultural and linguistic nuances; encourages self-reflection of researchers; and emphasizes cooperation *with*, as opposed to *for*, participants.

Critical consciousness is not a new idea, but an idea whose time has come to be applied to literacy research and policy. As critical theorizing continues to evolve and as current trends place emphases on the intersectional nature of oppression, there also is a call for social justice advocacy. Critically conscious analysis provides an approach that engages the complexities and depths needed to move the critical project forward, transform literacy research and praxis, and bring about positive social change.

Bibliography

Apple, M. W., Au, W., & Gandin, L., A. (2009). Mapping critical education. In M. W. Apple, W. Au, & L. A. Gandin (Eds.), *The Routledge international handbook of critical education* (pp. 3–19). New York: Routledge.

Crenshaw, K., Gotanda, N., Peller, G., & Thomas, K. (Eds.). (1995). *Critical race theory: The key writings that informed the movement.* New York: The New Press.

Delgado Bernal, D. (1998). Using a Chicana feminist epistemology in educational research. *Harvard Educational Review, 68,* 555–582.

Duncan, G. (2002). Beyond love: A critical race ethnography of the schooling of adolescent black males. *Equity and Excellence in Education, 35*(2), 131–143.

Dyson, A. H. (2003). "Welcome to the Jam": Popular culture, school literacy, and the making of childhoods. *Harvard Educational Review, 73*(3), 328–361.

Freire, P. (1973). Education and the practice of freedom, In P. Freire (Ed.) and Myra Bergman Ramos (Translator), *Education for Critical Consciousness.* New York: Seabury.

Freire, P. (1998). *Teachers as cultural workers: Letters to those who dare teach.* Boulder, CO: Westview.

Jiménez, R., Smith, P., & Martinez-León, N. (2003). Freedom and form: The language and literacy practices of two Mexican schools. *Reading Research Quarterly, 38*(4), 488–508.

Kincheloe, J. S. (1998). Critical research in science education. In B. Graser & K. Tobin (Eds.), *International handbook of science education* (pp. 1191–1205). Boston: Kluwer.

Ladson-Billings, G. (2000). Racialized discourses and ethnic epistemologies. N. Denzin & Y. Lincoln (Eds). *Handbook of qualitative research* 2nd ed. (pp. 257-278). Thousand Oaks: Sage.

Ladson-Billings, G., & Tate, W. (1995). Toward a critical race theory of education. *Teachers College Record, 97*, 47–68.

Prendergast, C. (2002). The economy of literacy: How the Supreme Court stalled the Civil Rights Movement. *Harvard Educational Review, 72*(2), 206–229.

Solórzano, D., & Yosso, T. (2002). Critical race methodology: Counterstorytelling as an analytic framework for education research. *Qualitative Inquiry, 8*(1), 23–44.

Strauss, A., & Corbin, J. (1990). *Basics of qualitative research: Grounded theory procedures and techniques.* Newbury Park, CA: Sage.

Tate, W. (1997). Critical race theory and education: History, theory, and implications. *Review of Research in Education, 22*, 195–247.

Willis, A. I., Montovan, M., Burke, L., Hunter, C., Herrera, A., & Hall, H. (2008). *On critically conscious research: Approaches to language and literacy research.* New York: Teachers College Press.

TEN

Nomadic Science: Lines for Conducting and Assembling Education Research and Practice

A. Jonathan Eakle

The times and spaces were emblematic of hopes for social change and justice: Paris 1968 and the great general strike of thousands of workers and students. Yet, what was anticipated as a social revolution fizzled. From that sputter, Deleuze and Guattari began work together that produced texts and concepts applied to various and diverse domains of study, such as political science, comparative literature, and cinema. The purpose of this essay is to briefly explore how the ideas they developed have, and could be, useful in education research and practice.

Deleuze and Guattari's project has been situated in what can be described as new social movement theory that examines "nomads of the present" who: (a) challenge dominant social structures and codes, (b) are concerned with events of everyday life (e.g., micropolitics) yet have broader social interests (e.g., global warming), (c) embrace and cultivate alternative lifestyles, and (d) are not interested in capturing or holding political power (Melucci, 1989). Moreover, although it may seem at first blush that Deleuze and Guattari's nomadology is set in opposition to a sedentary or fixed state, the nomadic and sedentary are "pure tendencies that are real, yet that are experienced *only in various mixed states*" (Bogue, 2004, p. 173, emphasis added).

A widely recognized concept from Deleuze and Guattari's (1980/1987) work that underscores the mixed and varied coexistence of the nomadic and sedentary is the rhizome radical, a figure they appropriated from botany. In iris species, for instance, rhizome stems move horizontally along the ground sending out multiple projections from nodes anywhere along its stalk. This horizontal movement and multiplicity is in contrast to how tree structures typically develop: vertically and through binary division. Deleuze and Guattari applied these principles to social structures, trees arranged hierarchically and by dualism (good vs. evil, male vs. female), which are archetypes that can be traced at least as far back as Genesis, wherein a purported tree of knowledge based on truth, justice, and wrath was situated. Importantly, their rhizome is *parasitic*, and it spreads like contagion to "arrive at a process to challenge all models" (p. 20).

In short, the rhizome, and its methodological analog rhizoanalysis, is a way to deconstruct power relations from below—the local—or aligned with rhizomes, the *ground* level. Further, rhizoanalysis stands against, but feeds off, scientific hierarchies of sedentary tree knowledge and its power effects. In fact, power for Deleuze and Guattari is dispersed in rhizomatic networks of relations rather than something that is held, dispensed, or surrendered, which in their view is a tattered model composed of worn notions such as sovereignty, serf, oppression, and liberation. Rhizoanalysis traces flows of power on the ground and at the same time as a tool of nomadic science, described subsequently, projects attack lines, or what one might call "shoots," that leap out and into institutional practices (e.g., education mandates, sedentary curricula) and pilfer and create new concepts that challenge conventional thoughts, actions, and power complexes.

Lines of Nomadic Science

Conventional science operates with particular rules and conditions in what Deleuze and Guattari (1980/1987) described as territorialized space, and dominant spaces are those of Majority—a "state of power and domination" (p. 105), which underscores common ground they share with Foucault (1975/1977); power is indivisible from knowledge, and it spreads by two principal means: spectacle, or what can be seen, and language, or what can be said (Deleuze, 1986/2000). From their perspective, typical science functions by slowing down phenomena, for example, with fixities such as mathematical constants (e.g., Planck's). Conversely, nomadology is about speed and movements, or in other words, it is "science on the run," where the nomad infiltrates sciences of convention from outside their territorialized, sedentary spaces. From convention, the nomad appropriates, discards, and transforms habits, rituals, signs, symbols, and so on, which in Deleuze and Guattari's terms, are processes of deterritorialization (breaks) and reterritorialization (reconstructions). Further, notions of spatial movement, capture, transformation, and release are related to their concept of creating a "nomadic war machine" (p. 17) and the likening of such creative assemblages (two or more disjunctive elements joined) to Genghis Khan and 13th-century Mongol hordes (Bogue, 2004), swarms, animal packs (Kamberellis, 2004), and so on. In following sections of this essay, I briefly unpack three broad elements of these nomadic processes: (a) language, (b) space, and (c) planes of composition.

Language Lines

Conventional scientific language and writing and discourses of education and social research insist on uniformity and conciseness. Yet, Deleuze and Guattari argue that language is far from homogenous, it "stammers" in multiple variations, which has been a notion appropriated by poststructural feminists, among others, to "trouble clarity" (e.g., Lather, 1996; see also Butler, 1995). Language vibrations are endemic to their rhizomatic notions of multiplicities, which, as Minor variants, deterritorialize Majority forms and shake roots of linguistic structures, then reterritorialize or construct new concepts, words, forms of expression, and so forth.

Minor variants of Deleuze and Guattari's language concepts have been the tools for education researchers to challenge rooted traditions. For example, St. Pierre (1997) used their views to "circle the text" in deterritorializing and reterritorializing fashions. As she described, words become "cartographic weapons that tear through the orderliness of humanist language; they prod and poke at positivities and foundations; and they perform curious transitions between disjunctive proximities" (p. 407). Indeed, words can be armaments in "war machines" of nomadic science that cannibalize and challenge state structures (Deleuze & Guattari, 1980/1987, p. 230). And, similar to nomadic war machines are the networks of so-called right and left—informal complexes that hurl militant statements through global communication systems, crisscross national borders, and attack without notice using makeshift weapons. Those network groups range from *Facebook* followers of explosive "death panel" statements (Palin, 2009) to jihadist complexes.

Volatile distortions and *terror*-torializing violence are revolting, yet means of such groups uncover possibilities of how nomadic science could function for education and social change. Nomadic statements can pry loose fixities of language and meaning. Words wobble around tenuous state centers (Derrida, 1996) that operate with particular games of truth (e.g., Annual Yearly Progress reports, accreditation, and scientifically based brandings and acronyms, such as NCLB, SBRR, etc.). Rather than play ordered truth games, education researchers can create war machines of nomadic science using cartographic stealth, words that strike at "truth" statements and shed light to what ends such statements are produced, for instance, economic and political gains attached to education programs (see Grimaldi, 2007). Similarly, researchers can deconstruct sedentary institutions and their apparatuses to elicit ethical social actions by applying "violence to thought…we search for truth only when we are determined to do so in terms of a concrete situation, when we undergo a kind of violence that impels us to such a search" (Deleuze, 1986/2000, p. 15). "Violence to thought" can induce a search for justice fueled by concrete brutalities present today in neoconservative and neoliberal global networks and cruel actions, both actual and virtual, that they promote or ignore (see Chomsky, 2009; Collins, 2009).

The practices of artists and their challenges to sedentary institutions are a touchstone for nomadic science, and the flows and stammers of aesthetic languages with variant meanings and usages provide cultural texts important to many young people. Sometimes these texts are composed of violent stutters as illustrated by the lyrics of *Soul Clap*, performed by hardcore rapper Styles P (2002, hear online midi sample; hardcore rap, is an urban music genre known for its "deviant" associations to drugs, sex, and violence, Miranda & Claes, 2004, p. 113), such as: "I got a flow you can hardly hear. And a gun with a silencer. Why? 'Cuz *they* hardly hear." Moreover, the title and sounds of Styles P's *Soul Clap* are somewhat of a historical reversal. At first blush, *Soul Clap* implies relations to Booker T. & the MGs' (1969) mellow instrumental refrain with the same title. In contrast, Styles P's *Soul Clap* is accompanied by sounds of shotgun rack loads; with its clap, a soul is held in balance. The rap feeds off, yet is detached and reversed from integrative, crossover music traditions, such as Gordy's 1960s Motown Sound; it is a fierce performance that occupies a recent space in the history and role of some radical lines of popular music in turning aback Majority (cf. Harper, 1989).

Soul Clap is likewise a theme of indie hip-hop group Strange Fruit Project (SFP, 2006). From rhizomatic perspectives, SFP, like Styles P, feeds off past and remixes language, among other sounds, in Minor variants that operate outside and against Majority. Nonetheless, SFP's *Soul Clap*, as is its companion piece *Liberation*, assumes a classic position of sovereign power and repression. Rather than violently turning aback Majority as does Styles P's music, their smoother song instead highlights those "on the bottom" and "on lockdown" attempting to make it in a Majority world. In this vein, SFP echoes past idealist alternatives (e.g., "love can conquer hate," Gaye, 1971) as opposed to works of militant musicians, such as Nina Simone (1964), who furiously attacked judicial and social actions such as desegregation and mass participation as simply "too slow."

Nonetheless, at its root, SFP is parasitic of literal tree structures. Strange Fruit feeds from Meeropol's (1936) poem of minorities lynchings, words formed after viewing photographs of corpses hanging from trees, later popularized in a Billie Holiday song (see Allen & Littlefield, 2005). Mapping such semiotic flows and patterns—how ideas and bodies are situated and move through spaces replete with multiple signs, symbols, and so on—affords researchers insights of how cultural concepts come into existence. And, comparative analyses of such local assemblages show a benefit of rhizoanalysis for mapping social change;

drawing from Bergsonism, it can untangle "differences in kind" (Bogue, 2004, p. 169; Deleuze, 1988).

Spatial Lines

Territorialization, deterritorialization, reterritorialization, and movement are part and parcel of Deleuze and Guattari's nomadic science and its notions of planes or plateaus. As noted earlier in this essay, such strata are crisscrossed by opposing lines of what can be said and what can be seen under certain conditions and in particular times and spaces; words and images are engaged in a battle of sorts where one forces the other to come into existence (Deleuze, 1986/2000). For example, once in public spaces, torture spectacles forced certain judicial statements leading to gentler forms of punishment and discipline (Foucault, 1975/1977). In reverse, lately, torture has taken place in shadows—set-apart spaces such as Abu Ghraib prison (Welch, 2009). And, when images of the U.S. "enhanced interrogation techniques" were brought to light, they forced legal statements into being, such as President Obama's executive orders purported to modify justice policies of terror suspects and the release of once secret documents that contain large redacted black blocks—dark panels among other order-words (Kern, 2009; U.S. Department of Justice, 2004). To some, nonetheless, the current U.S. justice agenda compared to previous neoconservative ones shows little difference in pure kinds of concepts and practices regarding individual freedom, war tactics, and so on (e.g., Chomsky, 2009; Hentoff, 2009).

Schools are also set-apart spaces where, like prisons, discipline and restraint are often interwoven in institutional culture and its words and images. Everyday performances exist within such structural conditions and involve speech acts and other forms of communication such as gesture and movement. Leander and Rowe (2006) used rhizoanalysis of such everyday performances in classrooms to show how multiple text forms are put in play, that "no single text provides a structure for the unfolding of the event, and as such it stutters, breaks, and moves in ways that are unpredictable to both performers and audience members" (p. 449). Further, their work displays other possibilities afforded by rhizomatics: how to map movement with language transcripts set against spatial figures.

In this vein of performance, Deleuze (2004) wrote that events are bound to values and dramatizations and "scientific knowledge, the dream, as well as things in themselves—these all dramatize" (p. 98). From this perfomitivity, Foucault's notions of power relations, and Deleuze and Guattari's (1980/1987, 1972/2003) nomadic operations, I conducted "space study" (Eakle, 2007a). Like Leander and Rowe, I positioned performance at the centers of the investigation. Further, using nomadic science, stage sets were created in research reports upon which data were to be displayed. These data included participant exchanges dramatized from verbatim language transcripts and also "blocking notes," a theatrical term and a reverse of redaction techniques mentioned earlier in the present chapter. These notes show how the investigation unfolded and how writing scientific reports can be parasitic on power structures and push against conventions. For instance, akin to added features of cinematic digital media, I added deleted scenes, outtakes, and director-like commentaries, as shown in the following blocking note:

> Dramatization is intended to convey spatial distances (gaps, ruptures, closeness) between things. First, it aims to make research spaces closer to the audience …Stage sets provide a spatial means to splice together texts, which is an assemblage technique taken to new levels through cinema…actor/participants can move forward in monologue…Of these monologues and insertions, some theater stages have an extended platform known as the apron…it is a space where players can speak to an audience without being "heard" by the other players, such as found in Shakespeare's *Othello*. (p. 489)

In this study, space was also threaded through data collection and analysis. Data walks were conducted and data maps created, using nomadic science to feed off traces left by the investigation (transcripts, observation notes, artifacts, etc.). To position space upfront rather than as backdrop is a reversal of sorts and an education research territory only recently traversed.

Lines on Compositional Planes

Whether on stage sets, music scores, or other paper pages suggested thus far in this essay are planes of composition. It is on these planes that images and word lines crisscross. Leaps and stutters allow people to shift from one plane to another, and artists are masters of such nomadic movement, which explains why Deleuze and Guattari used as touchstones Francis Bacon, and Nietzsche, among others of so-called anti-rational and unconventional streams of art and philosophy. For instance, Bacon painted stage sets on canvas into which he placed tortured figures to capture sensations—a pure difference in kind when compared to, for instance, Velásquez' (c. 1650) portrait of Innocent X from which Bacon drew; and, Nietzsche used notions of Greek theater to express values and counter values through his writings (Deleuze, 2002, 2004).

Paint on canvas and sculptural mass are compositions of space, and an archetype of how spatial relations have been deconstructed in art is cubist work (Eakle, 2007b). Related to such spatial manipulation are striking statements of how art is a lie that tells the truth—how art revolves about fantasies of certainty (Derrida, 1987). Alternatively, as Deleuze (2002) suggested, art is about sensation, nothing else. Researchers can, as artists, write, speak, image, and create such sensations (hear, for instance, Artaud, 1947) in ways that force things to be seen and represented and vice versa. Although imagery has been a focus of some education research, it is far less used as a tool for investigations in part because research culture has been dominated by attitudes that privilege science and language over art and image.

Some education researchers have, however, studied and sometimes used art in their work. Through museum studies, for instance, I have traced how art is designed and produced, displayed and transformed, and used by educators and young people (Eakle, 2007a). In one example, a painting with African imagery was produced, according to its creator, chiefly for affect—sensation. Nonetheless, it was taken up by a museum docent through oral presentations to teach notions of pantheism and African identity, among other things, to museum patrons. These same concepts were transformed by a faith-based schoolteacher to instruct students in religious doctrine, and adolescents used them to craft hip-hop lyrics similar to those of SFP mentioned earlier in the present essay. These leaps traverse ruptures between planes of observation and language, and mapping such lines and ruptures is key to nomadic science.

Lines of Escape, Closing Lines

Through this brief essay I showed ways by which Deleuze and Guattari's nomadic science can be used in education research and practice. It can provide escape lines from neoconservative and neoliberal sedentary agendas that seek to brand what counts as research and proper pedagogies or not. Nomadic science can be used to analyze pure differences regarding how languages and images evoke multiple interpretations and vibrations. It provides means to map semiotic flows and patterns and insights of how concepts come into existence. As such, nomadic science is a geo-philosophic lever to pry open games of truth and structures and institutional policies built on such games. Further, nomadic science is not only a way to collect and analyze data but also display it on planes of composition. Dramatizations, cartographic weapons, and creating images that battle with words are but a few of the means developed by Deleuze and Guattari that have begun to be explored by education researchers and can allow them to chart escape lines from conserving practices. In short, nomadology pushes creative productions into Majority spaces to form zones for possible social and political change.

Bibliography

Allen, J., & Littlefield, J. (2005). *Without sanctuary: Photographs and postcards of lynching in America*. Retrieved January 8, 2010, from http://withoutsanctuary.org/main.html

Artaud, A. (1947). *Pour en finir avec le jugement de Dieu* [audio file]. Retrieved January 8, 2010, from http://www.antoninartaud.org/god.html

Bogue, R. (2004). Apology for nomadology. *Interventions, 6*, 169–179.

Booker T. & the MG. (1969). *Soul clap '69* [multimedia file]. Retrieved January 8, 2010, from http://www.youtube.com/watch?v=9Rv-PD6TSZ8

Butler, J. (1995). For a careful reading. In S. Benhabib, J. Butler, D. Cornell, and N. Fraser (Eds.), *Feminist contentions: A philosophical exchange* (pp. 127–143). New York: Routledge.

Chomsky, N. (2009, May 11). *Obama recycles George W. Bush's plans*. Retrieved January 8, 2009, from http://www.youtube.com/watch?v=63HNuL2tfNc&feature=related

Collins, G. (2009, August 12). Gunning for health care. *The New York Times*. Retrieved January 8, 2010, from http://www.nytimes.com/2009/08/13/opinion/13collins.html

Deleuze, G. (1988). *Bergsonism*. New York: Zone.

Deleuze, G. (2000). *Foucault*. Minneapolis: University of Minnesota Press. (Originally published in 1986.)

Deleuze, G. (2002). *Francis Bacon: The logic of sensation* (D. W. Smith, Trans.). New York: Portmanteau. (Originally published in 1981.)

Deleuze, G. (2004). The method of dramatization. In D. Lapoujade (Ed.), *Desert islands and other texts* (pp. 94–116). Los Angeles, CA: Semiotext(e).

Deleuze, G., & Guattari, F. (1987). *A thousand plateaus: Capitalism and schizophrenia*. Minneapolis: University of Minnesota Press. (Originally published in 1980.)

Deleuze, G., & Guattari, F. (2003). *Anti-Oedipus: Capitalism and schizophrenia*. Minneapolis: University of Minnesota Press. (Originally published in 1972.)

Derrida, J. (1987). *The truth in painting*. Chicago: University of Chicago Press.

Derrida, J. (1996). *Archive fever: A Freudian impression*. Chicago: University of Chicago Press.

Eakle, A. J. (2007a). Literacy spaces of a Christian faith-based school. *Reading Research Quarterly, 42*, 472–511.

Eakle, A. J. (2007b). Museum literacy, art, and space study. In D. Lapp, J. Flood, and S. B. Heath (Eds.), *Handbook of research on teaching literacy through the communicative and visual arts* (pp. 177–186). Mahwah, NJ: Lawrence Erlbaum.

Foucault, M. (1977). *Discipline and punish*. New York: Vintage. (Originally published in 1975.)

Gaye, M. (1971). *What's going on?* [vinyl audio recording]. Written by A. Cleveland, R. Benson, and M. Gaye. Detroit MI: Tamla Records.

Grimaldi, J. V. (2007, December 20). A reading program's powerful patron. *The Washington Post*. Retrieved January 8, 2010, from http://www.washingtonpost.com/wp-dyn/content/story/2007/12/19/ST2007121902742.html

Harper, P. B. (1989). Synesthesia, "crossover," and blacks in popular music. *Social Text, 23*, 102–121.

Hentoff, N. (2009, October 22). *Obama as bad as Bush-Cheney*. Retrieved January 8, 2010, from http://www.cato.org/pub_display.php?pub_id=10693

Kamberellis, G. (2004). A rhizome and the pack: Liminal literacy formations with political teeth. In K. Leander & M. Sheehy (Eds.), *Spatializing literacy research and practice* (pp. 161–197). New York: Peter Lang.

Kern, G. (2009). Torture and intelligence in the global war on terror. *Intelligence and National Security, 24*, 429–457.

Lather, P. (1996). Troubling clarity: The politics of accessible language. *Harvard Educational Review, 66*, 525–546.

Leander, K. M., & Rowe, D. W. (2006). Mapping literacy spaces in motion: A rhizomatic analysis of a classroom literacy performance. *Reading Research Quarterly, 42*, 428–460.

Meeropol, A. (1936). *Strange fruit.* Retrieved January 8, 2010, from http://www.pbs.org/independentlens/strangefruit/film.html

Melucci, A. (1989). *Nomads of the present: Social movements and individual needs in contemporary society.* Philadelphia, PA: Temple University Press.

Miranda, D., & Claes, M. (2004). Rap music genres and deviant behaviors in French-Canadian adolescents. *Journal of Youth and Adolescence, 33,* 113–122.

Palin, S. (2009, August 7). Statement on the current health care debate. *Facebook.* Retrieved January 8, 2010, from http://www.facebook.com/note.php?note_id=113851103434

Simone, N. (1964). *Mississippi goddam* [vinyl audio recording]. Recorded live at Carnegie Hall. New York, NY: Phillips Records.

St. Pierre, E. A. (1997) Circling the text: Nomadic writing practices. *Qualitative Inquiry, 3,* 403-417.

Strange Fruit Project (2006). *Soul clap* [audio file]. San Francisco CA: Om Records. Retrieved January 8, 2010, from http://www.strangefruitproject.com/index2.html

Styles P (2002). *Soul clap* [audio file]. Yonkers, NY: Ruff Ryders. Sample retrieved January 10, 2009 from http://www.amazon.com/Gangster-Gentleman-Styles/dp/B000068TND

U.S. Department of Justice (2004). *CIA Memos with redactions.* Retrieved January 8, 2010, from http://www.aclu.org/safefree/torture/40832res20090824.html

Velásquez, D. (c. 1650). *Portrait of Innocent X* [oil on canvas]. Digital image retrieved January 8, 2010, from http://www.doriapamphilj.it/ukinnocenzox.asp

Welch, M. (2009). American painology in the war on terror: A critique of "scientific torture." *Theoretical Criminology, 13,* 451–474.

ELEVEN

Studying Literacy Practices in Classrooms Using Critical Discourse Analysis: From the Bottom Up

David Bloome, Stephanie Carter, & Ayanna F. Brown

Critical discourse analysis focuses attention on how discourse structures intersect with power relations among people and institutions. As van Dijk (1993) states, critical discourse analysis focuses

> on *the role of discourse in the (re)production and challenge of dominance.* Dominance is defined here as the exercise of social power by elites, institutions or groups, that results in social inequality, including political, cultural, class, ethnic, racial and gender inequality. This reproduction process may involve such different "modes" of discourse-power relations as the more or less direct or overt support, enactment, representation, legitimation, denial, mitigation or concealment of dominance, among others. More specifically, critical discourse analysts want to know what structures, strategies or other properties of text, talk, verbal interaction or communicative events play a role in these modes of reproduction. (pp. 249–250, original emphasis)

One hallmark of critical discourse analysis is the combination of a linguistic model for analysis of texts and communicative interaction with one or more critical/sociopolitical theories (although there are differences in the linguistic and critical/sociopolitical theories employed; see Gee, 2004). Because there are many excellent books providing introductions to critical discourse analysis (see Figure 11.1 for a select list) we do not describe the specific principles and techniques of critical discourse analysis here. Rather, we focus on the application of its logic-of-inquiry to the study of literacy practices in classrooms.

Figure 11.1 A Select List of Introductions and Overviews of Critical Discourse Analysis

Fairclough, N. (1989). *Language and power.* London: Longman.

Fairclough, N. (1995). *Critical discourse analysis.* London: Longman.

Fairclough, N. (2003). *Analysing discourse: Textual analysis for social research.* London: Routledge.

Gee, J.P. (1999). *An introduction to discourse analysis: Theory and method.* New York: Routledge.

Kress, G. (1990). Critical discourse analysis. *Annual Review of Applied Linguistics, 11,* 84–99.

Luke, A. (1995). Text and discourse in education: An introduction to critical discourse analysis. In M. Apple (Ed.) *Review of research in education,* 21 (pp. 3–48). Washington, DC: AERA.

Rogers, R. (2004). *An introduction to critical discourse analysis in education.* Mahwah, NJ: Lawrence Erlbaum Associates.

Titscher, S., Meyer, M., Wodak, R., & Vetter, E. (2000). *Methods of text and discourse analysis.* Thousand Oaks, CA: Sage.

Toolan, M. J. (2002). *Critical discourse analysis: Critical concepts in linguistics.* London: Routledge.

van Dijk, T.A. (1993). Principles of critical discourse analysis. *Discourse and Society, 4,* 249–283.

van Leeuwen, T. (2008). *Discourse and practice: New tools for critical discourse analysis.* New York: Oxford University Press.

Wodak, R. (2004). Critical discourse analysis. In C. Seale, G. Gobo, J. F. Gubrium, & D. Silverman (Eds.), *Qualitative research practice* (pp. 197–213). London: Sage.

Applied to classrooms, critical discourse analysis provides a way to investigate how instructional conversations, classroom texts, peer interactions, the curriculum, classroom displays (e.g., bulletin boards, pictures on walls), the arrangement of furniture, the architecture of the room itself, the social organization of the students (e.g., the number of students, their ages, gender, race, ethnicity, native languages, etc.), and other semiotic displays (e.g., the clothing worn by teachers and students) are all implicated in the control of knowledge (what counts as knowledge and what knowledge counts), who has access to what opportunities for social, economic, cultural, and symbolic capital (and their exchange), how personhood is defined (what it means to be human), how morality and ethics are defined (how good and evil are defined), who receives the benefits and rewards the social institution has to offer and who is marginalized (with accompanying happiness and suffering), how physical and mental health are defined (and who is defined as healthy and who sick), and how all of this structuring within the classroom and between the classroom and other social institutions is made to seem natural and reasonable (see Bloome, Carter, Christian, Otto, & Shuart-Faris, 2005; Luke, 1995; Rogers, 2004; Rogers, Malancharuvil-Berkes, Mosley, Hui, & O'Garro

Joseph, 2005). Educational researchers have used critical discourse analysis to investigate the use of lists in the promulgation of policies for the teaching of reading and writing (e.g., Bloome & Carter, 2001), tests and standards (e.g., Anderson, 2001), teacher-student interaction (e.g., Candela, 1998), the teaching of English to speakers of other languages (e.g., Kumaravadivelu, 1999), classroom literacy practices (e.g., Bloome et al., 2005; Lewis, 2001), adult literacy education (e.g., Rogers, 2004a), college composition (e.g., Ivanic, 1998), special education meetings (e.g., Rogers, 2002a), and family literacy (Rogers, 2002b) among others.

Fairclough (1989, 2003) outlines three levels of analysis: description, interpretation, and explanation. Description involves the linguistic analysis of the text (whether written or spoken). Such linguistic analysis includes the heuristics found in theoretical linguistics, sociolinguistics, sociolinguistic ethnography, rhetorical and composition studies, pragmatics, and speech act analysis, among other fields in linguistics and applied linguistics. Interpretation goes beyond description by focusing on the relationship between the text and the contexts and processes of production and consumption. That is, how the text positions people with regard to power relations. For example, interpretation might examine how nominalization, passive verb structures, and transitivity within a text hide agency suggesting "naturalness" to a particular worldview (as opposed to identification of agents who might benefit from the instantiation of a particular worldview). Explanation places the description and interpretation within broader social theory concerned with social reproduction, dominance, and resistance. Although there is some disagreement about these heuristic levels of analysis (see Toolan, 1997), in general the practice of critical discourse analysis has been dominated by how text and verbal interaction contributes to dominance by elite groups and social institutions. This has led van Dijk (1993) to criticize critical discourse analysis for emphasizing a top-down analysis; that is, an emphasis on how discourse processes are implicated in dominance rather than foregrounding resistance. But there is another way in which critical discourse analysis has also emphasized top-down analysis. Predominately, critical discourse analysis has been informed by macro social theories outlining the power relationships among classes; dominant social and cultural groups and nondominant ones; genders; social institutions such as government, law, religion, and education; and ordinary people. Rarely, are the insights from analysis at the levels of description and interpretation used to (re)constitute macro social theories including the categories of dominance and resistance themselves, nor to problematize the construct of social reproduction, nor to theorize how people through their verbal interactions and the texts they create and use form new spaces that eschew the structures of dominance existing elsewhere in their lives. We label such analytic efforts bottom-up critical discourse analysis.

In the rest of this chapter we will focus on bottom-up critical discourse analysis as our particular interest lies in how teachers and students (re)create literacy practices that enhance their opportunities and efficacy in creating a more just world and diminishing human misery. However, our focus here should not be interpreted as diminishing the importance of top-down approaches to critical discourse analysis. Top-down approaches provide opportunities to raise the critical consciousness of teachers and students and open up their social imagination for alternative ways of resisting dominance and social reproduction and for constituting new social relationships and ways of acting and being in educational settings.

Bottom-Up Critical Discourse Analysis

Bottom-up critical discourse analysis is concerned with the structure of power relations no less than top-down approaches; and, also similarly, it holds a definition of power as a productive process and not simply a coercive process (cf. Bourdieu, 1977, 1991; Foucault, 1980; de Certeau, 1984). It is also similar in bringing together linguistic models of analysis with critical/sociopolitical theories. In our view, bottom-up critical discourse analysis is distinguished by (a) an emphasis on the situated nature of the communicative event and text, (b) the historicizing of the analysis, and (c) a dialectical relationship between close analysis of texts and communicative interaction and macro social theorizing. We use an analysis of a few minutes from a seventh grade language arts lesson to illustrate and discuss each of the dimensions above. Although we present the analysis below, foregrounding first one and then the next of the three dimensions of a bottom-up critical discourse analysis, in actual practice these dimensions overlap and are inseparable. This methodological approach to critical discourse analysis is significant because it can unveil social justice in literacy instruction as a set of *in situ* opportunities for teachers and students to experience alternative approaches to sense making and for reconstituting learning in meaningful ways. To this end, we attend to how the engagement in learning enacts praxis and can be transformative where learning includes teachers and students seeing their lives and choices as dynamic and unbounded by circumstance or condition.

The teacher is leading the class in a discussion of the novel *Lottery Rose* (Hunt, 1976). For homework, the students had to highlight any section of the text they viewed as important or surprising. One of the students, Helen (all names are pseudonyms), has been asked to read the text she highlighted.

Transcription Symbols

T = Teacher	Underline = stress word or utterance
H = Helen	Italics = written text rendered orally
Sx = unidentified students	Items in parenthesis = nonverbal behavior and notes

J = Johnny   / = pause or hesitation

Ss = many students speaking | = place where a speaker was interrupted or overlap

xxxxx = undecipherable speech

+ = elongated vowel

1   T: <u>Read</u> that for us please

2   H: (reading from the passage she highlighted in her book): *Miss Preston didn't like Georgie much / she got mad at him for not doing his work/ she pointed to / the work she pointed to / when she wrote a long list on / the blackboard she especial she got mad / especially / |*

3   *Sx: | she got especially |*

4   H: | *she got especially mad at Georgie because he played hooky and lied xxxxx*

5   T: OK

6   T: Why was that / important enough for you to highlight or make note of

7   H: Because she didn't get that mad at the students but just at Georgie she got real mad at him

8   T: So you think she singled Georgie out

9   T: She displayed more anger toward him than she does the other kids

10   H: (nods head in agreement)

11   T: OK Johnny

12   J: She's mad because she she plays hooky and

13   J: talks bad and stuff and then xxxxxx he can't read

14   (1 second silence)

15   T: OK

16   T: Have any of you ever been the Georgie

17   T: In this |

18   T: | I'm not talking about the abuse part

19   Sx: Oh

20   T: But the being in class and not doing the work or not understanding and acting out and said

21   T: You said here are your damn X's and xxxxx up xxxxxx (makes big X in the air with her hand)

22   Ss: (Laughter overlaps hand gestures near end of the previous line)

23   T: OK

24   T: have any of you ever been the Georgie and mad at the rest of the world

25   T: Can I ask you a question

26   T: this this is just for my own personal professional development

27   T: How did you move out of the Georgie phase
28   T: How did you move away from the / being angry and / not doing the
      work and / move into the /
29   T: phase you're in now
30   Sx: who
31   T: Whomever
32   T: Who was once
33   T: OK
34   T: Johnny
35   T: How did you progress from being Georgie into being Johnny
36   J: Stop playing hooky
37   T: OK so your first step was to stop playing hooky
38   T: OK
39   T: Anybody else
40   T: I was once Georgie now I'm Helen
41   Sh: I xxxxxxxxxx if I didn't do my work and stuff xxxxxxxxxxxxx
42   S: (laughter overlaps last half of previous line)
43   So you are arguing that if you did not do the work then you would be
44   Sh: Yeah xxxxxxxxxx
45   T: OK
46   T: Terry
47   (1 second silence)
48   Ss: (soft laughter overlapping the previous two lines)
49   T: You learned Helen that if you did not do the work you would be a bad
      person.
50   T: Defi+ne a bad person
51   T: What's a bad person
52   H: a person who doesn't listen
53   H: Has no goal in life doesn't want to make anything of themself
54   T: OK a person who has no goal and doesn't want to make anything
55   T: So that's your definition of a bad person
56   H: Yes
57   T: OK a guy with no goals

The students are mostly African American and all of them come from work-ing class and low-income communities that make up the school's enrollment area. We note the students' race and socioeconomic class status not to invoke "at risk" factors derived from deficit model statistical studies; but to locate them, their classroom, and the event in U.S. history. Many of their families migrated to this urban area from rural areas and areas in the South several generations earlier, with earlier generations having been enslaved. This history of brutal racism and the resilience of their families and communities, coupled with a deep belief in the importance of education, is contextualized by an educational climate that views African American students and students from low-income families in deficit terms. They are framed as "at risk" students with low literacy and academic skills liable to drop out before graduating high school and unlikely to attend college. Such educational terms not only frame the students for their teachers and school administrators, but also for themselves as many of the students have low self-images of themselves as not academically and intellectually talented.

The teacher was a young, African American woman who received her teacher preparation with an emphasis on culturally responsive pedagogy; and whose personal history involves a strong family ethos for education despite her being a first generation college graduate. She viewed her teaching as part of a broader struggle against racism and for improving the lives of her students, their families, and the broader communities of African Americans and people from working-class backgrounds. As such, her teaching was influenced by African American educators such as Woodson (1933), Ladson-Billings (1994), and philosophical approaches to education that directly address issues of power, transformative praxis, and social analysis, such as Du Bois (1903) and Freire (1972).

We begin analysis by situating the event. By situating the analysis, we mean recognition that local, situational factors play a major role in understanding how power relations are being constituted (and reconstituted). That is, rather than viewing the specific, local situation and event merely as an instantiation of broader, macro social processes at work, the event needs to be viewed simultaneously as reflecting those broader macro social processes and as refracting them; and doing so through the specific texts and communicative interactions created by those particular people at that particular time in that particular place with their particular histories. While we would not describe the approach as emic (as reflecting the perspectives of the participants), it is nonetheless grounded in the event itself. Analysis needs to pay attention to the ways in which people act and react to each other (through their uses of language and other semiotic tools), how people index and reference their histories and social contexts, and how their uses of language and other semiotic tools bring the world outside the classroom inside and how they respond to that. Consider lines 12 through 16.

12 J: She's mad because she he plays hooky and
13 J: talks bad and stuff and then xxxxxx he can't read
14 (1 second silence)
15 T: OK
16 T: Have any of you ever been the Georgie

The teacher has called on Johnny to speak. Johnny's use of "talks bad," "stuff," and "he can't read" all reference a moral ideology associated with school as a social institution. Talking bad refers not to the use of obscene language but to the failure to show respect or deference to the teacher (and as such, represents a set of power relations taken to be natural and understood by all). There is also an implied assumption that there is "talking good" and "talking bad," a dividing practice separating out those who are good from those who are bad. At best, "stuff" is a vague reference to things Georgie did in the classroom. However, there is a great deal of ideological work being done by "stuff." Johnny assumes that everyone in the class understands what "stuff" refers to, so much so that he does not need to specify what the "stuff" is or why it is bad. By including not being able to read in the list, Johnny suggests that it is morally acceptable for a teacher to get mad at a student because s/he cannot read and that not being able to read is associated with being bad. Johnny presents this ideology as if it is common sense and a correct response to the teacher's opening of the topic of the teacher in the novel being mad at Georgie. Many of the students in the class have difficulties with reading, some of them have severe difficulties similar to those of Georgie. Indeed, the way in which Helen orally reads the text (lines 2 through 4) would suggest to most teachers that she is reading below grade level; and judging by his oral reading at other times, Johnny himself has difficulties with reading. The students espouse an institutional ideology that positions them as "bad" and although their own experiences would/should call that institutional ideology into question; that does not happen.

In response to most student turns at talk, the teacher either responds with a position evaluation (e.g., line 5), a question to keep the interaction going (e.g., line 6), or she revoices the student's response (e.g., lines 8–9). However, in response to Johnny, the teacher is silent (line 14). The lack of a verbal response could be interpreted as a negative or disapproving evaluation of Johnny's comment. But it is ambiguous as she says "OK" in line 15 suggesting either approval of Johnny's comment and/or a closure to that phase of the instructional conversation and the opening of another phase, initiated by the question, "Have any of you ever been the Georgie?" (line 16).

The tense of the verb in line 16, the past perfect, signals a state of being started and completed in the past; and as elaboration of the question in lines 17 to 29 makes clear, the teacher is soliciting personal narratives of a particular structure and content. The tense of the verb in line 16 positions students as no longer in the Georgie phase, as having moved from "bad" to "good." Johnny is the first person called to provide a narrative, and he does so consistent with the narrative structure requested. Subsequent student narratives all follow the same narrative structure. All of these narratives imply a particular chronotope (an ideology of movement through time and space, cf. Bakhtin, 1935/1981), from being bad to being good. Interestingly, the tone and prosody of the instructional conversation changes from line 14 to line 47. The teacher lowers the volume and raises the pitch of her speech, signaling a shift in the instructional conversation from recitation to conversation, from teacher as authority to teacher seeking personal information from the students. This shift is also signaled by lines 25 and 26, in which the rhetorical question, "Can I ask you a question?" is a polite form of signaling respect for the students' privacy and narratives as well as a shift in the teacher-student relationship. The use of the term "personal" in line 26 creates a different footing (cf. Goffman, 1981) for the instructional conversation at that particular moment.

The way in which the teacher framed the solicitation of student narratives—"Have any of you ever been the Georgie?"—connected the student narratives to the novel by asking the students to compare themselves with the protagonist. The reading practice shifted from discussions of what happened in the novel and what the students found important or surprising, to using the novel as a prop for reflecting on their own lives and for repositioning them in relationship to the institutional discourse of the school and education more generally. This goes beyond reading the word and the world (cf. Freire, 1972); it repositions and reframes who the students are in the world.

Historicizing the students and the teacher requires more than noting their history. It requires incorporating into critical discourse analysis theoretical perspectives that can provide counter-narratives and a set of heuristics that eschew deficit models. Two related theoretical frames provide one way to move toward such historicizing: Black feminist theory (cf., Collins, 1990; hooks, 1989, 1993) and critical race theory (cf., Bell, 1987; Crenshaw, Gotanda, Peller, & Thomas, 1995; Dixson & Rousseau, 2006; Ladson-Billings & Tate, 1995). (Given the limited space here, we cannot provide more than a very brief description of these theories; please see the authors cited for a more informative introduction to these theories.)

Black feminist theorists place Black women's experiences at the center of analysis suggesting that Black women are able to view the world around them in a "both/and" conceptual lens. Collins (1990) notes, "Viewing the world through a both/and conceptual lens of the simultaneity of race, class, and gender oppression and of the need for a humanist vision of community creates new possibilities for an empowering Afrocentric feminist knowledge" (p. 221). Collins and other Black feminists suggest that utilizing a both/and lens allows us to see race, class, and gender as interlocking systems of oppression. The notion of interlocking systems provides an opportunity to rethink social relations around dominance and resistance as they are grounded in particular histories, experiences, and contexts. Further, it begins to make visible different ways of knowing, allowing those who are oppressed to define and name their own experience. Collins notes that community is one example of how Black women have began to revision and name their own experiences. She suggests that Black women have used creative power to foster alternative communities to support and nurture those who are oppressed.

Similar to Black feminist theory, critical race theory is another lens that examines power relations and the intersections of race, gender, and class. Both critical race theory and Black feminist theory see dialogue/languaging as well as naming one's own reality as central to understanding and revisioning the lived experiences of marginalized groups. Each of these theories provides a set of heuristics useful for critical discourse analysis at all levels: description, interpretation, and explanation.

For example, consider lines 16–23 from the earlier transcript.

16. T: Have any of you ever been the Georgie
17. T: In this |
18. T: | I'm not talking about the abuse part
19. Sx: Oh
20. T: But the being in class and not doing the work or not understanding and acting out and said
21. T: You said here are your damn X's and xxxxx up xxxxxx (*makes big X in the air with her hand*)
22. Ss: (*Laughter overlaps hands gestures near end of the previous line*)
23. T: OK
24. T: have any of you ever been the Georgie and mad at the rest of the world
25. T: Can I ask you a question
26. T: this this is just for my own personal professional development
27. T: How did you move out of the Georgie phase

Using a Black feminist lens, one might argue that in line 16 the teacher invites students to place their experiences at the center. In lines 17–23 she elaborates by trying to create hypothetical examples "being in class," "not doing work," etc. In line 24, there is a shift, the teacher states, "have any of you ever been the Georgie and mad at the rest of the world." "Mad at the rest of the world" could be a loaded statement; but what it does is signal a particular type of relationship or experience between the individual and the "rest of the world" and serves as a marker for power relations. In line 25, the teacher poses a rhetorical question. Then, in line 26 she makes visible an epistemological understanding about knowledge that is not about competition and domination but "for [her]own personal professional development."

In brief, using a Black feminist lens one might argue that what the teacher has done is to provide a conceptual space for each student to engage in dialogue and name his/her reality, to theorize his/her reality from a both/and vantage point; she/he is *both* a member of multiple dominant groups *and* multiple subordinate groups. Ultimately, the teacher uses creative power to create an alternative community that makes students aware of their own realities while emphasizing personal responsibility.

Thus the historicizing of a communicative interaction or text requires the incorporation of other theoretical perspectives into critical discourse analysis. What theoretical perspectives are incorporated need to be justified and argued in terms of that perspective's grounding in that history and in terms of its orientation to the goal of making power relations visible and to pursuing a more just world. More simply stated, a bottom-up approach to critical discourse analysis is a logic-of-inquiry in search of a situated and historical grounded sibling theory(ies).

Although we have only provided a limited close analysis of the classroom communicative interaction above, nonetheless the analysis creates a dialectic with broader critical/sociopolitical theories. On one hand, there is linguistic evidence of broader critical/sociopolitical processes of dominance and social reproduction at play. In lines 2 through 4, Helen falters in her reading and is corrected by another student, indexing a social hierarchy and set of power relations grounded in oral reading performance. It also indexes the characterization of these students as having reading and academic difficulties that need to be remediated. In lines 12, 36, 41, and elsewhere, the students espouse an institutional morality that is taken as common sense, accepted by all, and natural; even though their life experiences would contradict such a morality. It is a direction for social reproduction of economically, politically, and culturally stratified society. On the other hand, that same close, linguistic analysis revealed that it was the teacher who repositioned the students' relationship to themselves and to the institutional ideology. And, she did this, in part, by redefining (reconstituting) reading; shifting reading from being a social practice of oral rendition and representing what happens in the text to the satisfaction of the teacher to the use of a text for reflecting on one's life and the worlds in which one lives. This practice is reflective of social justice in pedagogical action as described by Freire (1972), hooks (1994), and Ladson-Billings (1994). Through dialogue, the teacher and students positioned themselves as both members of multiple dominant groups and multiple subordinate groups while creating alternative epistemologies. Such repositioning, redefining, and reconstituting what counts as knowledge are not simply matters of resistance, but more so of supplanting a dominant institutional ideology with one grounded in African American history, culture, and life.

Final Comments

Critical discourse analysis is not a monolithic research methodology. Although similar in the goal of bringing together linguistic models of analysis with critical/ sociopolitical theories, critical discourse analysis varies in the linguistic models and critical theories employed, disciplinary perspectives foregrounded, and the emphasis on top-down versus bottom-up approaches. The application of critical discourse analysis to educational settings can be useful in large part because it is through language that education, teaching, and learning occur; and it is through language that dominant (and dominating) narratives and counter-narratives are created. Whenever people use language or any set of semiotic tools, they are always employing "motivated signs" (cf. Kress, 1993), structuring power relations. Making visible how people use language to establish these power relations as well as making visible how people reconstitute power relations have potential to inform curriculum and pedagogy for those who are interested in educational processes aimed at creating a more just world.

Bibliography

Anderson G. L. (2001). Disciplining leaders: A critical discourse analysis of the ISLLC National Examination and Performance standards in educational administration. *International Journal of Leadership in Education, 4, 3, 1,* 199–216.

Bakhtin, M. (1935/1981 trans.). *The dialogic imagination.* Austin, TX: University of Texas Press.

Bell, D. (1987). *And we are not saved: The elusive quest for racial justice.* New York: Basic.

Bloome, D., & Carter, S. (2001). Lists in reading education reform. *Theory into Practice. 40,* 3, 150–157.

Bloome, D., Carter, S., Christian, B., Otto, S., & Shuart-Faris, N. (2005). *Discourse analysis & the study of classroom language & literacy events: A microethnographic perspective.* Mahwah, NJ: Lawrence Erlbaum.

Bourdieu, P. (1977). *Outline of a theory of practice.* Cambridge, UK: Cambridge University Press.

Bourdieu, P. (1991). *Language and symbolic power.* Cambridge, MA: Harvard University Press.

Candela, A. (1998). Students' power in classroom discourse. *Linguistics and Education, 10,* 2, 139–164.

Collins, P. (1990). *Black feminist thought: Knowledge, consciousness, and the politics of empowerment.* Boston, MA: Unwin Hyman.

Crenshaw, K, Gotanda, N., Peller, G., & Thomas, K. (Eds.). (1995). *Critical race theory: The key writings that formed the movement.* New York: Routledge.

de Certeau, M. (1984). *The practice of everyday life.* Berkeley, CA: University of California Press.

Dixon, A. D., & Rousseau, C.K. (Eds.). (2006). *Critical race theory in education.* New York: Routledge.

Du Bois, W.E.B. (1903). *Souls of Black folk: Essays and sketches.* Chicago: A.C. McClurg and Company.

Fairclough, N. (1989). *Language and power.* London: Longman.

Fairclough, N. (2003). *Analysing discourse: Textual analysis for social research.* London: Routledge.

Foucault, M. (1980). *Power/knowledge: Selected interviews and other writings, 1972-1977.* (C. Gordon Ed.). New York: Pantheon.

Freire, P. (1972). *Pedagogy of the oppressed.* Harmondsworth, UK: Penguin.

Gee, J. (2004) Discourse analysis: What makes it critical? In R. Rogers (Ed.), *An introduction to critical discourse analysis in education* (pp. 19–50). Mahwah, NJ: Lawrence Erlbaum.

Goffman, E. (1981). *Forms of talk.* Philadelphia: University of Pennsylvania Press.

hooks, b. (1989). *Talking back: Thinking feminist, thinking Black.* Boston, MA: South End.

hooks, b. (1993). *Sisters of the yam.* Boston, MA: South End.

hooks, b. (1994). *Teaching to transgress: Education as the practice of freedom.* London: Routledge.

Hunt, I. (1976). *Lottery rose.* New York: Berkley Jam.

Ivanic, R. (1998) *Writing and identity: The discoursal construction of identity in academic writing.* Amsterdam: John Benjamins.

Kress, G. (1993). Against arbitrariness: The social production of the sign as a foundational issue in critical discourse analysis. *Discourse and Society, 4,* 2, 169–191.

Kumaravadivelu, B. (1999). Critical classroom discourse analysis. *TESOL Quarterly, 33,* 3, 453–484.

Ladson-Billings, G. (1994). *The dreamkeepers: Successful teachers of African American students.* San Francisco: Jossey-Bass.

Ladson-Billings, G., & Tate, W. (1995). Towards a critical race theory of education. *Teachers College Record, 97,* 1, 47–68.

Lewis, C. (2001). *Literacy practices as social acts: Power, status, and cultural norms in the classroom.* Mahwah, NJ: Lawrence Erlbaum.

Luke, A. (1995). Text and discourse in education: An introduction to critical discourse analysis. In M. Apple (Ed.) *Review of research in education,* v. 21. (pp. 3–48). Washington, DC: AERA.

Rogers, R. (2002a). Through the eyes of the institution: A critical discourse analysis of decision making in two special education meetings. *Anthropology & Education Quarterly, 33,* 2, 213–237.

Rogers, R. (2002b). Between contexts: A critical discourse analysis of family literacy, discursive practices, and literate subjectivities. *Reading Research Quarterly,* 37, 3, 248–277.

Rogers, R. (2004a). Storied Selves: A Critical Discourse Analysis of Adult learners' Literate Lives. *Reading Research Quarterly, 39,* 3, 272–305.

Rogers, R. (2004b). *An introduction to critical discourse analysis in education.* Mahwah, NJ: Lawrence Erlbaum.

Rogers, R., Malancharuvil-Berkes, E., Mosley, M., Hui, D., & O'Garro Joseph, G. (2005). Critical discourse analysis in education: A review of the literature. *Review of Educational Research, 75,* 3, 365–416.

Toolan, M. (1997). What is critical discourse analysis and why are people saying such terrible things about it? *Language and Literature, 6,* 2, 83–103.

van Dijk, T.A. (1993) Principles of critical discourse analysis. *Discourse and Society, 4,* 249–283.

Woodson, C. G. (1933). *The mis-education of the Negro.* [1990 reprint]. Trenton, NJ: Africa World Press.

TWELVE

Critical Ethnographies of Discourse: An Essay on Collecting Noise

David E. Kirkland

O ne cannot truly understand the conditions of culture without being able to listen to that culture's noise—its loud and exuberant screams of self-expression, cries to freedom, and documents of oppressions; its shouting limits and resounding possibilities. Insomuch as all human oppressions deal with the suppression of people's noise (i.e., silencing or restrictions of some sorts on the people's emancipated voices), then noise, as opposed to silence, is directly tied to all processes of human liberation. For those of us who have decided on the work of critical education inquiry, the question of noise—how it can be best captured without stripping it of its complexities or silencing its makers—sits at the fore of our research enterprise.

Indeed, we have learned much about noise from social and cultural sciences that analyze discourse. In the educational sciences, discourse is generally defined as symbolic forms of representation—what people say, write, or create in order to bring their realities into existence (Cochran-Smith & Fries, 2002). Discourse has also been described as symbolic ways of being, postures and dispositions toward things archived in a people's language or other textual productions that reveal those people's identity (Assaf, 2005; Gee, 2004; Kirkland, forthcoming; Rogers, 2004; Rogers, Malancharuvil-Berkes, Mosley, Hui, & Joseph, 2005). While it has been richly theorized and frequently analyzed by educational scholars, discourse remains an elusive concept to capture denotatively.

As a substance (or a culturally produced material artifact), discourse is perhaps more difficult to capture than define. When analyzed, researchers tend to take as discourse those available recordings of a people's noise—a kind of incidental method of data collection that relies heavily on the researcher's flawed ears. As an incidence of data, discourse—in line with more empirical traditions—is deductively (as opposed to inductively) taken up by researchers, who hear only what they can hear in the often muddled cultural situations of people. And yet, it seems to me that there are discourses that cannot be easily heard, either because of the untrained ear or because of strategic cultural codes that make some discourses unavailable to outsiders (Gee, 1996). Such deep flaws in perception deny us meaningful data, particularly the ability to capture the noises of the people, who are tied to a larger process of the people's liberation (Freire, 1970).

Further, the sciences of noise have too often dissolved into overly technical descriptions of the more dominant grammars, rhetorics, and poetics of the elite and have been successfully projected over the masses whereby the masses learn to consent to their own silencing. As such, the dominant discourses of the elite govern people's participation within mainstream structures such as schools. Rarely are the chaotic resonances of language that exist beyond the linguistic mainstream given calm by such sciences, nor are the silences that loudly erupt or quietly snore in the sleep of any cultural moment given due attention in the data collection process. Then, to truly liberate the people's voices in order to understand the people from the people's perspective, researchers must answer two important questions about noise: How can we hear and contextualize noise in order to understand the people from the people's perspective, and how can we begin to collect the people's noises in order to liberate these perspectives, their realities?

Contextualizing and Collecting Noise

Philosophers of language (Derrida, 1967; Foucault, 1970, 1972) and sociocritical linguists (Fairclough, 2003; Gee, 2004; Smitherman, 1977; Smitherman & van Dijk, 1988) have proposed several methodological approaches to analyzing noise. Chief among them have been the so-called critical discourse approaches (Fairclough, 1995; Gee, 2004; Rogers et al., 2005; Stevens, 2004; Wodak, 2008). While these approaches have been transformative in the study of language in educational research, they leave open the question of not how to analyze language, but how to capture it as a cultural artifact that carries the residue of a people's tensions, struggles, and hopes. Hence, a thorough understanding of language or literacy can never be fully achieved through analyses of discourse or communication alone. Surrounding communicative dialogue or discourses are what I call the silent noises, what Gee (1989) calls big "D" discourse—symbolic "ways of being" or "forms of life," that integrate language, ideas, values, beliefs, and various opportunities and motivations that aren't easily picked up by an analyst alone (Alim, 2005; Bakhtin, 1981; Smitherman & van Dijk, 1988). These systems of representation, of being and of living, carry within them unseen and often unheard elements of people, such as the intentions of others, desires and motivations, various and sometimes competing ideational limits (both constraining and expanding), and importantly power.

From this perspective, understanding people and their cultural artifacts such as literacy is much more than the product of understanding how people communicate. It is about capturing the people's noise, those sometimes heartrending, sometimes foreboding and unspoken dialogic artifacts of sound and chaotic symbiology (Defleur, 1991) that tell people's story. Therefore, researchers of language and literacy who intend to more fully understand the literate lives of individuals, particularly in relation to questions about what it means to be literate and in relation to questions about a people's literacy—in addition to analyzing discourse—must also explore ways to collect it. Failing to address the issue of how to capture people's voice makes us complicit in the ideological and repressive apparatuses that promote state-sanctioned oppression (Althusser, 1969; Bakhtin, 1986; Rogers et al., 2005).

However, I believe that much can be accomplished by collecting people's voice ethnographically, drawing not only on the ears of the researcher or the researcher's team. Rather, the researcher must work in cooperation with her or his participants, using the ears of the people and empowering their listening so that the people can know what to hear and how to report on those hearings in ways that provide rich, meaningful, and descriptive information about a cultural situation, or what Foucault (1970) has termed a *discursive field*. From a methodological standpoint, this approach is situated socially (Gee, 2001; Heath, 1983; Hymes, 1993; Street, 1995) and builds upon "the new literacy studies" (Alvermann, 2002; Hull, 2003; New London Group, 1996) and theories of dialogism (Bakhtin, 1981; Dyson, 2003, 2006; Fecho & Botzakis, 2007). It also draws from critical ethnography, which seeks to decenter the power of the researcher by disabling vertical relationships between the researcher and the researched (Foucault, 1977; McLaren, 1997, 2002).

Within the sociocritical sphere (Gutierrez, 2008), there are cultural, historical, and even geographical elements that complicate languages and literacies. Languages and literacies are yet alive, living intensely in the vicarious situations of individuals—both through mind and society in a complex tug of interests (Smagorinsky, 2007; Vygotsky, 2006). Research methodologies that account for these complications in the sociocritical study of literacy can also problematize uncomplicated assumptions that push to homogenize or decontextualize what literacy learning truly means to people. Further, all reductions of literacy are equally reductions of people since we, as language or language-related researchers, come to know the people through their productions of things, in this case; noise. Hence, divorcing the noise from its people does not give it or the people voice. However, in collecting the noise of the people, one must also collect the noisemaker—the people themselves.

Collecting the Noisemaker

Some might find the idea of "collecting the noisemaker" as farfetched. Some, who may have taken the comment more literally, might find the statement criminal, akin to promoting kidnap. However, I have no interests, here, in articulating pie-in-the-sky research ideologies or "gangsta" epistemologies. Rather, my goal is to suggest ways that research done in the service of justice can actually be more just and more acutely aware of the concerns of the people. This cannot be done without the people, who must stand on their own in our research. In standing, we must afford them a podium and a mic in our work—from theory to policy, from initial inquiry to the creation of our research designs—to express their realities in their own unique ways. Importantly, we must enlist their help in collecting the artifacts of noise (i.e., the people's interpretations, worldviews, theories, and reasons for being) that essentially constitute their voices.

In language and literacy, there have been several catchers of noise and noisemakers. Chief among them, Smitherman (1977)—a scholar who, I believe, has long captured the noise of people and, as a noisemaker herself, has made sense of its ordered chaos—has consistently enlisted "the contribution of the folk" (p. 103) in her research on African American language. Smitherman's critical cultural approach to discourse can be distinguished from other researchers who analyze discourse without considering "the contribution of the folk" or the silencing of them by mainstream elite ideological structures.

Smitherman's approach marks the early stages of what I call the *critical ethnography of discourse* (CED). In CED, discourse represents "folklore, folk utterances, songs and tales of folk expression" that make groups unique (Smitherman, 1977, p. 103). According to Smitherman (1977), discourse in this way comprises the cultural, social, and political history of language used and in use, which is derived from mutually understood "verbal strategies, rhetorical devices, and folk expressive rituals" (p. 103). Smitherman's approach follows CED in its search through a people's culture for its noise (e.g., its "expressive rituals"). Though it focuses on the people's noise—their critical discourses—CED borrows from other anthropological approaches to language and symbol that seek to understand people's "ritual" behaviors and "communicative" practices (Defleur, 1991; Hymes, 1962, 1974, 1993).

CED also holds open the possibility that people are not stable entities. The nature of "folk" is ever present but changing/amending in our thoughts, our actions, and our words. "Folk" and "folk expressions" (i.e., noises or discourses), then, are forever in flux. Therefore, at the center of social (inter)action are unresolved and dilemma-filled plays of meaning and symbolic activity that individuals negotiate as a result of conflict and sociocultural choices, choices that give rise to contingent forms of expression. These expressions, captured and re-presented in the vernacular or everyday voices of the people, liberate the people's realities. Moreover, CED is interested in capturing (as opposed to simply analyzing) and liberating (as opposed to having power over others through analysis) the voices of people, which mediate identity and power and embody the conflicting values and stances of a social group.

The ethnographic life of people, of the culture and conditions of its noisemaker, is tied to the idea that voice or discourse is a sociohistorical formation rather than a historical structure (Bakhtin, 1981). Hence, the noisemaker, when captured fully, becomes her or his own noise, which "lives, as it were, beyond itself, in a living impulse [*napravlennost*] toward the object" or the world it creates (Bakhtin, 1981, p. 292). For Bakhtin (1981):

> If we detach ourselves completely from this impulse all we have left is the naked corpse of the word, from which we can learn nothing at all about the social situation or the fate of a given word in life. *To study the word as such, ignoring the impulse that reaches out beyond it, is just as senseless as to study psychological experience outside the context of that real life toward which it was directed and by which it is determined.* (p. 292, emphasis in the original)

Bakhtin's understanding of noise, or discourse as he calls it, helps explain how noise is socially and historically configured in and in relation to selves, or what Smitherman (1977) calls the "folk." The noise of folks and the folks themselves (referred to here as noisemakers) emerge relative to the languages they use and the individuals and groups who have or still are using them. In this way, capturing noises in ethnography can be central to understanding human histories and human societies as they permeate cultural contexts both throughout the individual and the group.

Individuals and the groups to which they belong are consumed by, immersed within, vast oceans of circulating noises that transmit layers of ideas, desires, and motivations that are born out of the near or distant past. This is not to say that the noises of a people are at all random, neutral, or acting in some trivial way in the production of human societies. Rather, such noises are "populated—overpopulated—with the intention of others" (Bakhtin, 1981, p. 294). So while they function at social and historical levels, noises, in fact, carry fundamental political underpinnings that radicalize body and mind, reading and writing, silence and sound.

In this way, discourses—the scientific unit of noise—are united by a common object of study (e.g., law), a common methodology (e.g., logic), and/or set of common terms and ideas (e.g., justice). They are tied to various elements of cultural production—the production of knowledge, difference, or identity. They can be ordered by their functions: for instance, discourses that constrain the production of knowledge, difference, and identity, and those that enable new knowledge, differences, and identities.

Understanding discourse in this way has helped me to raise important questions concerning how power is enacted/negotiated in the languages and literacies of the youth I study (Kirkland, 2009; Kirkland & Jackson, 2009). In my observations of them, I have found—looking for noise—that discourses can be captured ethnographically in the contexts of youths' social performances and in the echoes of their cultural practices. Discourses in such places form and maintain sets of social competitions (privileging and marginalizing), influencing unequal power relationships that distinguish and create conflict among folk (e.g., literates and illiterates), folk groups (e.g., Blacks and Whites), and different folk practices of literacy (Kirkland & Jackson, 2009). Discourses, in effect, sanction power and simultaneously constitute the conflicted "nature" of the self (Foucault, 1976), the unconscious and conscious mind (Lacan, 1984), and the emotional life of the folk they seek to define, group, and govern.

Viewing discourse in this way has allowed me to raise important questions concerning the contested conditions under which literacies emerge and are practiced. It is within this larger light that I have begun to understand how discourses mediate power, legitimacy, and authority in the actual social situations of people and at the same time shape the conditions under which people are oppressed. Therefore, an ethnography that observes and examines discourse becomes a significant tool for understanding and uncovering the injuries of people because it reveals significant aspects of those people's lives. Locating such discourse(s), one listens for the people's noise. Moreover, listening to the people's noise has provided me with a way of capturing the people, themselves, in order to describe and explore, using their voices, un-proposed purposes and hidden meanings that cover their lives without stripping from them the thing that is most precious to their beings—their voices. It is in this way that CED acts as a method of social justice research. In my work, it helps to give the literacies practiced by the people meaning, voice, validity, identity, and connectedness.

Bibliography

Alim, H. S. (2005). Critical language awareness in the United States: Revisiting issues and revising pedagogies in a resegregated society. *Educational Researcher, 34*(7), 24–31.

Althusser, L. (1969). *For Marx*. New York: Vintage.

Alvermann, D. E. (2002). *Adolescents and literacies in a digital world*. New York: Peter Lang.

Assaf, L. C. (2005). Exploring identities in a reading specialization program. *Journal of Literacy Research, 37*(2), 201–236.

Bakhtin, M. M. (1981). *The dialogic imagination: Four essays* (M. Holquist & C. Emerson, Trans.). Austin, TX: University of Texas Press.

Bakhtin, M. M. (1986). *Speech genres and other late essays.* Austin, TX: University of Texas Press.

Cochran-Smith, M., & Fries, K. (2002). The discourse of reform in teacher education: Extending the dialogue. *Educational Researcher, 31*(6), 26–28.

Defleur, M. (1991). Ritual, anti-structure, and religion: A discussion of Victor Turner's Processual Symbolic Analysis. *Journal for the Scientific Study of Religion, 30*(1), 1–25.

Derrida, J. (1967). *Of Grammatology* (G. C. Spivak, Trans.). London: Johns Hopkins University Press.

Dyson, A. H. (2003). *The brothers and sisters learn to write: Popular literacies in childhood and school cultures.* New York: Teachers College Press.

Dyson, A. H. (2006). Literacy in a child's world of voices, or, the fine print of murder and mayhem. *Research in the Teaching of English, 41*(2), 147–153.

Fairclough, N. (1995). *Critical discourse analysis: The critical study of language.* London: Longman.

Fairclough, N. (2003). *Analysing discourse: Textual analysis for social research.* London: Routledge.

Fecho, B., & Botzakis, S. (2007). Feasts of becoming: Imagining a literacy classroom based on dialogic beliefs. *Journal of Adolescent and Adult Literacy, 50*(7), 548–558.

Foucault, M. (1970). *The order of things.* New York: Pantheon.

Foucault, M. (1972). *Archaeology of knowledge.* New York: Pantheon.

Foucault, M. (1977). *Discipline and punish: The birth of the prison.* New York: Pantheon.

Freire, P. (1970). *Pedagogy of the oppressed.* New York: Continuum.

Gee, J. P. (1989). What is literacy? *Journal of Education, 171*(1), 5–25.

Gee, J. P. (1996). *Social linguistic and literacies: Ideology in discourses* (2nd ed.). Bristol, PA: Taylor & Francis.

Gee, J. P. (2001). A sociocultural perspective on early literacy development. In S. B. Neuman & D. K. Dickinson (Eds.), *Handbook of early literacy research* (pp. 30–42). New York: Guilford.

Gee, J. P. (2004). Discourse analysis: What makes it critical? In R. Rogers (Ed.), *An introduction to critical discourse analysis in education* (pp. 19–50). Mahway, NJ: Lawrence Erlbaum.

Gutierrez, K. D. (2008). Developing a sociocritical literacy in the Third Space. *Reading Research Quarterly, 43*(2), 148–164.

Heath, S. B. (1983). *Ways with words: Language, life and work in communities and classrooms.* Cambridge, MA: Cambridge University Press.

Hull, G. (2003). Youth culture and digital media: New literacies for new times. *Reasearch in the Teaching of English, 38*(2), 229–233.

Hymes, D. (1962). The ethnography of communication. In T. Gladwin & W. Sturtevant (Eds.), *Anthropology and human behavior* (pp. 15–53). Washington, D.C.: Anthropological Society of Washington.

Hymes, D. (1974). *Foundations in sociolinguistics.* Philadelphia, PA: University of Pennsylvania Press.

Hymes, D. (1993). Toward ethnographies of communication. In J. Maybin (Ed.), *Language and Literacy in Social Practice* (pp. 11–22). London: Multilingual Matters.

Kirkland, D. E. (2009). The skin we ink: Tattoos, literacy, and a new English education. *English Education, 41*(4), 375–395.

Kirkland, D. (forthcoming). "Something to brag about": Black males, literacy, and teacher education. In A. Ball, & C. Tyson (Eds.), *Studying Diversity in Teaching and Teacher Education, Volume III*. Washington, DC: AERA.

Kirkland, D. E., & Jackson, A. (2009). "We real cool": Toward a theory of Black masculine literacies. *Reading Research Quarterly, 44*(3), 278–297.

McLaren, P. (1997). Decentering whiteness: In search of revolutionary multiculturalism. *Multicultural Education, 5*(1): 4-11

McLaren, P. (2002). *Life in schools: An introduction to critical pedagogy in the foundations of education*. New York: Longman.

New London Group. (1996). A pedagogy of multiliteracies: Designing social futures. *Harvard Educational Review, 66*(1), 60–92.

Rogers, R. (2004). An introduction to critical discourse analysis in education. In R. Rogers (Ed.), *An Introduction to Critical Discourse Analysis in Education* (pp. 1–18). Mahwah, NJ: Lawrence Erlbaum.

Rogers, R., Malancharuvil-Berkes, E., Mosley, M., Hui, D., & Joseph, G. O. (2005). Critical discourse analysis in education: A review of the literature. *Review of Educational Research, 75*(3), 365–391.

Smagorinsky, P. (2007). Vygotsky and the social dynamics of classrooms. *English Journal, 97*(2), 61–66.

Smitherman, G. (1977). *Talkin and testifyin: The language of Black America*. Detroit, MI: Wayne State University Press.

Smitherman, G., & van Dijk, T. A. (1988). *Discourse and discrimination*. Detroit: Wayne State University Press.

Stevens, L. P. (2004). Locating the role of the critical discourse analyst. In R. Rogers (Ed.), *An introduction to critical discourse analysis in education* (pp. 207–224). Mahwah, NJ: Lawrence Erlbaum.

Street, B. (1995). *Social literacies: Critical approaches to literacy in development, ethnography, and education*. London: Longman.

Vygotsky, L. S. (2006). *Mind in society: Development of higher psychological processes* (1st ed.). Cambridge, MA: Harvard University Press.

Wodak, R. (2008). The contribution of critical linguistics to the analysis of discriminatory prejudices and stereotypes in the language of politics. In R. Wodak & V. Koller (Eds.), *Handbook of applied linguistics: "The public sphere"* (Vol. IV). Berlin: de Gruyter.

THIRTEEN

Context and Narrative in Sociocultural Research

Bob Fecho & Janette R. Hill

When Bob, one of the authors of this essay, was doing research with the support of teens from working-class families, he conducted initial interviews in their homes, partly to allay fears of the parents about a relative stranger spending time with their son and partly to gain a sense of their home lives. Each boy—Isaac, Andy, and Jorge—lived in neighborhoods that differed markedly from the others and also from the northeastern U.S. row house in which Bob was raised. These differences were not lost on him. For example, as he climbed the stairs to the second floor of Jorge's apartment building, one in which all the front doors opened onto a terrace rather than an interior hall, Bob sought a sense of that space, taking in the textures, sounds, and nuances around him.

If, as Bakhtin (1981) suggested, all meaning is embedded in context, then Bob saw it as key to his work to have rich invocations of context and what it implies for our understandings. Freire (1970) argued that we read the world before we read the word and that the world—the particular context in time and space—in which we read the word deeply affects our understandings. The details of Jorge's home were telling Bob a story; he needed only to pay attention. As he was heading back to his home—a ranch house in an established subdivision—Bob was drafting the opening lines of the following poem in his head.

Cinderblocks
stacked
one on the other
forming two stories.
Cement stairs
metal-reinforced
with open risers
zig zag
to the narrow ledge
that runs the length.
Steel door
painted like red clay
after a rain
stings my knuckles
as I knock.
Car wheels grumble
on the gravel lot
Eyes
suspicious or disbelieving
watch me
from across the way.
Chains clatter
undone from inside

and the door groans open.
Warmth flows through
the rigid frame
into twilight chill
and voices
softly rounding syllables
pull me inside
to where
neons swim in
turquoise water.
An incandescent glow
lights the living room kitchen.
The TV murmurs
A wide-eyed baby coos
from the welcoming lap
of a smiling woman
Framed on the wall
the awards of childhood
(Where are mine?
In boxes maybe)
celebrate the future
through the past

To an extent, the poem Bob wrote narrates the transaction that was occurring between his and Jorge's worlds. It details the ways Bob was being shaped by what he was encountering. His choice to use a poem to convey context comes from a need on his part to create a more vivid sense of his immersion in the research and, in particular, to help him retain the preeminent understanding that research in general and particularly educational research are about crossing cultural borderlands, as Anzaldúa (2007) described. Those of us who cross those boundaries are affected by the transactions we encounter and we need to be more willing to tell the stories of those shaping experiences.

As researchers in educational settings, we enter people's lives. In doing so, we walk into their stories; we become audiences for, characters in, and shapers of the tales they tell about themselves. The students, teachers, and parents involved in our studies also enter our stories. They are present in the formal reports of our research as well as the anecdotal, off-the-cuff vignettes we tell in hotel lobbies at conferences. Sometimes we reduce the story to bare numbers or aggregated data, but they are stories nonetheless and breathing detail lurks behind every figure and table.

And, if we're honest, we accept that we are telling stories. It's either an occupational hazard or a goal to be sought, depending on your perspective. All research is fiction, at least to some extent. It's contingent on perceptions of a moment, of what occurred there, of what it all might mean. The emperor Marcus Aurelius (1997), writing in the 2nd century, suggested that "all is opinion" (p. 11). More recently, Bakhtin (1986) wrote that "When studying [humans], we search for and find signs everywhere and we try to grasp their meaning" (p. 114). Contemporary Africana philosopher Lewis Gordon (2000) argued that those most marginalized from the mainstream of society are those most wanting to make meaning of the stories of their lives.

In this essay, we—Bob and Janette—argue that narrative, the telling of story, is present in all that we do. In telling our research stories, we are involved in the continual re-construction and re-presentation of those narratives and that such work can never be divorced from historical, present, or future contexts. Furthermore, as researchers, we are always working cross culturally, with all the complications and rewards therein. Given those complications and rewards, we have a responsibility as researchers to construct and present the stories of our transactions with participants in all that complexity, knowing full well that no construction and presentation of data is ever complete. However, as context and narrative mutually shape each other, we gain new insight into the communities we research and ourselves as researchers.

In work outlining a dialogical approach to psychological therapy, Hermans and Kempen (1993) discussed the concept of contextualism, a central tenet of which dictates that a historical event "can only be understood when it is located in the context of *time* and *space*" (p. 14, emphasis in the original). Importantly, context is always shifting, as are the actors within the context. Citing the work of Sarbin (1986), Hermans and Kempen described the ways historians use chronicles and other primary material as foundation from which narrative is constructed. They further argued, "This reconstruction is not possible without imagination, since history can only be written on the basis of incomplete data" (p. 15). Nor does this reconstruction remain stagnant, but instead stays open to future transactions with readers who bring other contexts and thus new understandings (Rosenblatt, 1995).

Each of us, like historians, constructs personal narratives of our life events from the incomplete data available to us. Because those personal narratives are subject to shifting contexts, humans "are continually ordering and reordering the events that they consider relevant to their own lives (Hermans & Kempen, 1993, p. 15). As Bakhtin (1986) suggested, we derive meaning from response and response is ongoing, therefore, our life stories are never static, but remain in flux as we respond to new contexts, experiences, and other influences. Building on Bakhtin, Hermans and Kempen (1993) argued, "Changes in the situation may have direct repercussions to the story involved, and therefore both telling and retelling are essential" (p. 15). In doing so, we remain in constant transaction with the circumstances and conditions that bring meaning to our lives, maintaining what Bakhtin (1986) has described as an "active and also creative" (p. 142) trans-actional relationship between who we are becoming and the worlds we inhabit.

When we think about ourselves as researchers entering a community that has agreed to participate in a study, we need to remain aware that our life events, those of our participants, and the ones we mutually construct are complex narratives built on incomplete data and that they remain dynamic. In a similar way that Peshkin (1988) suggested we need to embrace and be aware of our subjectivities throughout the research process, so must we be cognizant of the limitations and limitlessness of the stories we construct. Rather than deterring us away from story, possibilities to continually re-construct and re-present our understandings of these stories enable us and the field to remain immersed in contexts that shape meaning making. An example taken from Janette's experience as a researcher and educator will better clarify this stance.

Janette's professional experience is grounded in instructional technology, a field in which narrative and story are not commonplace in scholarly work. In the fall of 2008, she taught a course in the instructional technology program related to the critique of teaching and learning. Freire's (1970) work served as a foundation for the course, along with a book of essays on critical perspectives on the teaching and learning process (McLaren & Kincheloe, 2007). Being a diverse group in terms of race, gender, generations, and sexual identity, the students and Janette decided to engage in an action research project with our class as the focal point. The purpose was to explore our perspectives toward teaching and learning as individuals and as a group, and to then look at the implications for others working in fields where such critique may not be embraced. In short, we constructed a context of critique.

To assist with data gathering, the class engaged in storytelling activities in the course, including periodic reflections on privilege and marginalization. In each of these activities, the students and Janette wrote about their experiences with self and other. During the exploration, the conversations and the storytelling were a central aspect of what happened during class meetings. Each story, created with the incomplete data described by Hermans and Kempen (1993), helped the students and Janette unpack their identities as educators and scholars. As the group used oral inquiry processes (Himley with Carini, 2000) to analyze the narratives, they brought their various contexts into the conversations in order to make meaning of the narratives.

Building on this foundation, Janette and the students wrote vignettes about events that were impactful for them during the course. This culminating activity was perhaps the most powerful as they all worked to gain an understanding of their perspectives related to the ideas of privilege and marginalization. Janette noted how there were many events in class that pushed her thinking on these issues, ranging from text rendering activities based on Freire's (1970) work to the sharing of poetry to the watching of video segments to gain new perspectives. One example is shared from Janette's vignette after a discussion of Freire:

> Connor shared with us how impressed he was that someone like Freire, an academic, would talk about love. *Dialogue cannot exist, however, in the absence of a profound love for the world and for people. The naming of the world, which is an act of creation and re-creation, is not possible if it is not infused with love.[4]Love is at the same time the foundation of dialogue and dialogue itself...love is an act of courage, not of fear, love is commitment to others....Only by abolishing the situation of oppression is it possible to restore the love which that situation made impossible. If I do not love the world—if I do not love life if I do not love people—I cannot enter into dialogue.* Freire, *Pedagogy of the Oppressed*, chapter 3, http://www.marxists.org/subject/education/freire/pedagogy/ch03.htm Connor went on to talk about how rare it is that we talk about love in higher education and that it seems remiss given how important it is. This led us into discussions about the importance of the whole person and how s/he can be recognized *even in* formal education contexts.

> I have thought a lot about our conversation from that day—and realized that "love" or the idea of the "whole person" (mind, body, spirit) have come up several times during our seminar this term, either in readings or in discussion. I realized...that the concepts of love and an interest in the whole person are at the foundation of what I try to do as an educator [and scholar]. I have tried in my classes, as well as in my one-on-one work with students, to come from a perspective of working with the whole person, coming from a center of love. I have been doing it naturally, but not really knowing that's what I was doing.

Writing the vignettes was important as doing so enabled something greater. In reflecting on the activities and then writing about them, Janette and the students came to realize how the sharing of and dialoguing around story were an important part of the process of developing understanding. As illustrated in Janette's sample vignette, the activity provided insight into her work as an educator, scholar, and person in the world. Janette ended her vignette with the following:

> I have also not been explicit about it [my belief in love and the whole person], but maybe I don't have to be...or maybe I should be now that I know that's at the core. So that is one pondering. Other questions that have come as a result of my thinking about this: How do you continue to pull this into formal learning settings—as well as informal interactions? Now that I know, how do I do more to extend it?

Janette has continued to ponder the questions she raised during the writing of the vignette; it was and remains a work in-progress. What also continues to grow is her understanding of the role that storytelling can play in developing understanding. After exploring storytelling beyond an everyday activity—indeed, as a way to develop understanding—Janette, like Bob, realized just how powerful it can be as a way to make meaning through narrative. Like Bob's work described earlier, Janette and the students' engagement with the vignettes illustrated that as we work and interact with our classes and our scholarship, more insight can be gained into who we are in the world, as individuals, educators, and scholars.

Bob and Janette explored the use of narrative in different ways, yet the results are similar: By unpacking the stories of our processes of collection and analysis, researchers remain immersed in an ongoing dialogue with those stories and processes. The evolution of Janette's identity as a scholar did not end when she saved her journal entry, when she shared it with the group, or when she added it to this essay. Rather, that identity and its transaction with that text remain in living dialogue as she continues to inquire within shifting contexts. Bob did not know what all there was to know about himself as a researcher having written the poem that brought Jorge's home life into focus, but it represents one more effort to do so, to gain another perspective and to rethink his sense of self given the shifting context. Transactions with narrative and context happen continuously, whether we as researchers acknowledge them or not. However, unless we find ways to call those transactions to the surface, our ability to construct meaning from them will be minimal. The story is never finished, nor should it ever be.

Bibliography

Anzaldúa, G. (2007). *Borderlands/La frontera: The new mestiza.* San Francisco, CA: Aunt Lute.

Aurelius, M. (1997). *Meditations.* Mineola, NY: Dover.

Bakhtin, M. (1981). Discourse in the novel. In M. Holquist (Ed.), *The dialogic imagination. Four essays* (C. Emerson and M. Holquist, Trans.) (pp. 259–422). Austin, TX: University of Texas Press.

Bakhtin, M. (1986). *Speech genres and other late essays* (V. McGee, Trans.) (C. Emerson & M. Holquist, Eds.). Austin, TX: University of Texas Press.

Freire, P. (1970). *Pedagogy of the oppressed.* New York: Continuum.

Gordon, L. (2000). *Existentia Africana: Understanding Africana existential thought.* New York: Routledge.

Hermans, H .J. M., & Kempen, H. J. G. (1993). *The dialogical self: Meaning as movement.* San Diego, CA: Academic.

Himley, M. (Ed.). (with Carini, P.F.). (2000). *From another angle: Children's strengths and school standards.* New York: Teachers College Press.

McLaren, P., & Kincheloe, J. L. (2007). *Critical pedagogy: Where are we now?* New York: Peter Lang.

Peshkin, A. (1988). In search of subjectivity—one's own. *Educational Researcher, 17*(7), 17–21.

Rosenblatt, L. M. (1995). *Literature as exploration* (5th ed.). New York: Modern Language Association.

Sarbin, T. R. (1986). The narrative as a root metaphor for psychology. In T. R. Sarbin (Ed.), *Narrative Psychology: The storied nature of human conduct* (pp. 3–21). New York: Praeger.

FOURTEEN

Irreducible Difference, Social Justice, and Autobiographical Qualitative Research: (Im)Possible Representations

Janet L. Miller

Prelude

Students who are interested in pursuing their advanced graduate degrees sometimes ask me, as they ask any potential faculty person with whom they might wish to study, for a quick description of my particular academic commitments and research interests. Most recently, that question was tossed across a hallway corridor as a student traipsed one way and I hastened in the opposite direction to one meeting or another. I lobbed a hasty reply that went something like this:

> I am a U.S.-born and educated English educator and feminist curriculum theorist. I most often work to challenge traditional, humanist versions of autobiographical inquiries within the broad fields of curriculum theorizing and qualitative research. I especially grapple with dilemmas of interpretation and representation in those endeavors.

Those sentences reverberated down to my toes as I tromped through the tangle of my institution's hallways. With such a visceral reaction, I (once again) realized that such a brief and seemingly definitive word sketch contradicts ways that, in my research, teaching, and writing, I attempt to disrupt and challenge such surface and essentialist summaries. I turned back, searching amidst the hallway bustle for that potential student who already had disappeared into the tunneled passageways. I longed for just another minute or two with her in order to complicate my hurried and seamless reply.

Framings

In hoping for a few moments to re-craft my response to the student's inquiry, then, I wished to describe some of the ways in which I constantly struggle with/in my refusals to construct any research representations that rest on universalized notions of "self" or "other," for example. I attempt to conceive of autobiographical forms of qualitative research and curriculum theorizing as working toward (im)possible representations of selves as always in flux, multiple and incomplete, as well as with conceptions of identities as always in the making. I posit such research attempts as one means of taking up the challenges of difference, a structuring principle that often suggests "ways of emphasizing and valorizing particular human traits over and above equally 'human' qualities that are devalued by decentering" (Peters & Burbules, 2004, p. 27). Thus, in co-conceptualizing a notion of "working difference," for example, I refer "to the possibility of engaging with and responding to the fluidity and malleability of identities and difference, of refusing fixed and static categories of sameness or permanent otherness" (Ellsworth & Miller, 2005, p. 181).

In my attempts at "working difference," I have focused my qualitative research studies for a number of years on engaging with teachers in autobiographical inquiries that challenge any unified and linear narratively rendered version of self, or curriculum, or qualitative research, or how we construct interpretations and representations of these. Further, I endeavor to situate partial and always incomplete research representations of selves in relation to analyses of political, social, historical, economic, discursive, and cultural contexts and events. Those myriad and contextualized moments as well as dominant discourses, in particular, are those that most directly frame, contain, or support which constructed identities might come into being at any one time and place.

Such studies toward which I strive are predicated, of course, on *challenges* posed in the past thirty years or so to forms of ethnographically oriented qualitative research that assume the ability of researchers to "capture" the essence and/or meaning of a particular culture or situation or individual. From the early segments of my academic career and beyond, I ascribed to a definition of qualitative research as

> a situated activity that locates the observer in the world. It consists of a set of interpretive material practices that make the world visible. These practices transform the world. They turn the world into a series of representations. . . . Qualitative researchers study things in their natural settings, attempting to make sense of, or to interpret, phenomena in terms of the meanings people bring to them. (Denzin & Lincoln, 2000, p. 3)

However, my ever-burgeoning research conundrums grew too big to ignore. I knew, after many faltering research attempts, that I never could make full sense of "the meanings" that any research participant might posit in relation to any one classroom situation or teacher identity, for example. These dilemmas came to the fore for me within what many ethnographically orientated qualitative researchers have identified as "the crisis in representation" in qualitative research (Clifford, 1988; Clifford & Marcus, 1986; Geertz, 1988; Marcus & Fischer, 1986). This crisis was prompted, in part, by the growing prominence of poststructuralist theories that broke with reflective theories of language; those reflective theories claimed that words label meanings that supposedly already exist in the external world.

Thus, the crisis in representation in qualitative research is briefly encapsulated as researchers' *inability* to continue to believe that we could directly "capture" lived experience if we just gathered enough supposedly transparent words—did enough interviews and observations of individuals in natural settings—and then "wrote up" our interpretations of such in what sociologist John Van Maanen (1988) termed "realist tales."

Instead, poststructuralist theories conceptualize language as an unstable system of referents: "language, far from reflecting an already given social reality, constitutes social reality for us. Neither social reality nor the 'natural' world has fixed intrinsic meanings which language reflects or expresses.... Meaning is constituted within language and is not guaranteed by the subject which speaks it" (Weedon, 1997, p. 22). Further, because language constitutes rather than reflects the individual's sense of self, poststructuralist theories conceptualize

> subjectivity (defined as our conscious and unconscious sense of self, our emotions and desires) as an effect of language. Rational consciousness is only one dimension of subjectivity. It is in the process of using language—whether as thought or speech—that we take up positions as speaking and thinking subjects. Language exists in the form of many competing and often contradictory discourses. . . .Some discourses, and the subject positions and modes of subjectivity that they constitute, have more power than others. (Weedon, 2003, p. 126)

Such theories, then, refute any possibility of researching and representing "the" meaning of an action, transcribed interview text, declared human intention, or precategorized and static identity.

Thus, the crisis in representation requires qualitative researchers to attend to how and why we construct versions of our research in the ways that we do. "[I]t is in the writing—about qualitative research, subjectivity, language, data and so forth—that I learn refusal. So I write and then I analyze my writing to see what I've done and not done" (St. Pierre, 2008, p. 329). Further, that crisis also requires that qualitative researchers attempt to resist "the pulling together of temporally distributed, disparate events and supposedly intentional actors into the coherent comfort of narrative....Narrative is always already interpretation piled upon interpretation" (pp. 324–325).

In pointing to how the gathering of data and the writing up of qualitative research consists of such interpretation "piles," then, the crisis in representation forces all variously epistemologically-oriented qualitative researchers to attend to how meaning is produced within language rather than reflected by language. That crisis also points to the understanding that

> individual signs do not have intrinsic meaning but acquire meaning through the language chain and their difference within it from other signs....Once language is understood in terms of competing discourses, competing ways of giving meaning to the world, which implies differences in the organization of social power, then language becomes an important site of political struggle. (Weedon, 1997, p. 23)

Were I able to return to that crosscurrent moment in the hallway with that anonymous student, I certainly would want to complicate my seemingly fixed narrative of my academic positionings and research passions by articulating how aspects of the crisis in representation have changed my academic work over the years. But more important, I would want to describe how my graduate students, whose own interests and concerns have provided vivid exemplification of how language indeed becomes an important site of political struggle, have infinitely challenged my research and its representations.

"Local" Challengers

Many doctoral students with whom I work, teach in a variety of public and private greater New York City–area schools at the secondary and collegiate levels. In their doctoral research, some wish to focus on their own or other teachers' accounts of what they often describe as professional tensions. Several describe these as primarily located between unitary- and mass-produced versions of school reform, national policy mandates, or local school enactments of such, and their daily classroom, counseling, or administrative experiences of and struggles with difference. I agree with many of my students' pedagogical and research concerns: sameness—in terms of who, how, and why educators should be engaged in their practices—characterizes many current and dominant discourses of school reform initiatives, educational policies, and the educational research often attached to such processes and projects.

Undeniably, predetermined versions of educational policies and school reform efforts often ignore educators' disruptive autobiographical accounts. Within conceptions of language as a site of political struggle, some doctoral students wish to examine ways in which varied discursive constructions of gender, sexual orientation, age, race, ethnicity, for example, shape and inform our lives and work. With such pressing concerns framing their doctoral research interests, then, many of these doctoral students are committed to concerted research attempts that could illuminate, challenge, and disrupt the normalizing language of educational policies that prescribe and often standardize teachers' pedagogies in relation to linear, sequential, and universalized versions of curricula that sometimes essentialize what and whose knowledge counts.

Further, schools, colleges, and universities in the U.S. are dealing with increasing surveillance prompted by governmental mandates contained, for example, within No Child Left Behind. President Obama's continuing reinforcement of initial aspects of the George W. Bush administration's legislation is reflected in the current administration's recently funded program entitled Race to the Top. This program is comprised of a series of competitive grants totalling over $4 billion that are designed to both provide support for struggling educators and to motivate educators and students to outperform one another on the already in-place series of high-stakes testing. These government mandates and competitive grant programs, among others, contain similar presses for curriculum standardization and measurable teacher and student accountability performances.

Given this continuing emphasis on the measurable, the quantification of what counts as effective teaching and learning, many of the graduate students with whom I work especially toil to conceptualize forms of autobiographical qualitative research that gesture toward (im)possible representations of the un-knowable, the diversity, and the variety of social, cultural, and discursive contexts and identities with and in which teaching and learning daily take place. In such forms of autobiographical research, the emphasis often centers on how, why, and by whom difference gets constructed within language contained in dominant educational discourses as well as processes and contexts.

Thus, to continue to develop autobiographically situated inquiries that support such goals also requires that we, as practitioner-researchers, raise challenges to humanist versions of narrative forms of autobiographical inquiry. Those humanist versions, as noted above, posit unified, singular, prefigured, and es-sentialized versions of self, experience, other, and voice—as well as analyses of normative cultural scripts for these.

Indeed, I approach possible versions of autobiographical educational inqui-ry from feminist poststructuralist perspectives in order to draw attention to the multiple and often contradictory meanings, subjectivities, and power relations that circulate in any research account of constructions of curriculum, pedagogy, school reform strategy, or educational policy. Because of my various qualitative and often collaborative and long-term research projects over the years (see Miller, 1990, 2005), I obviously have come to embrace theoretical as well as method-ological research stances that *challenge* any autobiographical representations that result in naturalizations, essentializations, or compartmentalizations of identities and their constructions. Amidst all these persuasions, I still attempt, in self-reflexive methodological moves, to maintain as primary what feminist philosopher Jane Flax (1993) describes as "certain visceral beliefs about justice and how people should be treated" (p. 7).

Thus, I maintain that to advocate for "social justice" in education, *writ large*, and within English education and research, in particular, requires forms of qualitative research that interrogate any representations of whole and complete and thus often static, stereotypic, and normalizing representation of educators' selves. In particular, I posit, with my students, that qualitative researchers need to address complexities raised by feminist poststructuralist theorists who, in working toward an inclusive social imaginary based on difference, create transgressive versions of qualitative researching, theorizing, and writing in relation to educators' lives in and out of school (St. Pierre & Pillow, 2000). Such work has potential to shatter versions of research on teacher learning and development or school change or social and culturally responsive pedagogies and curricula, for example. Those versions often assume knowledge of and access to, for example, the teacher's true self, to the fully knowable nature of her students—some of whom may be coded as different—and to her classroom as a transparent canvas upon which the autobiographical lives of the teacher and her students are similarly encoded.

I share with my doctoral students my passion for such critiques because of my convictions that persons engaged with and in education can overtly benefit from such perspectives that both analyze and work to change dominant and positivist versions of school language and normalized policies that mandate certain behaviors and outcomes that supposedly characterize all versions of good teacher and student. Such policies often limit educational possibilities and instead enable difference to be viewed primarily in deficit ways.

Working autobiographically can enable us to thus potentially imagine possibilities for constructing alternative versions of our selves in these roles, selves who resist current educational policies that mandate measurable and standardized versions of what counts as good teaching and learning, as well as to respond to the divergent, the paradoxical, and the unanticipated in classroom life. In particular, then, I share with my students my commitments to counter-practices and generative qualitative research methodologies that register a possibility and mark a provisional space in which a different sort of inquiry might take form (Lather, 2004, 2007).

"International" Challengers

At the same time that I am working with students who teach in U.S. contexts, I also am forging pedagogical, theoretical, and research relationships with a number of doctoral students labeled "international" by our university. A number of those doctoral students with whom I work, who are classified as "international"—students born in Nigeria, Taiwan, Scotland, Japan, Zimbabwe, South Korea, Italy, Colombia, China, Lebanon, for example—choose to remain in the U.S., others to leave when they complete their doctoral studies. In these varied processes, some of my international students "become variously decentered from their cultural bearings and, in the U.S., seek different forms of identity as politics rather than as an inheritance" (Ong, 1995, p. 351).

These students, in particular, often choose to engage in forms of autobiographical qualitative research that interrogate rigid and immutable conceptions of national and international, for example. We together glean perspectives from postcolonial cultural theorist and philosopher Gayatri Spivak (2003), for example, who in choosing the term *transnational*, contributes to this disruption of rigid categories by developing the idea of "transnational literacy." This concept in its broadest sense refers to a reshaping of colonial systems of education and institutional knowledge away from (European) nation-based formations. Spivak argues that transnational literacy would involve a study of the multiplicity of languages and cultures in the world, and describes how reading can serve as one way of thinking with and through concepts of nation that currently are being troubled by the cultural and economic effects of globalization. Here, reading refers not just to reading-based literacy, but literacy more generally, as an interpretive act.

By extension, paying attention to intersections of knowledge and power in pedagogical practices, curriculum constructions, and qualitative research, for example, conceptions of transnational literacy could be instrumental in challenging qualitative research representations that recuperate "the originary narrative of diversity without questioning the 'very processes by which 'othering' is fabricated in American society" (Alarcon, Kaplan, & Moallem, 1999, p. 14), especially as they appear in autobiographical forms of qualitative education research.

Indeed, many feminist poststructuralist qualitative researchers now often locate educators within a

> complex understanding of the rise of the educational state, shifts in the global economy, and continuing patterns of racial and western privilege. [We are] conscious of the ways in which history very often rests on first person narratives, on representations and claims to truth that are laden with assumptions of power, privilege and subordination that underlie social relationships. (Weiler & Middleton, 1999, p. 6)

In light of the heterogeneity and rapid flux that now characterize global flows of people, technologies, commodities, ideas, culture, and capital through and across constantly changing borders, discourses, and subjectivities (Castells, 2000), many of my registered and pre-labeled "international" doctoral students have refused this homogenizing category affixed to them by our shared university. These students have taught me, again and again, how language indeed must be understood as systems of competing discourses that imply differences in the organization of social power. Through struggles with the label "international," for example, as a potentially othering discourse in a U.S. university, some of these doctoral students have demonstrated to me how the meaning of international is both socially produced and variable between and among different forms of discourse. Thus, as qualitative educational researcher, I too must now not only acknowledge but also move across, between, and with/in spatial and temporal as well as varying historical, social, and cultural discourses of self, "other," literacies, and difference.

Further, transnational flows and mobilities create varied effects on our differing and yet intertextually constructed subjectivities as we research between and across destablized versions of nations, cultures, literacies, and languages. Such intertwined complexities especially bring difference to the fore of our deliberations. Thus, in a feminist poststructuralist way, I currently use autobiography to trouble essentialized notions of uniform, stable, always coherent "selves" or socially constructed versions of relationships of any kind in order to highlight limitations of local/global binaries and tensions that permeate persons' diversely embodied realities.

So, I certainly agree that difference and the other, for example, cannot be conceived as static concepts and constructions in and of themselves, each cannot be detached from its embeddedness in language and thus in social, cultural, historical, geographic, epistemological, and power relations, among others. At the same time, I watch and I feel too the embodied conflicts, the struggles with displacement, with translation of both identities and languages, with assigned homogeneous identity constructs and knowledge products that some of my international students encounter as they attempt to rework their selves across the flows and mobilities of new relationalities in their graduate student lives:

> My research develops from my personal and professional experiences, both as a high school English teacher and student in Los Angeles and as an immigrant woman from Colombia. As a teacher, my literature anthologies and set curricula, designed by the state, the district and the school, established and maintained the literature canon. U.S. Latino authors seemed to be sprinkled in the literature selections to represent THE Latino experience....This created a limited and often erroneous account of what it means to be Latino not only for non-Latino students but also for those who identified as Latino themselves. (Rojas, 2006)

This doctoral student's challenging of homogeneous labels that in turn constitute a portion of the literary canon in the U.S. prompts me to think that engaging in the constant translation of and interactions not only with versions of transnational literacy but also with irreducible differences could be another point of autobiographical educational qualitative research. It's certainly the labor that

I see this student and others engaged in every day. Such engagements now take place especially in relation to the absence of any singular or permanently fixed center and peripheries in the new global order (Appadurai, 1990). These fluxes and flows force us to question any versions of autobiographical narratives that attempt to reify unitary versions of subjects in static and binary versions of local/global narratives from which they previously have been excluded.

I thus explore, with my doctoral students, ways in which we might construct autobiography as a form of qualitative narrative research—not as a static place of cross- or trans-cultural exchange of research stories across predetermined borders, but rather as lived spaces wherein subjectivities, difference, curricula, and place are embodied, mobile, and always in the making.

Further, taking into account now unavoidable influences of transnational flows and mobilities, we conceptualize autobiographical and narrative methodologies as shifting spaces of negotiation where we constantly are kneading categories and separations, again attempting to position ourselves as "engaging with and responding to the fluidity and malleability of identities and difference…refusing fixed and static categories of sameness or permanent otherness" (Ellsworth & Miller, 2005, p. 181). In doing so, we clearly wish to disrupt autobiography as both genre and research practice based only on humanist assumptions. Those assumptions often contain rigid categorizations, such as "other," and binaries, such as "insider/outsider" or "center/margin." One goal, then, is to disrupt any notion of a "self" (and by extension, any fixed, reified, and thus comparative version of nation and its educational research practices, for example) already known and made. Further, we believe that such disruptions potentially open possibilities for "syncretic, 'immigrant,' cross-cultural, and plural subjectivities, which can enable a politics through positions that are coalitions, intransigent, in process, contradictory" (Grewal, 1994, p. 234).

Because all students teach their teachers, I thus am more committed than ever in my academic career to creating and working with/in forms of autobiographical educational inquiry that welcome the paradoxical, the unknowable, the always shifting discursive and material constructions of subjectivities and literacies that no longer can be labeled, captured, identified, or represented in any static and immovable ways. Such versions of autobiographical educational qualitative research draw upon as well as forge theories and methodologies that could possibly enable normative and stereotypic representations of "self/other," "national/international," "border/center," and "abnormalized different/normalized same" to be unfixed, mobilized, destabilized, and released. Therein lies hope, I believe, for commitments to "certain visceral beliefs about justice and how people should be treated" to be realized and enacted in qualitative educational research. Such realizations and enactments in turn possibly could influence educational policies that now deny social, cultural, historical influences on discursive constructions of difference that frame the core of all educational endeavors.

These are the examples that perhaps I could have elucidated to that potential student, had I lingered with her for a while in the hallway. I have learned, again from a student, that in order to complicate and challenge any normative representations, I must attend to the unanticipated, the unknowable, the momentary, the fragmented, and the un-representable in all educative interactions and inquiries. I still look for that student in order to thank her.

Bibliography

Alarcon, N., Kaplan, C., & Moallem, M. (Eds.). (1999). *Between woman and nation: Nationalisms, transnational feminisms, and the state*. Durham, NC: Duke University Press.

Appadurai, A. (1990). Disjuncture and difference in the global cultural economy. *Public Culture, 2,* 2.

Castells, M. (2000). *The rise of the network society (The information age,* Vol. 1, 2nd ed.). Oxford: Blackwell.

Clifford, J. (1988). *The predicament of culture: Twentieth-century ethnography, literature, and art.* Cambridge, MA: Harvard University Press.

Clifford, J., & Marcus, G. E. (Eds.). (1986). *Writing culture: The poetics and politics of ethnography.* Berkeley, CA: University of California Press.

Denzin, N. K., & Lincoln, Y. S. (Eds.). (2000). *Handbook of qualitative research* (2nd ed.). Thousand Oaks, CA: Sage.

Ellsworth, E., & Miller, J. L. (2005). Working difference in education. In J. Miller, *Sounds of silence breaking: Women, autobiography, curriculum* (pp. 179–196). New York: Peter Lang.

Flax, J. (1993). *Disputed subjects: Essays on psychoanalysis, politics and philosophy.* New York: Routledge.

Geertz, C. (1988). *Works and lives: The anthropologist as author.* Stanford, CA: Stanford University Press.

Grewal, I. (1994). Autobiographic subjects and diaspora locations: *Meatless Days* and *Borderlands.* In I. Grewal & C. Kaplan (Eds.), *Scattered hegemonies: Postmodernity and transnational feminist practice* (pp. 231–254). Minneapolis, MN: University of Minnesota Press.

Lather, P. (2004). This IS your father's paradigm: Governmental intrusion and the case of qualitative research in education. *Qualitative Inquiry, 10*(1), 15–34.

Lather, P. (2007). *Getting lost: Feminist practices toward a double(d) science.* Albany, NY: State University of New York Press.

Marcus, G. E., & Fischer, M. M. J. (1986). *Anthropology as cultural critique: An experimental moment in the human sciences.* Chicago: The University of Chicago Press.

Miller, J. L. (1990) *Creating spaces and finding voices: Teachers collaborating for empowerment.* Albany, NY: State University of New York Press.

Miller, J. L. (2005). *Sounds of silence breaking: Women, autobiography, curriculum.* New York: Peter Lang.

Ong, A. (1995). Women out of China: Traveling tales and traveling theories in postcolonial feminism. In R. Behar & D. A. Gordon (Eds.), *Women writing culture* (pp. 350–372). Berkeley, CA: University of California Press.

Peters, M. A., & Burbules, N. C. (2004). *Poststructuralism and educational research*. Lanham, MD: Rowman & Littlefield.

Rojas, M. A. (2006, March 3). Generative possibilities of performative exchange in qualitative research. Performance/presentation at The Ways of Knowing Conference, Teachers College, Columbia University.

Spivak, G. C. (2003). *Death of a discipline*. New York: Columbia University Press.

St. Pierre, E. (2008). Decentering voice in qualitative inquiry. *International Review of Qualitative Research 1*(3), 319–336.

St. Pierre, E. & Pillow, W. (Eds.). (2000). *Working the ruins: Feminist poststructural practice and theory in education*. New York: Routledge.

Van Maanen, J. (1988). *Tales of the field: On writing ethnography*. Chicago: University of Chicago Press.

Weedon, C. (1997). *Feminist practice and poststructuralist theory* (2nd ed.). Malden, MA: Blackwell .

Weedon, C. (2003). Subjects. In M. Eagleton (Ed.), *A concise companion to feminist theory* (pp. 111–132). Malden, MA: Blackwell.

Weiler, K., & Middleton, S. (Eds.). (1999). *Telling women's lives: Narrative inquiries in the history of women's education*. Houston: Open University Press.

Closing Comments: The Politics of Social Justice Representations: *Right-ing* and Re-searching

Obtaining truth in any form is difficult. Yet in the pursuit of truth, research-ers have long sought to deny the impact of the human mind in shaping what that truth might be or eventually become. By contrast, feminist scholars have adamantly maintained that truth can never be found in denying the presence of the human hand on the things we humans touch (Acker, Barry, & Esseveld, 1983; Hawkesworth, 1989). Rather, all truths bear the brandings of their manu-facturers. To call such politics into question and to be more honest in our pursuits of truth, we believe that researchers should follow the advice of Alsup (in *Section 2*), and move past the mythologies of data analysis and toward more transforma-tive data analysis processes.

The idea of transformative data analysis might strike some as odd or even il-legitimate in sciences that strive for objectivity. However, as we and countless oth-ers have noted (Acker et al., 1983; Gage, 1989; Hoff, 1988; Lather, 2001; Rosaldo, 1989), the pursuit of objectivity in social research is futile. It is not likely to be accomplished by a subjective human mind, which imposes its own views on data, views that mostly go unbeknownst to the researcher (Hawkesworth, 1989). Of course, the subjective mind is part of a much larger politics of truth. Therefore, acknowledging our positionalities (Milner, 2007) in our research is a first step to tempering the mind toward imagining social justice in education.

To this point, Willis (in this section) suggests that the consequences of mind in method carry greater effects for certain populations than for others. Usually the groups most at risk of being harmed by the dysconscious mind and "neutral" research practices are those who rarely wield power to conduct research themselves, either because their frames for inquiry are not legitimated in mainstream contexts or because other forms of inquiry have been successfully imposed upon them. Yet, we know that even marginalized individuals, including marginalized youth, have consistently fashioned their own modes for understanding the world (Farganis, 1989; Kinloch, 2009; Moje, 2004; Morrell, 2004).

For Eakle (in this section), there are a number of delicate ideological fault lines that lie at the epicenter of ways of knowing. As he has maintained, a critical process of inquiry privileges a careful negotiation not only along lines of differences, but along invisible lines of space-time categories particularly in the parsing of data. To transgress the lines of historic social inequities that prop up the injustices that have fully hidden behind so-called scientific boundaries is simply just. And the question remains as to how to bend boundaries in the name of justice. After all, there are many ways to understand social and cultural data. Finding just ways to represent research remains a daunting challenge. Still, we must rise to the noble endeavor of justice, always searching for answers to difficult questions about equitable representations in research.

Indeed, many books have been written on the topic and many others remain to be written. However, there is an unwritten urgency that looms in the margins of every written research report and in the vacuous yet glaring silences of all noble acts of inquiring. These silences beg their own series of speculations, chiefly: How do we researchers achieve quality in research and representation without imposing unjust descriptions of, or marginalizing, certain groups (Gutierrez & Orellana, 2006)? Addressing this question requires that researchers engage in a continual process of acknowledging the human element in researching and writing research as well as the related human consequences that grow out of what we claim to find.

Nonetheless, we have been quite ambitious in this section, staging a conversation among critical scholars interested in moving the field further into the new millennium and a step closer to justice. In the course of the conversation, we have found it hopeful that concepts such as democracy, for example, be redefined. Critical theorists, who have long-defined democracy consistent with the attributes of equality, are now beginning to redefine the concept, resolving that democracy defined simply as equality is limiting (Ayers, Hunt, & Quinn, 1998; Guinier, 1970; Sandel, 1996). We too believe that democracy defined simply as equality mystifies the ideal. By its basic definition, democracy seeks inequality, more over less, to establish compromises and rule of law. For minority groups, the notion of democracy as mystified in unquestioned ideals has too often lead to disappointing ends and a deepening of oppressions. At many crucial junctures in history, democracy that does not insist on fair and full representation of people has sadly promoted what Lani Guinier (1970) sees as the tyranny of the majority.

The theory of democracy on which the chapters in this section converge is rooted in the idea that democracy, in its most prodigious sense, guarantees equal representation—a kind of inclusive ethos that promotes diversities, pluralisms, and multifarious etchings of the effervescent human experience. This definition of democracy does not necessarily lead to equality of means *per se*. Rather, it seeks equality of ends in so far as all voices, experiences, and perspectives have an equal chance of being heard in the chambers of our deliberations. Democracy of this stripe, democracy that fairly represents the people, promotes greater equity and seeks to ensure that all people are heard.

This is true for Fecho and Hill (in this section), who include art in their writing of research to represent the poetics of human experience, a presence that is well captured in verse. They also use song to promote the people's voices over the authoritative voices of the songless and the rigidity of the technocratic research industrial complex. For Janet Miller (in this section), it means enabling our personal stories so that the dearth and value of nuance can be realized and compared to other tells of who we are and are capable of being. How do we learn from the perspectives of Fecho, Hill, and Miller so that we can more accurately simulate reality in research to show the authentic lives of people without hurting them or subjecting them to our own intellectual and moral limits? How do we expand upon what science has already learned and learn from the tragedies of science to enable a more just, more prosperous science that fuses humanity and art? Of course, the answer lies in the seat of policy stain with the impressions of social justice thought: How do we not do all of these, hone our wisdom to formulate a policy for critical inquiry that is fluid, meaningful, and full of purpose. In the next section, we discuss how such policies might look.

Bibliography

Acker, J., Barry, K., & Esseveld, J. (1983). Objectivity and truth: Problems in doing feminist research. *Women's Studies International Forum, 6*(4), 235–423.

Ayers, W., Hunt, J. A., & Quinn, T. (Eds.). (1998). *Teaching for social justice: A democracy and education reader.* New York, NY: New Press.

Farganis, S. (1989). Feminism and the reconstruction of social science. In A. Jaggar & S. Bordo (Eds.), *Gender/Body/Knowledge* (pp. 207-223). New Brunswick, NJ: Rutgers University Press.

Gage, N. L. (1989). The paradigm wars and their aftermath: A "Historical" sketch of research on teaching since 1989. *Teachers College Record, 91*(2), 135–150.

Guinier, L. (1970). *Tyranny of the majority: Fundamental fairness in representative democracy.* New York: Free Press.

Gutierrez, K. D., & Orellana, M. F. (2006). The "Problem" of English Learners: Constructing Genres of Difference. *Research in the Teaching of English, 40*(4), 502-507.

Hawkesworth, M. E. (1989). Knowers, knowing, known: Feminist theory and claims of truth. *Signs, 14*(3), 533–557.

Hoff, L. A. (1988). Collaborative feminist research and the myth of objectivity. In K. Yllo & M. Bograd (Eds.), *Feminist perpectives on wife abuse* (pp. 269–281). Newbury Park, CA: Sage.

Kinloch, V. (2009). Suspicious spatial distinctions: Literacy research with students across school and community contexts. *Written Communication, 26*(2), 154–182.

Lather, P. (2001). Validity as an incitement to discourse: Qualitative research and the crisis of legitimation. In V. Richardson (Ed.), *Handbook of Research on Teaching* (4th ed., pp. 241–250). Washington, DC: American Educational Research Association.

Milner, H. R. (2007). Race, culture, and researcher positionality: Working through dangers seen, unseen, and unforeseen. *Educational Researcher, 36*(7), 388–400.

Moje, E. B. (2004). Powerful spaces: Tracing the out-of-school literacy spaces of Latino/a youth. In K. M. Leander & M. Sheehy (Eds.), *Spatializing literacy research and practice* (pp. 15–38). New York: Peter Lang.

Morrell, E. (2004). *Becoming critical researchers: Literacy and empowerment for urban youth.* New York: Peter Lang.

Rosaldo, R. (1989). *Culture and truth: The remaking of social analysis.* Boston, MA: Beacon Press.

Sandel, M. (1996). *Democracy's discontent.* Cambridge, MA: Harvard University Press.

Subject of the Transformation: Policy and Possibility

Many well-intentioned scholars and researchers are beginning to abandon the critical educational enterprise because, while they believe it can offer a powerful critique of unjust policies, it too rarely makes an impact on policy or offers realistic policy alternatives (Ellsworth, 1994; North, 2008). It is one thing to point out what is wrong with our systems of education and how they contribute to chronic cycles of injustice, yet it is quite another thing to posit fruitful suggestions for improving educational conditions and thereby challenge social equities. Of course, we are blessed when ideas surface that can improve schools, classrooms, research agenda, and practices. However, fomenting ideas that can bring us closer to solutions without limiting reform to such shrill transactions that swap one grand narrative for another seems elusive. Further, the orthodoxy of cynicism that has become the critic's roost reinforces the problems of inequity instead of resolving them.

This is not to say that finding answers to problems trumps finding the problems themselves. Exposing injustice in any way helps to transform the foundational logics that ground harmful policies and practices. Rather, our point in this section is to begin the policy conversation, making good on the book's promise of priming social justice for the policy world. Indeed, we felt it important to consider that state of social justice in English education, from theory to practice, from conception to research. But now we are in a position to move beyond the products of thought, practice, and inquiry into the place where we believe change must matter most: policy. In this way, we believe that policy and controlling the political theater in which it is staged should matter as much, if not more, to the social justice–minded educator/researcher as does the change we seek from policy. We must begin to ask: What are the concrete ideas that can be applied to education and educational studies that will enable the change we want to see in the world? How might we docket our ideas in ways that promote freedom, justice, understanding, and tolerance; but also educational excellence, innovation, and accountability?

These items need not be bifurcated along political lines. Rather, we point out the tensions here, anticipating the folly of the current and overly partisan conversation, which toils from one end of the political spectrum to the other. In our political discourse, equality has been presented as the arch nemesis of quality, and vice versa. Items such as accountability have been co-opted by the political extremes through questionable policies in divisive ways, and the architects of such divisions have prompted split reactions between the political poles.

In spite of the political climate, it is more than fair, however, to acknowledge that we cannot have quality education without having equality in education. Moreover, we cannot have justice in education without holding injustice in education accountable. It is upsetting, then, that arguments in educational policy have increasingly become entangled in the political web of ideological positions, where neither side wishes to cede ground in the futile but ongoing debate. In this mercurial process, millions, if not more, of our young people languish in the wait, needing us to affirm more righteous grounds where change matters not as a condition of intellectual leisure, but more desperately as a prerequisite to human salvation.

We need policies in education today that are shaped from the social justice ideas, practices, and modes of inquiry we have discussed throughout this book. Before we can achieve these ideas, we must address several questions critical to framing policy: How do socially just policies look? How are they written? Whom shall they serve? How might they get implemented? There are perhaps hundreds of other questions that we can add to these; however, no one question will lead us closer to the change we wish to see. In spite of the multitude of questions that will be left unanswered, we too seek some form of resolution.

Contributors to this section find a starting point in interrogating policy, its sometimes broken relationship with theory, research, and practice, and the language (i.e., metaphors) upon which most educational policies today are based (cf. Cochran-Smith, 2002). The through line of their essays suggests that dismantling gross metaphors that stake meaning in competition (e.g., No Child Left Behind and Race to the Top) can expose very troubling impulses. In the case of American educational policy, contributors work to expose a discourse of incredulity that props up theoretically fallow arguments about success versus failure. They reveal a set of man-made convections that build upon histories of educational documents that promote oppression, stratification, inequity, and unnecessary competition.

In this way, penetrating critiques of failed educational policies continue in this section, as we, and our contributors, believe that it is folly to abandon the work of exposing injustice in any form. As we have alluded to in the introduction of this text, exposing injustice can raise consciousness about justice, and raised consciousness about justice can lead to transformative social change. Notwithstanding, contributors attempt—the best they can—to offer alternatives to match their critiques when such alternative may be found. Neither we nor our contributors purport to have found all the answers. There is no holy grail in education to heal the sick or take away our social ills. Indeed, if change is going to happen, we must work at it; we must write it into existence. Further, we are too wise to believe in cure-all. That is, if a holy grail existed, it too would be stained, marred by the flaws of the human hand. So we simply offer a conversation, a decent dialogue that we hope might impact in some important way how policy gets shaped in education. In this conversation, contributors do their best to offer a portrait of how social justice in education policy, specifically English education policy, might look.

Bibliography

Cochran-Smith, M. (2002). Editorial: The research base for teacher education: Metaphors we live (and die?) by. *Journal of Teacher Education, 53*(4), 283–285.

Ellsworth, E. (1994). Why doesn't this feel empowering? Working through the repressive myths of critical pedagogy. In L. Stone (Ed.), *The education feminism reader* (pp. 300–327). New York: Routledge.

North, C. E. (2008). What is all this talk about "social justice"? Mapping the terrain of education's latest catchphrase. *Teachers College Record, 110*, 1182–1206.

FIFTEEN

The Debate About Teacher Quality: Policy, Politics, and Social Justice

Marilyn Cochran-Smith

In countries all over the world, there are now major efforts to improve the quality of schooling with the goal of meeting raised social and economic expectations. Teachers are regarded as central to improvement efforts, and teacher quality has become a major public policy issue at the highest levels of governance. In the U.S., at a time that there is heightened attention to teacher quality, there is also excoriating criticism of teaching and intense controversy about teacher quality policies.

Teacher Quality: A Politicized Policy Issue

In this essay, I consider contemporary U.S. policy proposals regarding teacher quality in terms of social justice. I suggest that many teacher quality debates can be understood in terms of two agendas, which are demarcated by differing assumptions about schooling, equity, educational purposes, and the impact of out-of-school factors on achievement.

My perspective on social justice stems from acknowledgement of significant disparities in the educational opportunities and outcomes between minority and/or low-income students and their white, middle-class counterparts and identifies one goal of schooling as challenging inequities. In contemporary political philosophy, however, the central question in theorizing social justice is the relationship between liberalism's notion of distributive justice, on one hand, and the politics of identity and difference, on the other (Fraser & Honneth, 2003; North, 2006).

From this perspective, failure to recognize social groups and their knowledge traditions (King, 2008) is a central dimension of injustice, and thus the goal of recognition, rather than simply redistribution, is central (Honneth, 2003; Young, 1990). Although the inherent tensions between the dual goals of redistribution and recognition are often glossed over by contemporary theorists (Gewirtz & Cribb, 2002), in this analysis, I try to account for both by taking what Fraser (2003) has called a "multi-perspectival" approach. (See Cochran-Smith [2008, in press] for further discussion of a theory of social justice for teacher education.)

Teacher Quality Policy: What's Social Justice Got to Do with It?

Given space limitations, I consider what social justice has to do with teacher quality policies by focusing on two agendas—the "Broader, Bolder Approach to Education" (Economic Policy Institute, 2008) and the "Education Equality Project" (Education Equality Project, 2008). Released just days apart in June of 2008, both proposals were intended to influence the reauthorization of the Elementary and Secondary Education Act as well as the education agendas of the 2008 presidential campaigns and then the Obama administration.

Dueling Education Policy Agendas

The "Broader, Bolder Approach to Education" (BBA), issued by the Economic Policy Institute, is co-chaired by Duke University economist Helen Ladd, NYU education policy professor Pedro Noguera, and former Boston Public Schools superintendent Tom Payzant. It boasts a long list of signatories, primarily social scientists, education researchers, and policy experts. The agenda of the "Education Equality Project" (EEP), issued by a new civil rights coalition, is co-chaired by clergyman-activist Al Sharpton and NYC Schools chancellor Joel Klein. This proposal also has prominent signatories, primarily civil rights activists and urban educators. Although each proposal has Republican supporters, both are led by Democrats and are regarded by many as "dueling" Democratic policy agendas for education (Hoff, 2008).

In short, the BBA argues that standards, teacher quality, and high-stakes tests alone cannot offset the impact of poverty on school outcomes. This is supported by background papers on the connection between social class and student achievement; the impact of class size, teacher quality, and accountability systems; expanded preschool and health programs; and the importance of youth development as educational goals. The proposal asserts that NCLB-type frameworks cannot succeed because they work from two false premises: that school factors are the major reason for low achievement and that policies targeting standards, testing, and teacher education can overcome the impact of low socioeconomic status. Instead, the BBA agenda argues, we need a bolder approach that focuses on school and teaching reforms at the same time it targets early childhood and health programs and incorporates new development goals and ideas about accountability. The goal of this agenda is "to produce a large reduction in the current association between social and economic disadvantage and low-student achievement" (Economic Policy Institute, 2008).

In contrast, the EEP calls for tough accountability for teachers, principals, school systems, and parents and for confronting teacher management contracts. This agenda is supported by a report titled "The Economic Impact of the Achievement Gap in America's Schools" (McKinsey & Company, 2009) and a position paper on teacher quality (Education Equality Project, 2008). The McKinsey report concludes that four distinct gaps in education (between the U.S. and other countries; between White students and Black and Latino students; between students from different socioeconomic groups; and between students attending different school systems or regions) have the impact of "the economic equivalent of a permanent national recession," and serious consequences in earnings, health, and incarceration rates for individuals. The EEP agenda argues that policy makers must "address head-on crucial issues that created this crisis: teachers' contracts and state policies that keep ineffective teachers in classrooms…; school funding mechanisms…; and enrollment policies that consign poor, minority students to our lowest performing schools" (Education Equality Project, 2008).

What's Social Justice Got to Do with It?

Both these agendas are committed to radically improving public education. Although they mean different things by the words used the agendas share some rhetoric about challenging the status quo and eliminating injustice. EEP's website features Joel Klein's words: "Every day that our nation refuses to do the work necessary to eliminate the racial and ethnic achievement gap, we are perpetuating an injustice on our children and their future" (Education Equality Project, 2008), while BBA's website declares: "It is a violation of the most basic principles of social justice that a country as wealthy as ours denies the opportunities that come with a high-quality education to a substantial proportion of our young people" (Economic Policy Institute, 2009). Despite the shared goal of eliminating injustice, these agendas are based on different theories about the reasons for low student achievement, and they advocate sharply contrasting policies.

The EEP agenda identifies school issues as both the root cause of educational inequality and its fundamental solution. Here, the premise is that the cause of achievement gaps in the U.S. is the unequal and unjust distribution of effective teachers and leaders in schools that serve disadvantaged students; this system of inequality is exacerbated and sustained by teachers' union contracts and other "anti-performance structures" that preserve a "failed system" (Education Equality Project, 2008). EEP wants to upturn the current system of recruiting, re-warding, and retaining teachers by implementing a "progress-based" rather than an "inputs-based" system with seven policy initiatives, including: lowering entry barriers to teaching, state data systems tracking teacher impact on achievement, outcomes-based school effectiveness measures at all grades and areas with test scores the key, immediate assessment of new teachers' impact on achievement with mentoring and development, tenure based on achievement gains, large bo-nuses for effective teachers in high poverty schools, and periodic reassessment of tenured teachers (Education Equality Project, 2009).

As these seven suggest, EEP's distributive notion of justice applies only to the distribution of school personnel who know how to boost achievement scores. There is nothing in the EEP materials about the impact of contextual fac-tors on achievement, which I discuss below, or the need for revised curriculum or instructional goals. As Joyce King (2006) has argued, however, "if justice is our objective" (p. 337) in education, then we must recognize the ways "ideologically distorted knowledge sustains societal *in*justice" (p. 337). Nor is there anything in the EEP agenda about the justice of recognition, indicated by the lack of strate-gies for participation by all social groups in the discourse about what is funda-mental in education, including those historically marginalized. Unfortunately, as King points out, this can lead to the untenable situation in which "equal access to a faulty curriculum" (p. 337)—or, I would add, equal access to teachers governed by a faulty accountability system—is assumed to constitute justice.

The BBA agenda asserts that the cause of the persistent association between disadvantage and low student achievement is the failure of policymakers to act on school improvement in conjunction with improvements in the social and eco-nomic conditions of young people's lives. The BBA proposal targets the unequal distribution of quality schooling in tandem with the unequal distribution of qual-ity pre-school and health programs, development goals, out-of-school programs, and immigrant experiences. BBA's report on school accountability (Economic Policy Institute, 2009) explicitly rejects the idea that test scores alone capture the effectiveness of teachers and schools. Instead it proposes a new accountability that includes the "broad range of knowledge and skills" needed to succeed in a pluralistic society. The report proposes collection of state NAEP data (or other low-stakes surveys) on a range of skills and disaggregated on contextual fac-tors as well as new accountability systems with multiple indicators. This would be coupled with improved assessments and school inspections of multiple out-comes, including citizenship, health, the arts, a full curriculum, professional de-velopment, and coordination with communities and parents.

The BBA agenda is animated by both redistribution and recognition justice goals. Within the distributive paradigm, injustice is defined as inequalities rooted in the socioeconomic structure of society (Fraser, 2003), and the remedy is redistribution of goods, including opportunity, power, and access. As Will Kymlycka (1995) suggests, "According to this principle, injustice is a matter of arbitrary exclusion from the dominant institutions of society, and equality is a matter of non-discrimination and equal opportunity to participate" (p. 59), which is consistent with BBA's focus on context and outside-of-school learning. In addition, however, the BBA demands a "balanced" curriculum (i.e., not controlled by high-stakes tests), to prepare students for a pluralistic society along with strong connections to parents and communities. These aspects are consistent with the recognition paradigm where justice is not reducible to distribution, since even distributional injustices reflect "the institutional expression of social disrespect—or unjustified relations of recognition" (Honneth, 2003, p. 114).

In terms of social justice, it is worth noting that neither the BBA nor the EEP explicitly addresses the larger conditions and policies that sustain educational injustices. Jean Anyon (2005) names these specifically: "minimum wage statutes that yield poverty wages, affordable housing and transportation policies that segregate low-income workers of color in urban areas, and industrial and other job development [initiatives] in far-flung suburbs where public transit does not reach" (p. 2). However, the ideas behind the BBA agenda are consistent with recognition of these societal factors. Alternatively the EEP agenda explicitly rejects the contention that factors outside schools cause achievement disparities and injustices.

Teacher Quality Policy: Where Are Things Headed?

Although it is clear that President Obama's agenda targets teacher quality (as evidenced by the Title II funds in the recovery act and by his many public statements about the centrality of teachers in determining educational outcomes), it remains to be seen where U.S. teacher quality policies are headed. In a highly politicized and controversial decision, Obama selected Arne Duncan over Linda Darling-Hammond as secretary of education. Interestingly, while Darling-Hammond was a signatory of BBA, Duncan was the sole signer of both the BBA and EEP proposals, which perhaps reflects Obama's strategy of seeking common ground between opposing ideas. Along these lines, the president's educational agenda incorporates funding for initiatives that are central to each of the two proposals, including early childhood programs, services to families, higher standards, and better assessments of educational progress. In addition, when the president debuted his healthcare agenda, Duncan was present to emphasize the connection between improving healthcare and improving educational outcomes.

In many of Duncan's speeches about education, the rhetoric of "no excuses" has been prevalent, as it was during Duncan's tenure as CEO of the Chicago Public Schools. This language has come to be code for the dual positions that school factors—especially teachers, principals, and union contracts—are responsible for achievement disparities and that emphasizing contextual factors constitutes an "excuse" for poor teacher performance along with tacit support for a failed system. The prominence of the "no excuses" theme may suggest that teacher quality policies are moving in the direction of a narrow view of justice, which focuses only on the distribution to low-performing schools of teachers who can up test scores. Unfortunately, this ignores both the unjust distribution of broader access, power, and opportunity and—just as bad—also ignores the unjust omission from curricula and educational goals of the knowledge traditions and assets of diverse social groups.

Short of the magic that some attribute to Obama, it is hard to imagine teacher quality policies situated in the common ground between the social justice orientations of BBA-like and EEP-like agendas. One hopeful indicator, however, is that unlike the privatization agenda, both of the Democratic agendas seek to preserve, rather than dismantle, the American covenant to provide public education for all. My own hope is that the Obama administration will expand and strengthen health and out-of-school resources for disadvantaged youth at the same time it supports radically improved preparation and professional development for all teachers and will also lead efforts to truly reinvent assessment. All the while, however, to move social justice into policy, the administration will have to keep its eye on the prize of building on the knowledge traditions and the cultural and linguistic resources of traditionally marginalized groups.

Bibliography

Anyon, J. (2005). *Radical possibilities: Public policy, urban education, and a new social movement.* New York, Routledge.

Cochran-Smith, M. (2008, April). *A theory of teacher education for social justice.* Paper presented at the meeting of the American Educational Research Association, New York.

Cochran-Smith, M. (In press). Toward a theory of teacher education for social justice. In M. Fullan, A. Hargreaves, D. Hopkins, & A. Lieberman (Eds.), *The international handbook of educational change* (2nd ed.). New York: Springer.

Economic Policy Institute. (2008). *A broader, bolder approach to education.* Retrieved March 1, 2009, from http://www.boldapproach.org.

Economic Policy Institute. (2009). *School accountability: A broader, bolder approach.* Retrieved July 1, 2009, from http://www.boldapproach.org/report_20090625.html.

Education Equality Project (2008). Home website. Retrieved March 1, 2009, from http://www.educationequalityproject.org.

Education Equality Project. (2009). *On improving teacher quality.* Retrieved June 1, 2009, from http://www.educationequalityproject.org/content/pages/position paper

Fraser, N. (2003). Social justice in an age of identity politics: Redistribution, recognition, and participation. In N. Fraser and A. Honneth (Eds.). *Redistribution or recognition: A political-philosophical debate* (pp. 7–109). London: Verso.

Fraser, N., & Honneth, A. (2003). *Redistribution or recognition: A political-philosophical debate.* London: Verso.

Gewirtz, S., & Cribb, A. (2002). Plural conceptions of social justice: Implications for policy sociology. *Journal of Education Policy, 17*(5), 499–509.

Hoff, D. J. (2008, August 22). Democrats air dueling ideas on education. *Education Week*, pp. 1–5.

Honneth, A. (2003). Redistribution as recognition: A response to Nancy Fraser. In N. Fraser & A. Honneth (Eds.), *Redistribution or recognition: A political-philosophical debate* (pp. 110–197). London: Verso.

King, J. (2008). Critical and qualitative research in teacher education: A blues epistemology, a reason for knowing for cultural well-being. In M. Cochran-Smith, S. Feiman Nemser & J. McIntyre (Eds.), *Handbook of research on teacher education: Enduring issues in changing contexts* (pp. 1094–1135). Mahwah, NJ: Lawrence Erlbaum.

Kymlycka, W. (1995). *Multicultural citizenship*. Oxford: Clarendon.

McKinsey & Company, (2009). *The economic impact of the achievement gap on America's schools.* Retrieved June 1, 2009, from http://www.mckinsey.com/clientservice/socialsector/achievementgap.asp

North, C. (2006). More than words? Delving into the substantive meaning(s) of "social justice" in education. *Review of Educational Research, 76*(4), 507–535.

Young, I. M. (1990). *Justice and the politics of difference*. Princeton: Princeton University Press.

SIXTEEN

Language Education and Social Justice in English Education Policy

Leslie David Burns

A t least since the late 1960s and early 1970s, the National Council of Teachers of English (NCTE) has worked to develop a consistent commitment to social justice via its professed value for linguistic diversity in modern society. Over the past forty years it has continually emphasized that value as a cornerstone of its policies, and used those policies to frame language arts instruction as a project for enlightenment regarding culture and power relations. In 1974, and again in 2003, NCTE's affiliate Conference on College Composition and Communication (CCCC) affirmed the policy statement "Students' Right to Their Own Language" (SRTOL) for use by the profession at large to institutionalize its commitments to democracy, equity, and social justice. SRTOL states,

> We affirm the students' right to their own patterns and varieties of language—the dialects of their nurture or whatever dialects in which they find their own identity and style. Language scholars long ago denied that the myth of a standard American dialect has any validity. The claim that any one dialect is unacceptable amounts to an attempt of one social group to exert its dominance over another. Such a claim leads to false advice for speakers and writers, and immoral advice for humans. A nation proud of its diverse heritage and its cultural and racial variety will preserve its heritage of dialects. We affirm strongly that teachers must have the experiences and training that will enable them to respect diversity and uphold the right of students to their own language. (p. 4)

The SRTOL position calls for teaching students "effective" and "appropriate" language use (p. 3), and has consistently informed other NCTE policies and position statements ever since. In the last decade especially, NCTE has utilized the language of SRTOL in numerous contexts as a response to national standardization of language education.

One example of NCTE's continuous reliance on the SRTOL's explicit social justice mission is its 1999 "Resolution on Diversity." That policy text states that standardization of curriculum and assessment in schools has led to reproducing rather than transforming the dominant culture at the expense of marginalizing valuable minority groups and individuals. It goes on to argue that such reproduction fails to recognize the complexity of language. The organization resolved to study and communicate "the relation of dominant forms of language, knowledge, and culture to the democratization of expression, articulation, and access" in schools. Its purpose in doing so was to "resist racism, sexism, homophobia, Eurocentrism, the privileging of English, economic injustice, and other forms of domination" (NCTE, 1999, Resolutions 2 and 3). As a part of the policy ecology (Weaver-Hightower, 2007) for English education, NCTE's Resolution on Diversity framed future policy work.

Similarly, the Conference on English Education's (CEE) position statement "Supporting Linguistically and Culturally Diverse Learners in English Education" (2005) recognizes the social justice mission of ELA teachers by stating "teachers need to foster ongoing and critical examinations with their students of how particular codes came into power, why linguistic apartheid exists, and how even their own dialectical and slang patterns are often appropriated by the dominant culture" (para. 37). CEE's policy statement stipulates that "All students need to be taught mainstream power codes and become critical users of language while also having their home and street codes honored" (Belief 2). More globally, it states, "students have a right to a variety of educational experiences that help them make informed decisions about their role and participation in language, literacy, and life" (Belief 4).

The notion that students have a right to use their own languages in shaping their educations and identities manifests most profoundly in NCTE's overarching policy text *Guidelines for the Preparation of Teachers of English Language Arts* (2006), which states that the goal of teachers and teacher educators should be to "foster diverse students' abilities to shape both their own identities and their understanding of the larger world in which they live through the study and practice of the language arts" (p. 13). While the document is not explicit about teaching and honoring students' cultural and linguistic diversity as matters of social justice, references to the imperative of students' rights in literacy education utilize SRTOL discourse. This usage is apparent as the foundation for language instruction and teacher preparation in the 21st century and generates a *discourse of appropriateness* in which teachers are obligated to ensure their students learn that some forms of English are more powerful than others, at least when it comes to access and achievement in school and society at large. However true those notions may be from dominant cultural and linguistic mainstream perspectives, they set the stage for an ironic undercutting of the very linguistic knowledge and values for diversity NCTE embraces. The discourse of appropriateness leads to an instructional focus on the very "correctness" NCTE deems illegitimate and which scholarship in literacy and English education demonstrates is misleading (Fecho, 2004; Nieto, 2002).

The SRTOL discourse of teaching effective and appropriate language use to students is readily apparent in NCTE's *Guidelines*. According to NCTE, teachers must value "the responsibility to assist students in learning about many forms and uses of language and how to use these *effectively* and *appropriately* for different purposes…" (p. 13, emphases added). They are expected to "respect the language and dialect that each student brings to the classroom," and recognize that "all language varieties have an *appropriate* context" (p. 15, emphasis added). NCTE consistently emphasizes that teachers must honor "all forms of language" (p. 15), and that they must ensure their personal biases do not shape expectations for student achievement in ways that marginalize students' home languages. The *Guidelines* stipulate that teachers must encourage "creative and *appropriate* uses of language" (p. 16, emphasis added), and that they must help their students recognize "the *appropriate* levels of *correctness* in diverse kinds of communication" (p. 24, emphases added). They must teach students distinctions between "*formal* and *informal* structures that may guide *appropriate* usage" (p. 24, emphases added), and support students' use of "*nonacademic* as well as *academic* English" so they can learn when to use formal or informal structures (p. 25, emphases added). ELA teachers should ultimately explain to their students how "using *appropriate* and *effective* communication strategies can lead to the enhancement of relationships and resolution of conflict" (p. 27, emphases added). The language of SRTOL is woven throughout NCTE's teacher preparation guidelines as the primary justification for contemporary curriculum and instruction.

Despite using rhetoric from SRTOL that apparently supports and values diversity, the cumulative effect of discourse in NCTE language education policies is the establishment of four interconnecting binaries that marginalize students' right to their own language even as those policies are intended to make students' rights central in classroom practice. Foremost among these binaries, NCTE proposes that all ELA teachers must learn and teach appropriate versus inappropriate language use. Superficially, this approach honors linguistic diversity by acknowledging that all languages are valuable and useful depending on context and situation. However, policy further dictates that teachers must be prepared to teach students academic versus nonacademic English, a binary that is tied to prescriptions for when students are allowed to use formal versus informal structures in communication. These are all ultimately tied to a conception of language use in which there are varying "appropriate levels of correctness" for language use depending on context and situation, which leads inevitably to a binary of correct versus incorrect language use that governs curriculum, instruction, and evaluation in ELA classrooms.

Although the establishment and interrelation of these binaries is almost certainly unintentional, their articulation in policy results in an unjust framework for curriculum that perpetuates a negative status quo with regard to achieving social justice. Students are required to learn appropriate language use for classroom achievement, which by definition suggests certain dialects are *in*appropriate for classroom use and will lead students who speak nonacademic forms to fail or at least struggle in school. In particular, students must learn to distinguish between academic and nonacademic language, wherein nonacademic language is sometimes acceptable in the classroom—but only for informal purposes in the service of learning academic registers. Such a practice marginalizes minority speakers and sends a clear message to all classroom participants that certain languages (and therefore certain identities) are better than others. Academic English is aligned with formality, and nonacademic English and other languages are aligned with informality, leading to a linguistic hierarchy in which certain English dialects are treated as correct while others are at best deemed less correct for use in school. Accepting that all American English dialects are linguistically systematic but also constantly evolving, they are all therefore, by definition, correct (Wolfram & Schilling-Estes, 2005; Bauer & Trudgill, 1998; Gee, 1996). The tacit implication in NCTE policies that some language varieties are better than others and thereby rewarded in school poses serious obstacles to teaching language for social justice.

Given the well-established finding that academic English reflects the dialects of middle- and upper-class White speakers—variously labeled Formal Standard English (FSE), standardized English, or "the Language of Wider Communication" (Smitherman, 2000)—it is difficult to escape the conclusion that NCTE's policies for language education violate its professed support for students' right to their own language. Student dialects that do not closely align with the Language of Wider Communication are most likely to be deemed nonacademic, informal, inappropriate, and ultimately incorrect for use in school and other powerful sectors of society that determine access to opportunity and life outcomes. If their dialects are honored at all in the classroom, they will not be honored in relation to formal assessment situations and grades, but at best in nonevaluative situations where students are allowed by teachers to use their own dialects only in subordination to the imperative that they learn the dominant academic form. That Language of Wider Communication alone meets the criteria inadvertently set forth by NCTE that students must learn to use language that is academic, formal, appropriate, and correct according to the values of the dominant White culture in order to achieve in school and society.

Perhaps the most telling instance of marginalization for socially just language education is a statement in the *Guidelines* in which teachers are obligated to "monitor their instruction in ways that honor…language diversity while helping all students achieve academic success through acculturation" (p. 15). Acculturation is the "cultural modification of an individual, group, or people by adapting to or borrowing traits from another culture" (Merriam-Webster, 2009). NCTE's phrasing in its *Guidelines* profoundly contradicts its desire to honor diversity and teach language for social justice. If NCTE truly values cultural and linguistic diversity in U.S. and global society, then supporting academic success through acculturation and explicitly modifying certain individuals and groups for adaptation to a dominant linguistic form in school pose serious obstacles to supporting students' right to their own language. Although NCTE is careful to state that "ELA teacher candidates should…be able to explain how language usage varies as affected by linguistic, social, cultural, and economic diversity in society" (p. 24), the treatment of education as a matter of acculturation voids value for diversity of any kind.

By definition, education through acculturation explicitly attempts to *eradicate* diversity, at least in academic contexts. It marginalizes and subordinates students whose languages fall outside the mainstream. By treating them as objects for modification toward the traits of the dominant culture, this approach to language education takes a decidedly *unjust* turn by signaling to students and teachers alike that there is only one legitimate dialect that leads to success in school and society—the Language of Wider Communication. All other dialects are less valuable and in fact less correct, even though they should be honored, respected, valued, and so on. Despite numerous instances in which NCTE policy superficially reflects an orientation to equity and justice, its discourse masks a conservative tendency that reproduces the dominant society and maintains an exclusive language of power—whether intentional or not.

One response to this analysis is that it amounts to quibbling over semantics. However, in educational policies and politics, semantics matter (Stone, 2002). A single word, be it "appropriate," or "correct," or "acculturation" can determine whether and how a particular policy element will be implemented. Sometimes, it may be difficult to predict how a policy will manifest, and it is necessary for participants to continually monitor, analyze, and revise those governing texts and treat them as temporal, fallible, and contingent (Apple, 1990; Cherryholmes, 1988, 1999). It is almost certainly true that the professional educators, linguists, and other scholars involved with NCTE policy construction over the years emphatically did not intend the use of a word like *appropriate* to undercut their sincere value for cultural and linguistic diversity, let alone their genuine desire and passion to achieve social justice. Rather, the progression of appropriateness as a discourse for framing language education over the past forty years indicates a need for more careful attention to precise language choices in policy formation, as well as the need to carefully analyze policy documents and ensure that various positions, guidelines, and standards produced over time are clearly articulated with one another, consistent, and supportive of NCTE's actual knowledge and values (Stone, 2002; Bardach, 2005).

Consistency and alignment matter in English education because of NCTE's considerable influence on national policy. Its 1996 guidelines (which also strongly reflect the discourse of appropriateness) were the central document used by the National Council for Accreditation of Teacher Education (NCATE) to generate its standards for program accreditation and teacher candidate performance assessment. With forty-eight states adopting NCATE's framework, it cannot be denied that NCTE's guidelines function as a powerful policy vehicle. Unfortunately, their transformation from guidelines to "standards" by NCATE created a standardized accountability system with extremely high stakes (McCracken & Gibbs, 2000). At this time, the use of the discourse of appropriateness in program and candidate standards for English teacher education accreditation precludes implementation of NCTE's social justice mission. One can argue that the discourse of appropriateness in English education policies perverts that mission by using the language of diversity and equity in ways that mask an antithetical orientation.

NCTE is currently translating its 2006 guidelines for teacher preparation into a revised set of national standards for use by NCATE in the evaluation of participating English education programs and teacher candidates. As such, NCTE has an opportunity to remedy what amounts to a profound series of semantic glitches in its policies and institutionalize a social justice mission in teacher education curriculum, instruction, and policy. To do so, NCTE must carefully synthesize its available research on culture, diversity, linguistics, and students' right to their own language to make its knowledge explicit via consistent referencing and careful composition in its policy texts. Using articulated research and policy syntheses to systematically communicate professional knowledge, NCTE can position teacher education programs, classroom teachers, and K–12 students to think about language education as a project of *strategic* rather than *appropriate* language use. It can move beyond treating ELA as a project for *acculturation* of children and consider how language can be taught in more equitable, sophisticated, and complex ways that lead to an *assimilated*, blended society where people with diverse languages interact productively through the deliberate use of multiple dialects and discourses that are treated as assets rather than obstacles. In this way, NCTE (2006) can meet its professed goal of helping citizens "consider their language in different real-world contexts" and "create new language possibilities" that enrich our society and truly reflect the dynamic nature and richness of English in its totality (p. 43).

Shifting NCTE's language education policies toward a discourse of *strategic language use* does not preclude the imperative to teach all children how to use the codes of power and the Language of Wider Communication as they navigate school and society (Delpit, 1995; Delpit & Kilgour Dowdy, 2003). Rather, it enables all children to use those codes toward ending linguistic apartheid and fully participating in the shaping of their own identities, subjectivities, and critical thinking skills during their educations. Doing so is not only more appropriate than teaching children to speak and write *appropriately*. It is representative of our professional commitments to value students' right to their own language. It is not only appropriate, it is just.

Bibliography

Apple, M. (1990). *Ideology and curriculum.* New York: Routledge.

Bardach, E. (2005). *A practical guide to policy analysis: The eightfold path to more effective problem solving, 2nd ed.* Washington, D.C.: CQ Press.

Bauer, L., & Trudgill, P. (1998). *Language myths.* New York: Penguin.

Cherryholmes, C. (1988). *Power and criticism: Poststructural investigations in education.* New York: Teachers College Press.

Cherryholmes, C. (1999). *Reading pragmatism.* New York: Teachers College Press.

Conference on College Composition and Communication. (1974/2003). *Students' Right to Their Own Language.* Downloaded October 8, 2009, from http://www.ncte.org/library/NCTEFiles/Groups/CCCC/NewSRTOL.pdf

Conference on English Education. (2005). *Supporting linguistically and culturally diverse learners in English education.* Downloaded October 8, 2009, from http://www.ncte.org/cee/positions/diverselearnersinee

Delpit, L. (1995). *Other people's children: Cultural conflict in the classroom.* New York: The New Press.

Delpit, L., & Kilgour Dowdy, J. (Eds.). (2003). *The skin that we speak: Thoughts on language and culture in the classroom.* New York: The New Press.

Fecho, B. (2004). *"Is this English?" Race, language, and culture in the classroom.* New York: Teachers College Press.

Gee, J. P. (1996). *Social linguistics and literacies: Ideology in discourses.* London: Routledge.

McCracken, H. T., & Gibbs, S. E. (2000). *Final report: NCTE/NCATE research project on the preparation of teachers of English language arts.* Urbana, IL: National Council of Teachers of English.

National Council of Teachers of English (1996). *Guidelines for the preparation of teachers of English language arts.* Urbana, IL: NCTE.

National Council of Teachers of English. (1999). *Resolution on diversity.* Downloaded October 8, 2009, from http://www.ncte.org/positions/statements/diversity

National Council of Teachers of English. (2006). *Guidelines for the Preparation of Teachers of the English Language Arts.* Urbana, IL: NCTE. Downloaded October 8, 2009, from http://www.ncte.org/store/books/middle/126639.htm?source=gs?source=gs

Nieto, S. (2002). *Language, culture, and teaching: Critical perspectives for a new century.* Mahwah, NJ: Lawrence Erlbaum.

Smitherman, G. (2000). *Talkin that talk: Language, culture and education in African America.* New York: Routledge

Stone, D. (2002). *Policy paradox: The art of political decision making.* New York: W. W. Norton & Company.

Weaver-Hightower, M.B. (2007). An ecology metaphor for educational policy analysis: A call to complexity. *Educational Researcher, 37*(3), 153–167.

Wolfram, W., & Schilling-Estes, N. (2005). *American English (2nd ed.).* Malden, MA: Blackwell.

SEVENTEEN

Discourse-Oriented Research and Democratic Justice

Mary M. Juzwik & Matt Ferkany

Discourse-oriented (DO) educational researchers have long been seen as advocates for some notion of "social justice in education." This designation seems to be given, and accepted, when DO researchers (a) give voice to previously marginalized voices and discursive practices in educational research and/or (b) show the logic and artfulness of discursive practices that many consider "deficient" or illogical. Dyson's line of scholarship (e.g., 1993, 1997, 2003) studying primary-aged child writers in urban schools is a prime example of research that sets out to do both, although Dyson seems to style herself less as someone doing "social justice in education" and more modestly as a researcher and scholar of writing. Other examples of work in language and literacy that do one or both (a) and (b) above include Gee's (1985) influential analysis of the storytelling and literacy practices of one African American child; Shaughnessy's (1977) also influential study of the logics of error-filled writing made by college students who many considered to be "unprepared" for college work; and more recently Kirkland's (Kirkland & Jackson, 2009) analysis of the masculine literacy practices of African American youth. Calabrese-Barton (2003), a scholar of science education, quite explicitly claims to be advocating "teaching for social justice" through her research on after-school programs for urban youth that would similarly fit the criteria delineated above.

Although not focusing specifically on educational research, Bourdieu (1998) dismissively labeled this body of social science research "populist aesthetic" and critiqued it on the following grounds: although researchers may celebrate the logic and artfulness of marginalized discourses and voices (and we might add, by extension, literacy practices), such research fails to change the way those voices are figured in the broader fields of social practice. By ignoring, or backgrounding, the broader fields of social practice, researchers may (unwittingly) participate in reproducing the very social inequities they are trying to expose and work against.

Perhaps confirming Bourdieu's (1989) criticism, much DO research fails to make a difference in refiguring fields of social practice at the policy level. This is equally true of DO work that goes beyond the "populist aesthetic" work described above and is furthermore (c) critical of structural configurations of practice and power tends not to be taken up by policy makers. For example, we have in mind the work of critical discourse analysts such as the studies presented in the volume edited by Lewis, Enciso, and Moje (2007).

One reason for this may be that policy makers—that is, professional politicians—and their aides do not welcome such research accounts, which tend to complicate rather than simplify trenchant problems in education. Another reason may be that discourse research—even large-scale DO work, such as that conducted by Marty Nystrand and colleagues as part of the (now defunct) OERI-funded Center for English Learning and Achievement (e.g., Applebee, Langer, Nystrand, & Gamoran, 2003; Nystrand with Gamoran, Kachur, & Prendergast, 1997; Nystrand, Wu, Gamoran, Zeiser, & Long, 2003)—tends not to make certain, universal, causal claims about "what works in education."[1] However, themes of "scientific research" (i.e., research designs that yield causal inferences) and teacher accountability (with accompanying testing regimes) currently ground public discourse about education in the U.S. This status quo appears to have bipartisan support. Given this contemporary political reality, research making claims grounded in primarily descriptive and/or theoretical work (e.g., in-depth case studies with just a few, or one, focal participant[s]) fails to be taken up by professional politicians.

We do not endorse this state of affairs; to the contrary we think policy makers should take such research into consideration. Nonetheless, we wonder whether social justice–minded DO researchers might enjoy more success influencing policy by pursuing research that either goes beyond or outright departs from the sort characterized by points (a), (b), and (c) above. In particular, we advocate that DO researchers consider pursuing the following actions:

1. Seeking to highlight through their research points of commonality and shared experience, values, and practices among diverse people and relating to this in a way explained later in this chapter.

2. Pursuing longer term comparative studies.

3. Fashioning larger-scale studies that—when relevant—address issues of student learning and achievement.

Consider point #1. From the standpoint of social justice, it matters greatly that citizens, especially diverse ones, share a range of background experiences, values, and practices. Being able to *articulate* these shared experiences, values, and practices also matters. The main reason for this is that just societies are democratic societies and democratic societies cannot function well without, among other things, a minimum of background social unity. Without minimum social unity, the will to engage in reasoned deliberation and to seek compromise when disagreements arise may be wholly lacking. Shared experiences and values also enable a capacity to see the reason and sense in views we might personally reject, which again facilitates reasoned deliberation and compromise.

To say that democratic societies require background social unity is not to endorse an assimilationist political ideology, one according to which all social differences should be arbitrarily eradicated or absorbed into some dominant socio-cultural system (e.g., "English-only" policies in various U.S. states). We view promoting social unity and celebrating difference and diversity as not incompatible undertakings. To value social unity is simply to proscribe *needlessly divisive* policies or practices and to promote a sense of shared mission whenever possible.

Reasoned debate, deliberation, and a will to compromise seem sorely lacking in current political processes; as we write this piece, the so-called debate about healthcare reform in the U.S. offers a prime example of this failure. Such fractiousness may in part be owing to the countless injustices perpetrated against various disempowered segments of American society and the ongoing resistance of the advantaged to social change. But we wonder whether social justice–minded DO research might, on the one hand, risk perpetuating the situation by focusing exclusively on elucidating cultural differences across diverse persons while, on the other hand, having potentially significant influence in undoing unjust policies by giving more attention to what is common and shared among persons.

To flesh this argument out, we now turn to a sustained example: DO research focused on narrative and narrative practices. One of the interesting characteristics of narrative study is that researchers have looked to narrative both for (a) universal understandings about how humans recapitulate and construct experience across cultural or other social groups (e.g., Gee, 1991) and for (b) particular understandings of how narrative practices differ across sociocultural groups (e.g., Hymes, 1972). Narrative researchers doing work in education, then, face choices. One option is to seek out and highlight accounts of sameness in narrative practices across cultural groups, for example as Spector (2007) does in her analysis of "narratives of redemption" that two very different cultural groups (one suburban, one urban—both in the metro area of the same U.S. city) of high school students brought to, and sustained throughout, their study of Elie Wiesel's memoir *Night*. Another option, which seems to be the current preference for many DO researchers, is to seek out and highlight accounts of difference in narrative practices across groups (Heath, 1983; Michaels, 1981) or to describe the particularities of a single group or individual (e.g., Juzwik, 2009; Martinez-Roldan, 2003; Rymes, 2001). We believe that, given the importance of social unity to well-functioning democracy, social justice–minded researchers have good reason to sometimes choose the former and not exclusively focus on the latter.

To account for cross-group similarities, as well as differences, DO researchers interested in narrative practices might take on more comparative work (for example, designs in the tradition of Heath [1983]), rather than continuing currently popular practices of conducting "deep" case studies focused on single groups, context, or individuals. This undertaking would likely involve studying narrative practices of social and cultural groups over longer periods of time, again following the example of Heath (1983). We acknowledge that this path could be difficult to follow, especially for early career researchers, who may feel compelled by institutional demands to pursue relatively fast-track publications programs after accepting positions in order to be awarded tenure. Further, given the political environment outlined above, funding for time-consuming, long-term work is much needed, yet quite scarce, especially in language and literacy studies (as opposed to Math or Science education, areas of research that enjoy ample opportunities for large-scale [e.g., millions of dollars] funding from such sources as the National Science Foundation).

In addition to pursuing longer-term comparative studies that have capacity to highlight similarities as well as differences across sociocultural groups, DO narrative researchers—at least those doing work in classrooms—might further inform policy decisions by working toward *larger-scale* designs that account, again in comparative ways, for student learning beyond the single case context. It may be instructive to consider a recently published study that did this sort of thing, a collaboration undertaken by Juzwik, Nystrand, Kelly, and Sherry (2008). The goal of the study was to account for a set of narrative practices that the team discovered in classroom discussions about literature, a phenomenon we labeled "conversational narrative discussion," when teacher or students' narrative talk co-occurred with discussion talk. The study built on previous correlational work by Nystrand and colleagues (e.g., Applebee et al., 2003; Nystrand et al., 1997) that linked discussion discourse with student achievement. Following this prior research, we defined "discussion discourse" as at least thirty seconds of open-ended talk, not controlled by the teacher, among at least three people (see Nystrand et al., 1997).

What was unusual about this case study of narrative practices in a single classroom setting was the choice to embed it within a large-scale study of other classrooms and teachers. This design allowed us to determine that, relative to other similar classrooms (both participating in, and not participating in, the large-scale intervention study), the focal classroom was (a) high discussion and (b) high achievement, even after such variables as family income, and other student characteristics were controlled for. The choice further allowed us to contextualize our case study of narrative classroom discourse practices within large-scale discourse practices (e.g., practices across many classrooms) and state-level achievement data.

We ourselves do not believe that state literacy tests always offer comprehensive determinations of student literacy learning. Researchers are capable of developing, and have perhaps designed, stronger learning measures. However, the measures we used—mandated by state-level educational policies—do (we think, regretably, in some cases) have some currency in the national discussions about education currently being led by Arne Duncan. Therefore, we made a pragmatic decision to use these test data because we believed that this research design might speak to an audience that included professional politicians and their staff personnel.

Our research became possible because DO researchers (Juzwik, Nystrand, & Sherry) collaborated with a non-DO researcher (Kelly), a sociologist who does large-scale statistical analysis of educational phenomena such as student engagement (Kelly, 2008). This sort of research collaboration can, as ours did, lose some of the fine-grained description that is the hallmark of much outstanding DO work. Yet a study like this may have potential for reaching broader audiences, including policy makers who want certain information that our study provides. For example, is the classroom phenomenon described in a case just idiosyncratic or can it be placed within a larger context that speaks to achievement growth? Even if the study cannot make causal claims about discourse practices and achievement growth, DO studies with larger scale can yield more generalizable claims. We are, however, aware that the work may not influence policy without further advocacy efforts by us as researchers, or lobbyists representing our interests (e.g., colleagues or others who are in positions of political influence). Although we have perhaps belabored this example to make our point about rethinking case study designs, we see few examples of DO studies—at least in language and literacy—that attempt such designs.

We have made some tentative suggestions for DO researchers in language and literacy with an interest in the ends of democratic justice to consider. We do not claim here to be definitive or comprehensive. This exploration has, however, suggested to us the need for careful, systematic, and precise theorizations and definitions of what researchers mean when they claim "teaching for social justice" or "education for social justice" as the goal of their work. We believe that researchers in education could be assisted in this endeavor, by becoming familiar with current definitions, positions, and debates about justice amongst contemporary political philosophers.

Note

1. For this observation, we are indebted to Christina Berchini and Laura Jimenez, who collaboratively and orally developed it in a Discourse Analysis seminar Mary taught at Michigan State University in Fall 2009.

Bibliography

Applebee, A., Langer, J. A., Nystrand, M., & Gamoran, A. (2003).Discussion-based approaches to developing understanding: Classroom instruction and student performance in middle and high school English. *American Educational Research Journal 40* (3), 685–730.

Bourdieu, P. (1998). *Practical reason*. Stanford, CA: Stanford University Press.

Calabrese-Barton, A. (2003). *Teaching science for social justice*. New York: Teachers College Press.

Dyson, A. Haas. (1993). *Social worlds of children learning to write in an urban primary school*. New York: Teachers College Press.

Dyson, A. Haas. (1997). *Writing superheroes: Contemporary childhood, popular culture, and classroom literacy*. New York: Teachers College Press.

Dyson, A. Haas. (2003). *The brothers and sisters learn to write: Popular literacies in childhood and school cultures*. New York: Teachers College Press.

Gee, J. (1985). The narrativization of experience in the oral style. *Journal of Education, 167* (1), 9–35.

Gee, J. P. (1991). A linguistic approach to narrative. *Journal of Narrative and Life History, 1*(1), 15–39.

Heath, S. B. (1983). *Ways with words: Language, life, and work in communities and classrooms*. Cambridge, UK: Cambridge University Press.

Hymes, D. (1972). Models of the interaction of language and social life. In J. Gumperz & D. Hymes (Eds.), *Directions in sociolinguistics: The ethnography of communication* (pp. 35–71). New York: Holt, Rinehart & Winston.

Juzwik, M. M. (2009). *The rhetoric of teaching: Understanding the dynamics of Holocaust narratives in an English classroom*. Cresskill, NJ: Hampton.

Juzwik, M. M., Nystrand, M., Kelly, S., & Sherry, M. B. (2008). Oral narrative genres as dialogic resources for classroom literature study: A contextualized case study of conversational narrative discussion. *American Educational Research Journal, 45*(4), 1111–1154.

Kelly, S. (2008). Race, social class, and student engagement in middle school English classrooms. *Social Science Research, 37*, 434–448.

Kirkland, D., & Jackson, A. (2009). "We real cool": Toward a theory of black masculine literacies. *Reading Research Quarterly, 44*(3), 278–297.

Lewis, C., Enciso, P., & Moje, E. (Eds.). (2007). *Reframing sociocultural research on literacy: Identity, agency, and power*. Mahwah, NJ: Lawrence Erlbaum.

Martinez-Roldan, C. (2003). Building worlds and identities: A case study of the role of narratives in bilingual literature discussions. *Research in the Teaching of English, 37,* 491–526.

Michaels, S. (1981). Sharing time: Children's narrative styles and differential access to literacy. *Language in Society, 10,* 423–442.

Nystrand, M., with Gamoran, A., Kachur, R., & Prendergast, C. (1997). *Opening dialogue: Understanding the dynamics of language and learning in the English classroom.* New York: Teachers College Press.

Nystrand, M., Wu, L. L., Gamoran, A., Zeiser, S., & Long, D. A. (2003). Questions in time: Investigating the structure and dynamics of unfolding classroom discourse. *Discourse Processes, 35*(2), 135–198.

Rymes, B. (2001). *Conversational borderlands: Language and identity in an alternative urban high school.* New York: Teachers College Press.

Shaughnessy, M. (1977). *Errors and expectations.* London: Oxford University Press.

Spector, K. (2007). God on the gallows: Reading the Holocaust through narratives of redemption. *Research in the Teaching of English, 42*(1), 7–55.

EIGHTEEN

Embodying Socially Just Policy in Practice

Gerald Campano & Lenny Sánchez

"A finger is useful for pointing to the moon, but woe to him who mistakes the finger for the moon."— Zen Aphorism

The invitation to think about the relationship between practitioner research and policy immediately conjures an antagonism. For many of us who work on the ground with teachers and students and consciously cultivate an inquiry stance (Cochran-Smith & Lytle, 2009) in our endeavors to generate collaborative local knowledge, policy is often thought of as the problem or, in critical parlance, a dominant hegemonic force that impinges on our efforts to create educational arrangements more conducive to fuller student flourishing. The interpretive breadth of the word "flourishing" is intentional because we are committed to an enlarged vision of educational justice: one that involves, among other aspirations, the cultivation of democratic citizenship, universal access to higher education and beyond, a deeper appreciation of human variance, and an understanding that adequate material and intellectual resources should be a precondition, not a reward, for educational development. More often than not, it seems, literacy policy is driven by an impoverished understanding of progress, fueled by a failed testing paradigm which narrows curriculum and measures, classifies, and sorts students, thereby reproducing inequalities. In fact, the educational practices that constrain student flourishing—e.g., tracking, standardization, labeling, assessments that conform to the ideology of the bell curve, etc.—are frequently the very points of critical inquiry: What drives the research agendas of many teacher and action researchers is the felt urgency to resist and enact alternatives to these policies.

Practitioner research thus exists in a type of parasitical relationship with dominant policies; ultimately it hopes to "act" its way out of existence, to create conditions where its identity as both an intellectual and social movement isn't predicated solely on oppositional impulses. Of course, many teacher and action researchers do not need to be versed in a poststructuralist's skepticism of millenarianism to realize that an education system free from domination is a working, rather than a fully achievable, ideal. In our own experiences immersed in classrooms and communities, it is rather obvious that injustices—subtle and brazen, attitudinal and structural in nature—are woven into the fabric of almost every aspect of schooling. It feels quixotic to imagine not being skeptical about policy.

This being said, recent events in our state of residence have compelled us to attempt to add more nuance to our position. Upper administration—being advised by a right-wing educational "think tank"—tried to push through "reforms" in teacher credentialing that would have the potential effect of eliminating "early childhood certification and bilingual education, mandate caps that reduce teacher education programs by 50–75%, and enforce a narrow interpretation of reading and language arts instruction" (Wohlwend & Medina, personal communication). Part of the goal was to dilute the amount of education courses required for credentialing. This assault on the discipline doesn't surprise us; it is part of a nationwide effort by some in power to deregulate public education, and with it the professional autonomy of teachers and college faculty. What does catch us off guard—a function of our own naïveté—is the fragility of a number of *socially just* policies which we had taken for granted. These policies, the result of hard-won political struggles and sacrifices, are partially symbolized by banners draped in the atrium of our school of education building, which colorfully highlight our stated mission to principles such as "embracing diversity," "reflective teaching," and "dynamic partnerships." Usually we debate if in practice we are approximating our own principles. If the proposed policy changes were to go through, it would be structurally impossible to live up to our institutional ideals. Seemingly overnight, the banners which have informed so many of our policy decisions may be blown away.

The lesson we are learning is therefore about the illusory and ephemeral nature of policies, whether they are progressive or reactionary. The caution, not to conflate illusion with reality—the finger pointing to the moon with the moon itself—is, of course, one of the central tenets of Buddhism. It was perhaps most notably invoked on a global level in 2001, after the Taliban dynamited the Buddhas of Bamyan. While there seemed to be almost universal condemnation of an act which destroyed what was considered a treasure to all of humanity, there were also Buddhist scholars and laypeople who suggested that, despite the unequivocal tragedy of the loss, it's important to remember that the statues themselves did not embody Buddhism: Buddhism is in the heart.

As we contemplate how to respond to the destructive forces that seem to be crumbling progressive policies before our eyes, we too are reminded that any codifications of what education should be—whether inscribed into credentialing reforms, articulated in a mission statement, or hung on banners—are ultimately fragile abstractions, once removed from the heart of our work. What then is the heart of work? It's the equitable human relationships we strive for on a day-to-day basis with students and colleagues. Practitioner research is—not unlike Buddhism or even the principles that motivate many activist communities—an ethics of practice. It is less concerned with imposing a totalizing theoretical formulation of pedagogy onto reality, and more about theorizing from the situational practice of responding to students in their full humanity, dignity, and intellectual promise. This is an ongoing cultural work that involves humility and reflection. Policy may be helpful in pointing to the direction of this work, but it is not the work itself. The heart of teaching is where theory and practice merge in relationships—becoming as indistinguishable as Yeats' dancer and dance—as communities collaboratively inquire into student educational self-determination and flourishing.

The Miller and Kirkland vision for this book is thus of utmost importance; it encourages us to think beyond antagonism toward a constructive understanding of policy that will promote more egalitarian and humane educational relations and practices that might have life beyond any particular policy's (inevitable) expiration. What cautions and advice would we give critical educators who are interested in "moving social justice theory into policy"? We believe the key term in this formulation is "moving," with its valences of lived, active experience and inspiration. The methodological perspective of practitioner researcher would shift attention away from delineating and prescribing particular policies to thinking about the conditions and *processes* by which policies may be collectively conceived and enacted. Drawing on our own attempts to embody our principles in our practice of partnering with faculty and students at a boys academy in northwest Indiana, we briefly sketch four interrelated dynamics to be mindful of when striving for social justice: troubling top-down notions of policy; regarding everyone as a public intellectual; fostering multiplicity in the curriculum; and creating non-hegemonic educational alternatives within and alongside dominant structures.

Unsettling Hierarchical Policies

While policies should take into account the complexities of schools and the daily lives of its members, too often, reform efforts view schools as "problems" and prescribe policies to "fix" them, ready to issue penalties when they are not adequately carried out. Devon, a sixth grader at the Boys Academy, implicitly troubles this hierarchical notion of policy in his opening speech at his sixth grade graduation ceremony:

> This year has been a challenge...We've been tested in many ways....Our spirits have sunken at times and soared again, only to rise again. We have certainly accomplished many feats...At least 6 of us, including myself, exceeded the top scores in the state. We've been tested over and over again...but we will continue to keep our stride so that it will lead us into a great future.

Devon's words illustrate what feminist theorist and educator Chandra Talpade Mohanty (2003) might call the need to "read up the ladder of privilege" (p. 231), a phrase which calls attention to the unique epistemic insights of those who are most vulnerable in a power calculus. In a speech that alludes to Maya Angelou, Devon bears firsthand witness to those unfairly burdened by a testing-paradigm that induced social suffering and reproduction. The students at the Boys Academy were required to participate in multiple remediation and evaluation protocols due to their aggregate "failure" to meet Annual Yearly Progress (AYP). In fact, during Devon's time in sixth grade, the school was subjected to biweekly state monitoring on mandated computerized reading and math tests. As realized by Devon, these testing policies were relentless and interfered with the opportunities for teaching and learning that he rightfully deserved, including an intellectually rigorous and meaningful curriculum.

Devon was not alone in his school in voicing concerns with top-down policies. Teachers often discussed how external bureaucratic pressures threatened their professional autonomy and judgment. An administrator even expressed at a faculty meeting how "fed up" she was with the testing, commenting, "It's just plain embarrassing when you're one of the schools in the state that have to do these kinds of things, and go to state meetings, sitting there...having everyone look at you, having to defend what you are doing, all because you missed your AYP goal by 6%." The effects that "one-size-fits-all" policy can have on its stakeholders are quite devastating. Many local educators felt that the real unaddressed problem in the neighborhood was poverty, and the heavy-handed remediation and high-stakes testing only exacerbated the school's challenges and stigmatization. Policy can never be understood apart from the immediate context. For these teachers and students, mandates which neglected to consider the relational dimensions in how policies, people, and places come together ultimately failed them.

Regarding Everyone as a Public Intellectual

Our second point of mindfulness concerns the need to view *everyone* as a public intellectual. Devon's comments clearly demonstrate that even schoolchildren have the capacities to critically discern and interpret their conditions, if afforded the space and opportunity to do so. In the field of critical pedagogy and social justice education, we believe it is important to keep in mind the inter-subjective process of knowledge construction. While there are many critiques of vanguard-ism both within and outside the academy, Mohanty (2003) self-reflectively articulates the links between ideas and popular social movements: "In the end, I think and write in conversation with scholars, teachers, and activists involved in social justice struggles. My search for emancipatory knowledge over the years has made me realize that ideas are always communally wrought, not privately owned" (p. 1). While we may always be inspired by leaders in the field, it is important to not overly mythologize particular people as the true heirs and embodiments of a critical tradition, which in many ways reinforces the bourgeoisie notion that change can be pressured through an exertion of an individual's will. Change that matters is always collective in nature.

One of the most powerful outgrowths of our work with the Boys Academy has been a renewed sense of interconnection. A recent workshop on "moving beyond the standards" involved fourteen faculty members and staff in the school, including classroom teachers, administrators, the speech therapist, instructional aides, a local grandmother, and the school nurse: a genuine assembly of community members interested in culturally engaging pedagogy. Everyone with the passion to participate took their first two days of summer vacation to move beyond their own institutionally assigned roles and collectively forge a new literacy vision for the upcoming year. Conscious of their own role in the policy process, this group came together in solidarity to be seen as viable contributors to the decisions that concerned their lives. As stated by one of the group members, "We have the strength within ourselves to say this is what we are going to do and then bring in more community to help."

The idea of the public intellectual is necessary to help people think beyond their immediate and often insular professional interests and to engage the world. But from the methodological perspective of practitioner research, we can only endorse the term if all participants are thought of as potential knowledge producers whose insights and perspectives are taken seriously. Otherwise, we risk reproducing the very intellectual hierarchies we may hope to challenge.

Fostering Multiplicity

If socially just projects are worked out at the local level under a framework which values a more expansive and egalitarian understanding of the public intellectual, then differences of policy implementation should be embraced rather than viewed as problematic. For example, critical literacy might vary considerably between Los Angeles, rural Tennessee, and Hawaii. But we would go even further to endorse a radical multiplicity at the classroom and student level as well. Just as there are different legacies of both knowledge production and activism across regional and cultural boundaries, each particular learning context would have its own alchemy and potential. Who is to say what tools a student may employ to engage her or his world? In the field of literacy it may be the "classics," new media, hiphop, opera, storytelling, political theater, everyday observation and conversation, etc.—a seemingly endless array of options and combinations (Beach, Campano, Edminston, & Borgmann, in-press). In our zeal to create new policies, we should be wary of replacing one form of standardization and hegemonic conformity with another. Instead, we need to ensure that both educators and students are provided the autonomy to cultivate their own critical lenses and have access to a wide range of social and linguistic resources. We have discovered that when our teaching is at its best, our students' work will be unpredictable, not easily conforming to preconceived categories, and irreducible; each piece unlike the other. For example, the elementary students we have worked with wrote realistic fiction in the spirit of Richard Wright, personal essays that could be likened to the genre of Magical Realism, utopian science fiction about better worlds, multilingual migration stories, and biographies of heroes such as Dolores Huerta, José Rizal, and the fictional character Heidi.

We advise against any policy or pedagogical approach that suppresses difference, even in the name of an agenda that promotes change. The challenge for critical educators is not so much to reproduce themselves in their students, but instead to look for affinities across a multiplicity of perspectives in order to forge a common vision of a better world that honors human variance and equality.

Creating Non-hegemonic Arrangements

There is little doubt that socially just education needs to be fought for at the level of policy. In addition to taking up positions in legislation and administration, in order to articulate a counter-hegemonic policy strategy, critical educators can also embody socially just policy by prefiguring and creating alternative spaces "alongside" and "within" dominant structures (Day, 1995). These alternatives may take many forms, including after-school programs (e.g., Fisher, 2007; Hill, 2009; Kinloch, 2009; Wissman, 2007), "second classrooms" (Campano, 2007) within the regular school day, and progressive schools that offer inspirational models of how to live equitable relations (e.g., Simon, 2005). Although these relational forms will look different across contexts, what may be similar is their ultimate focus on the intellectual flourishing and social well-being of students, something that is best understood in the local and everyday by participants—students, teachers, parents, and college and university faculty alike—who have the freedom to engage in autonomous collaborative inquiry. Perhaps Devon and his peers offer us an example of what it means to embody policy in practice in their planning and facilitation of their entire sixth grade graduation ceremony: They took on the roles of Masters of Ceremony, handed out the awards, directed the singing, wrote and performed dramatizations and musical selections, led the pledge, and presented speeches. For the students, the act of creating policies is also a process of creating community from the ground up.

Because of the coalitional work of concerned educators and community members, the proposed legislation for altering credentialing in our state seems to be losing steam. This provisional victory reminds us to vigilantly participate in the Realpolitik of educational reform. At the same time, we need to prefigure alternative educational and social relations that aspire to be non-hierarchical. We have recently documented our own efforts to create a university-school partnership based on consensus models of decision-making that emphasize local knowledge, multiple perspectives, and reciprocity (Campano, G., Honeyford, M., Sanchez, L. & Vander Zanden, S., 2010). This is challenging work that often exposes our vulnerabilities and limitations. But it is also the work that sustains us: the process, lived experience, and "heart" of social justice beyond its official manifestations and representations. These alternative professional relations are psychically nourishing while simultaneously assuring that not all our energy is spent reacting to a dominant hegemonic agenda. Woe to us if, in our urgency to try to both resist and seize hold of power, we confuse policies with the heart of socially just practice in education.

Bibliography

Beach, R., Campano, G., Edminston, B., & Borgmann, M. (in-press). *Literacy tools for critical inquiry*. New York: Teachers College Press.

Campano, G. (2007). *Immigrant students and literacy: Reading, writing, and remembering*. New York: Teachers College Press.

Campano, G., Honeyford, M., Sánchez, L. & Vander Zanden, S. (2010). Ends in themselves: Theorizing the practice of university-school partnering through horizontalidad. *Language Arts, 87*(4), 277-286.

Cochran-Smith, M., & Lytle, S. (2009). *Inquiry as stance: Practitioner research for the next generation*. New York: Teachers College Press

Day, R. (1995). *Gramsci is dead*. London & Ann Arbor, MI: Pluto.

Fisher, M. T. (2007). *Writing in rhythm: Spoken word poetry in urban classrooms*. New York: Teachers College Press.

Hill, M. L. (2009). *Beats, rhymes, and classroom life: Hip hop pedagogy and the politics of identity*. New York: Teachers College Press.

Kinloch, V. (2009). *Harlem on our minds: Place, race, and the literacies of urban youth*. New York: Teachers College Press.

Mohanty, C.T. (2003). *Feminism without borders: Decolonizing theory, practicing solidarity*. Durham, NC: Duke University Press.

Simon, R. (2005). Bridging life and learning through inquiry and improvisation: Literacy practices at a model high school. In B. Street. (Ed.), *Literacies across educational contexts* (pp. 124–144). Philadelphia: Caslon.

Wissman, K. (2007). This is what I see: (Re)envisioning photography as a social practice. In M. L. Hill & L. Vasudevan (Eds.), *Media, learning, and sites of possibility* (pp. 13-45). New York: Peter Lang.

Closing Comments: Subject of the Transformation: Policy and Possibility

As each of us, both individually and collectively, continues in our efforts to prime social justice for policy, our efforts benefit when we name what needs to change. Even though we might vote, campaign, or even make systemic change through our teaching and our research, this may only have minimal effect on the principles upon which any given democracy governs its people. If we want to have a far-reaching and sustainable impact, we must stay committed in our efforts to not only challenge egregious standardized testing practices and accrediting institutions that perpetuate social and cultural inequities, but we must also remain committed to identifying oppressive actions in schools that disempower students and teachers. The educational community grows more compassionate and formidable as we reconcile such elitist elements in our enterprise.

We have written this book mindful of our work with current and future teachers. They remind us that our commitment to social justice truly matters. This commitment helps us remember that our work to prime social justice for policy can have an indomitable impact on future generations of teachers and students. Our sensitivity toward what teachers inherit through haphazard and reckless interpretations of constitutional battles that can render students as victims, can help all stakeholders in this timely quest for change. With that said, whether in the field conducting research or in our methods courses or in our heads, by continuing to unpack the paradoxes and myths of democracy, we can candidly forefront the potential impact that academic inequities have had on students. We can heighten people's understanding about social inequities as we induct our pre-service teachers into these dialogical dilemmas and invite our colleagues through our work to understand what social justice means in the context of their own lives. However, we must also be mindful not to inculcate preservice teachers or would-be critical researchers to believe solely in what we may deem as socially just, but that we make our classrooms as exploratory as possible, inviting contro-versy and curiosity while supporting students in creating and sustaining practices that speak to our most valuable principles and socially just habits. We can offer preservice teachers perspectives that invite them to embody socially just teach-ing pedagogies, yet at the same time, we must be candid that those identities and stances may be positionally challenged by anti-activism in the classroom, in the school, the district or even in policy.

In spite of our own principles, we cannot readily leave our identities checked at the entrance to the school. We can hope, though, as we begin to institutionalize social justice theory, to understand that, by definition, it is fluid. Then, we grow stronger in our efforts to develop policy that can become an essential part of the democracy under which we live. Though idealistic, it might behoove our field to renew our commitment to social justice by unveiling and then rearticulating with-in our respective communities the roots of any and all forms of moral, social, cultural, economical, gendered, political, and historical oppression and reflect on the manifestations of injustice. From there, schools of education can build upon what is accessible to their own students, taking into account students' historical deficits, and build such contexts into critically relevant research agendas, into our methods courses, and ultimately into our English language arts classrooms. As with the question posed earlier by Beach and Lindahl (2000), *should there be a fundamental right to an education in the U.S.*, we extend their efforts as we continue in our efforts to build a more solid theoretical, methodological, and empirical foundation around social justice work, and codify and reify its tenets, so that we can pivot these efforts closer to policy. *Should there be expressed social justice tenets in English education?*

The essays by our contributors have continued to steer us toward bringing social justice into contexts of English education, from theory to policy. So, as we move forward and continue to candidly reveal how each of our own habituses (e.g., education, spiritual beliefs, ethnicity, age, size, gender and its expression, ability, social class, political beliefs, marital status, sexual orientation, language, and national origin) intersect with the principles by which we live and how they position us in our work, we open to even greater possibilities of how we can use our own self-understandings to strengthen our collective power to enact social justice authentically. When we invite others around us on a similar journey, we are better prepared to build bridges with colleagues, teachers, and methods course students toward enacting social justice as reality for all.

The contributors of this collection know well how important it is to have social justice policies not only in English education but in all of education. We hope that these essays will be noted by policy makers who can and will begin to craft policy based on empirical studies—where empirical promotes more than just quantitative research designs. Based on the arguments made in this collection and suggestions from our contributors, we provide specific recommendations to policy makers that are pertinent for those crafting social justice policy in English education. To this end, we resolve the following:

1. New English education policies must recognize the existing reform and policy efforts put forth by NCTE. Currently, *standards* are being updated for the teaching of English along with the many English cultures and communities that pepper the globe. These standards must account for the cross-cultural, intercultural, and transcultural comparisons that reflect the dearth and value of resources and differences within various populations as they are set against one another. Specific examples for writing new standards for language can be found in the *CEE Position Statement: Beliefs about Social Justice in English Education,* http://www.ncte. org/cee/ positions/socialjustice, which offers a set of seven beliefs that suggest key research, theory, and pedagogical applications on social justice that can be drawn from drafted policy.

2. New English education policies must reflect the vital connection between how accrediting mandates' specific wording around social justice affects colleges of education teacher preparation candidates and how that has a direct effect on students' dispositions in the classroom. These policies must strive to challenge how accrediting agencies include and exclude particular populations of students in their reviews so that accrediting can be fair and just for all populations of students.

3. New English education policies must draw from social justice research frameworks (broadly conceived) to shape decisions that challenge inequitable schooling practices.

4. New English education must call for site-based reform to develop social justice policies and hold schools of education accountable for the integration of social justice theory and research into English teacher education programs. The U.S. government must offer incentives and funding for curriculum development and assessment practices related to social justice in schools so that not only will English educators have a grasp for how to prepare teacher candidates to adopt dispositions related to social

justice in English education programs, but also that they will have clear indicators and notable observations for what it means to have a classroom that is framed by equitable practices.

5. New English education policies must consider how to make the distribution process of access, power, and opportunity equitable across all schooling communities.

6. The U.S. government should draft a Student's Bill of Rights on social justice in schools that outlines in enumerated detail the individual rights of every student to be entitled to an education regardless of any difference, and emphasizes that each student has a right to learn in an environment free of prejudice and harassment in any form.

In the *Introduction* to the book, we retold the story of the group of five-year-olds who were given a test of skills in schools. Recall, that one of the results showed that Black students performed highest in all baseline assessments. Then as students progressed through schools, these testing results went down and White students' scores went up. It has been our hope that nonsensical, insensitive, and outrageous schooling practices can be eliminated over time. Each student has rights and those rights must be guaranteed from the second a student walks onto school property. It is beneath our moral dignity to allow school inequities to go unchecked. As such, we must now more than ever ask: What is our national commitment to social justice in schools? How might we develop policies that endorse that commitment, and how might we achieve them sooner rather than later? These questions are essential to bringing about a timely change that can help our society grow richer, deeper, and more united than it has even been.

Other possible changes for social justice are in the midst of review by organizations such as the Conference on English Education Executive Committee and the NCTE executive committees. The Conference on English Education, for example, unanimously approved the belief statement about social justice in English education at the Annual Meeting of the National Council of Teachers of English in Philadelphia, 2009. A next move is forthcoming, a request to NCTE to pass a resolution for moving social justice into policy. Efforts are also being made to create a set of NCTE/IRA standards on social justice related to K–12 classrooms. In the process, we hope to ally with the NCTE/NCATE standards task force to create official standards related to teacher preparation and teacher education. Such efforts form a lattice onto which our hopes about social justice in English education are currently hanging. While we eagerly await the outcomes during this critical time of change and possibility, we keep our eyes turned toward the future, reminding ourselves daily that not only are we on the precipice of change but that change is actually happening.

Bibliography

Beach, R., & Lindahl, R. (2000, September). Can there be a right to education in the United States? *Equity & Excellence in Education, 33*(2), 5-12. Retrieved October 1, 2007, from Education Abstracts database.

Conference on English Education Commission on Social Justice. (2009). CEE position statement: Beliefs about social justice in English education. *First Biennial CEE Conference*. Chicago: CEE.

Matters Change: And Why Change Matters

Peter McLaren

Arguably it is the case today that corporate greed constitutes the epochal spirit of our times. But to my thinking it is not the central antagonism at this current juncture in world history that is witnessing the ongoing trauma of capitalist formation within national security states such as the U.S. The problem is not entrenched corporate interests. This is merely the symptom that we mistake for the disease. The main problem—dare I say it?—is not that corporations and the banking industry (what used to be called the "Big Mules") are mulcting the public. The problem is global or transnational capitalism itself. Capitalism is the very Eye of Sauron, the Hammer of Havoc, a heinous blight upon the planet that sees all, consumes all, and destroys all in its path. We, the people, are lodged fast in the fetid bowels of the capitalist state, buried deep inside a monological regime of untruth, ensepulchured within the monumentalism and U.S. exceptionalism of the dominant culture—spread-eagled in the vortex of conflict that Bakhtin calls the authoritative discourse of the state and the internally persuasive discourse of our own making that expresses our values and our aspirations. The discourse of the state—that positions the "other" as irredeemably evil, as a monolithic alien species that is so barbaric as not to merit the rule of law—along with the functional existence of the state as an instrument of exploitation and repression, clearly need to be overcome. How will this be possible? Cold War ideology prevails and U.S. citizens in the main bear the ideological marks of their times. The term "American empire" is being championed by the right out of a sense of noblesse oblige—to be part of an empire is a duty and a responsibility that comes with being the leader and protector of the "free" world. With their paternalistic toy trumpets and their willingness to jettison their critical faculties in favor of embracing an iron certainty and ineffable faith that the U.S. has a providential mission in the world, the far right boasts that free market democracy has to be delivered to the far corners of the earth (by bombing runs, if necessary) if civilization is to prevail on the planet.

One path out of this mess—socialism—continues to be demonized, having long since been culturally amputated by the mass media as a form of political gangrene. Has socialism been superannuated and already seen its day? Irretrievably so, I'm afraid, although for some—like myself—its previous glow still excites. For the popular majorities, socialism is not seen as the opened eyes of democracy which have remained closed under capitalism. Which brings to mind a saying by the great American sociologist, poet, writer, anarchist, and public intellectual Paul Goodman: "in America you can say anything as long as it doesn't have any effect."

It would take some changes in the Constitution and a mass uprising of the people to even make a dent toward progress. It doesn't seem likely in today's climate that the Constitution can serve a people bent on a democratic socialist transformation of capitalist society. The Constitution works, rather, to forestall such an eventuality. The central antagonism, of course, is the contradiction between political democracy and economic servitude. America's citizens historically have been unable to use political democracy to obtain economic democracy. It almost seems like it can't be done. Human rights in the U.S. systematically exclude economic democracy. In fact, it makes economic servitude for the majority of U.S. citizens an inevitability. Critical pedagogy conceived as a revolutionary social movement is one possible (although insufficient) way of achieving such a goal. At least, that's my educational wager.

I am interested in educational change, and like the editors and authors of this prescient and powerful collection of essays, *Change Matters*, I believe that change matters. But matters also change. What has changed so much, and what in my mind makes education matter so much, is that public education has been all but destroyed by capitalist forces of privatization and corporatization. Nothing can save public education—not even a powerful book such as this one—unless capitalism itself is overcome. We won't be able to sweep capitalism away with a corn-shuck mop, but we can begin the long struggle of imagining together an alternative to capital's value form, and fighting tooth and nail to bring it about. Again, that is my political wager. And it is a wager that I will try to elaborate throughout this *Afterword*.

My work is largely atypical of the North American academy in that I work from a Marxist humanist perspective, largely influenced by the work of Raya Dunayevskaya. That I am mostly interested in educational works of Marxist inspiration—which some critics believe are a throwback into the age of dinosaurs—is not the same as me embracing the opinion that non-Marxist works are uninteresting or unimportant. I am an educational ecumenist. I believe that the critical tradition in education, and in particular the social justice tradition in which *Change Matters* is firmly located, is of signal importance in the long and perilous road towards educational transformation. But I don't believe that we will get very far in our collective struggle for educational change unless at the same time we work towards economic justice. And in this respect the editors and authors of this volume would, I am sure, agree with me. After all, you can't have human rights without economic rights and in this climate you can't say that without being derided as un-American. And for me to encourage educators to engage in the struggle for an alternative to capitalism and towards a postcapitalist future is well considered and downright seditious. But the big debate is not about whether we need economic justice in the U.S. The big debate centers around the question: How do we bring about real economic justice in the U.S. that moves beyond piecemeal reform? Is that even a viable question?

I'd like to share with readers some basic principles and positions that I have developed since I began my work in critical pedagogy, and why I have decided to add the adjective "revolutionary" to the term. What exactly is revolutionary critical pedagogy? Is it merely some grandly baptized new phrase? Or an outdated adjective shackled to a still fecund term? The question is a little more complex than it might seem at first blush. I will try to offer an answer throughout the pages that follow. To a large extent, revolutionary critical pedagogy has to do with developing a philosophy of praxis that can escape the Kantian dualism of mind and world. I don't see them as separate. That's important. In this regard, I have found that a Hegelian-Marxist reading of the word and the world is the most helpful framework I have discovered in developing such a pedagogy in what I would describe as a very long and arduous journey that began for me when I started teaching in an elementary school in my native Toronto, Canada, in the mid-1970s.

I hope that classroom teachers and teacher educators will forgive me for this, but I locate the *differentia specifica* of revolutionary critical pedagogy within a wider optic than classroom teaching, or popular education that takes place in community settings. I define it as the working out of a systematic dialectic of pedagogy that is organized around a philosophy of praxis. This praxis begins with an immanent critique of conventional pedagogies in order to see if its assumptions and claims are adequate to the type of praxis needed to both understand and challenge and eventually overcome capitalism's expansionistic dynamic. So we need both a philosophy of praxis that is coherent and forms of organization—horizontal and democratic—that best reflect our praxis. Now it is a praxis of being and becoming, of mental and manual labor, of thinking and doing, of reading and writing the word and the world (in the Freirean sense); in short, it is a practice of the self, a form of self-fashioning but not simply in the Foucauldian sense or in the Nietzschean "will to power" sense.

Revolutionary critical pedagogy, then, is both a reading practice where we read the word in the context of the world, and a practical activity where we write ourselves as subjective forces into the text of history—but this does not mean that making history is only an effect of discourse, a form of metonomy, the performative dimension of language, a rhetorical operation, a tropological system. No, reality is more than textual self-difference. Praxis, as I am using the term, is directed at understanding the world and the world dialectically as an effect of class contradictions. As Teresa Ebert (2009; see also Ebert & Zavarzadeh, 2008) argues, the medium of meaning is language; but the meaning of meaning is not necessarily linguistic, it is social—and it is directly linked to the social relations of labor. So revolutionary critical pedagogy then is a philosophy of practice lived in everyday life that attempts to uncover the congealed, abstract structures that constitute social life materially. Revolutionary critical pedagogy, then, is a way of challenging the popular imaginary (which has no "outside" to the text) that normalizes the core cultural foundations of capitalism and the normative force of the state. In other words, it tells us that there is no alternative to capitalist social relations. So then critical pedagogy is a reading of and an acting upon the social totality by turning abstract "things" into a material force, by helping abstract thought lead to praxis, to revolutionary praxis, to the bringing about of a social universe that is not based on the value form of labor, that is a socialist alternative to capitalism. Here I am looking at critical pedagogy as a social process, a social product, and a social movement that is both grounded in a philosophy of praxis and partakes of democratic forms of organization. And, after Ranceire (1991), it considers equality and equal intelligence as a starting point rather than a destination.

Critical pedagogy deals with the becomingness of human beings, which is tautologically the defining feature of education (the ontological quest for becoming human), but it does so with a particular political project in mind—anti-capitalist, anti-imperialist, anti-racist, anti-sexist and pro-democratic and emancipatory struggle. It works against what Anibal Quijano and Michael Ennis (2000) call the "coloniality of power." Here critical pedagogy serves to make the familiar strange and the strange familiar (i.e., refiguring how we discern the relationship between the self and the social so that we can see both as manufactured, as the social construction of multiple dimensions, and, at times, as the observer of each other, and the suppressed underside of each other); in addition, it attempts to bring out the pedagogical dimensions of the political and the political dimensions of the pedagogical and to convert these activities to a larger, more sustained and focused project of building alternative and oppositional forms of sustainable environments, of learning environments, of revolutionary political environments, where capitalism can be superceded by socialism.

Revolutionary critical pedagogy is about the hard work of building community alliances, of challenging school policy, of providing teachers with alternative and oppositional teaching materials. It has little to do with awakening the "revolutionary soul" of students—this is merely a re-fetishization of the individual and the singular under the banner of the collective and serves only to bolster the untruth fostered by capitalist social relations and postpone the answer to the question: Is revolution possible today? Can we organize our social, cultural, and economic life differently so as to transcend the exploitation that capital affords us?

Yes, ideas and reason have an important role to play in a meaningful account of life. We need to understand our place in the rational unfolding of the world, but more important, we need to play an active—and indeed, protagonistic—role in the unfolding of history. As critical educators we can't move history through ideas alone, we need to transcend the capitalist law of value and the social relations that constrain us. We transcend the alienation of this world by transforming the material world. Revolutionary critical pedagogy is illuminated by an insight made foundational in the work of Paulo Freire: that politics and pedagogy are not an exclusive function of having the right knowledge via some kind of "ah-ha" awakening of the revolutionary soul. Critical consciousness is not the root of commitment to revolutionary struggle but rather the product of such a commitment. An individual does not have to be critically self-conscious in order to struggle. It is in the act of struggling that individuals become critically conscious and aware. This is the bedrock of revolutionary critical pedagogy's politics of solidarity and commitment. While radical scholarship and theoretical ideas are important—extremely important—people do not become politically aware and then take part in radical activity. Rather, participating in contentious acts of revolutionary struggle creates new protagonistic political identities. Critically informed political identities do not motivate revolutionary action but rather develop as a logical consequence of such action. And the action summoned by revolutionary critical educators is always heterogeneous, multifaceted, protagonistic, democratic, and participatory—yet always focalized—anti-capitalist struggle. The ideas and beliefs that are derivative from the practical—and yes, often messy—aspects of life are those that drive history. They do not depend upon a prophet to lead the people to the promised land—it is the people that will lead themselves. As Eugene Debs once said: "I am not a Labor Leader; I do not want you to follow me or anyone else; if you are looking for a Moses to lead you out of this capitalist wilderness, you will stay right where you are. I would not lead you into the promised land if I could, because if I led you in, some one else would lead you out. You must use your heads as well as your hands, and get yourself out of your present condition."

I have taken the position over the years that transcendence must always remain within the immanence of human possibilities. There's a saying that goes something like this: "If you don't know where you want to go, any road will take you there." I agree with Michael Lebowitz (2010) that this saying is mistaken. If you don't know where you want to go, it is pretty clear that no road will take you there. What we need in critical pedagogy is an understanding of the goal and a vision of the future that is gleaned from understanding how we are made to be unfree within the larger social totality of capitalist social relations.

Marx's vision of a society was one that would permit the full development of human beings as a result of the protagonistic activity of human beings in revolutionary praxis—the simultaneous changing of circumstances and human activity or self-change. This key link in Marx was the concept of human development and practice. In other words, as Marx makes clear, there are always two products as the result of our activity: the change in circumstances and the change in people themselves. Socialist human beings produce themselves only through their own activity (Lebowitz, 2010). Which is why I have always made the distinction between *abstract utopian praxis* and *concrete utopian praxis*. I have always stressed a concrete utopianism that is grounded in the creative potential of human beings living in the messy web of capitalist social relations—in the here and now—to overcome and transform their conditions of unfreedom. When I say that we need to strive as educators toward a concrete utopia and not an abstract utopia, I mean here what Santos (2009) means when he talks about *acto in proximis* and *acto in distans*. Knowledge production as a liberatory act must include an *acto in proximis* meaning that the epistemology in question must have a practical effect in the world. This echoes Walter Benjamin's argument that if we merely contemplate the world we will only arrive at knowledge of evil (see McNally, 2001). Knowledge of the good is knowledge of a practice designed to change reality, it derives from action, from contemplation. We judge the truth of our actions in their effects on the lives of the oppressed. But an epistemology of everyday praxis is not enough, because such acts or forms of praxis need a larger rudder, something to give the emancipatory act not only ballast but direction. That is, it must also be implicated in an *acto in distans*, or the utopian aspect of knowledge production, which, in our case, is part of our struggle to diminish exploitation and suffering and promote justice. An *acto in proximis* is very much like a form of emancipatory praxis whereas the *acto in distans* is the larger movement within these forms of praxis toward a utopia built upon the principles of equality and participatory democracy. It is precisely the double valence, or mixture of the two acts, that prevents the utopia from becoming abstract and metaphysical and prevents everyday acts of emancipatory praxis from becoming free floating and directionless, detached from the larger project of global emancipation. It directs the praxis toward a concrete utopia, grounded in everyday struggle. The question that I think is lacking in critical pedagogy is the ideologeme of distance. Frantz Fanon asked how to negotiate a correct distance from both the colonial power and the nativist past so as to avoid the triumphalism of Western master narratives and resistance motored by racialist separation. Here Hal Foster's model of deferred action is important. If subjectivity, as Lacan notes, is structured on a relay of anticipations and reconstructions of traumatic events, and if one event (disruptive) is only registered through another that recodes it (restorative), we come to be who we are only in what Foster calls deferred action. If the struggle of revolutionary critical pedagogy constitutes, therefore, a complex relay of anticipated futures and reconstructed pasts, as a form of deferred action, then we can see that this struggle acts on capitalist social relations as it is acted upon by it.

The repressed part of revolutionary critical pedagogy returns but it returns from the future. And, it is this delay, this deferral of action, that allows us the space for dialogue, a dialogue that can serve as the conditions of possibility for a new beginning. So revolutionary critical pedagogy is a trauma that can be acted out hysterically with the sufficient distance. It was Lévi-Strauss, who as a Jew left European fascism, was exploring the concept of distance (Foster writes that it was the ethnological equivalent of Lacan's mirror stage). Lévi-Strauss saw a danger in the fascist extreme dis-identification of the "Other" and also the extreme over-identification of the surrealists who would appropriate the "Other." In the twentieth century, Lévi-Strauss envisioned the Polynesian Islands being turned into aircraft carriers and Asia and Africa becoming slums. In our quest for the lost unity of our being, what is the necessary distance between the self and the "Other," a distance that will produce neither dis-identification nor over-identification and appropriation—a distance that can result in relative equanimity? Of course, there are those critics who say that we cannot have critical distance today since the society of the spectacle necessarily subsumes criticality under distraction, given the nature of the new technologies and the media, where separations are concealed by an imaginary unity (Foster, 1996).

So the question becomes: How do we transcend the conflicts today that lead to over-identification and dis-identification? According to Marx, transcendence means not only abolishing the dehumanizing conditions of human life under capitalism but also going beyond the given to create the conditions of possibility for individuals to shape their own destiny—always, of course, recognizing at the same time that they live in conditions not of their own making. Of course, it is impossible to create a classroom free of the totality of social relations that make up the social universe of capital such that students or teachers can take charge of the rudder of history. Pedagogical struggle will always be contingent, and provisional, and relational as well as disciplined and most certainly at times mutinous! It plays a necessary but not sufficient role in the struggle for socialism.

We struggle to negate social structures and social relations that negate us as human beings. This includes aspects of classroom life. But such a struggle will not be absolute, a once and for all moment—or even a series of moments. It is a protracted struggle waged every day in the schools, the factories, the board rooms, and the churches, and community centers. The self-transcending formation of the meaning and values of our lives isn't restricted to the realm of ideas. It is an exigency and a demand. Our future has to be fought for through our projects, in the various realms of class struggle itself, in the productive dimension of history, within history's process of humanization as we become more and more conscious of ourselves as social beings—that is, within all dimensions of human creativity.

The ideas of critical pedagogy—as well as its practices—are never independent of the social conditions of the actions and processes that produced them. The concept of a revolutionary critical pedagogy implies some form of relation between knowledge of a domain formally constituted as "the social setting" in which learning takes place (such as classrooms) and another domain formally constituted as "the pedagogical" or where "teaching" occurs in the most general sense (and this includes venues other than classrooms). Revolutionary critical pedagogy analyzes pedagogical practices with protocols that are specific to the humanities and social sciences in general and Marxist and critical theory in particular. Depending on the level of detail at which analysis takes place, the object of critical pedagogy may take the gross form of a totality (capitalist society in general), or it may exist in nuanced forms: specific classroom practices or sites of knowledge production such as the media, community centers, conferences, etc., or some subset of pedagogy as such (i.e., definitions or generalizations about teaching and learning found in encyclopedias or handbooks of education). But critical educators recognize that pedagogical acts of knowing and engagement can neither be given in advance nor arbitrarily constructed by an analytic choice, but are, rather, necessarily implicated in and derived from particular interpretations that are grounded in our social life, that is, in our everyday experiences. They have an experiential existence, a social existence, before they have an analytic existence. Experiences are never transparent, and they require a critical language that can interpret them as part of the larger struggle against social relations of capitalist exploitation.

Indeed, revolutionary critical pedagogy seeks to challenge the core cultural foundations of capitalism that normalizes the idea that there is no alternative to capitalist social relations and no way of challenging the status quo. Revolutionary critical educators question capitalist concepts—such as wage labor and value production—alongside their students to consider alternative ways of subsisting and learning in the world. It seeks new democratic visions of organizing our schools and our communities through conscious praxis that self-reflexively examines the historical context of our ideas, social relations, institutions, and human relationships while opening space for the possibilities of the popular imaginary. As such, revolutionary critical pedagogy calls for a movement that is anti-capitalist, anti-imperialist, anti-racist, anti-sexist, anti-heterosexist, and pro-democratic.

This movement to challenge capitalism requires that we question normative ways of thinking about the world that corporate advertising and consumer-based culture continuously push upon us. We must look beyond Western, Euro-/U.S.-centric ways of knowing the world that are based in capitalist wastefulness and a lack of regard for the planet, in order to consider alternative and oppositional ways of thinking about and acting toward/against the imperialism of free-market, neoliberal, global capitalism.

Following the footsteps of women's studies, critical race theory, indigenous studies, ethnic studies, and other fields that have been labeled as "Other" or nondominant, revolutionary critical pedagogy urges us to be self-reflective enough to examine the ways in which it may unconsciously uphold mainstream ideologies at the expense of nondominant conceptualizations of the world, so that we may seek solidarity with nondominant groups in bringing together of the creative imaginaries of all people.

Rather than fall into the epistemologies of empire that designate certain knowledges as normative and nondominant knowledge as "Other," radical critical pedagogy must find creative purpose and protagonistic agency in embracing all epistemologies by acknowledging how all people engage in a reciprocal relationship with the world from their own sociohistorical contexts. It is through such a process of denying epistemologies of empire and recognizing the entirety of diverse human lifeways and thought that a new social order can be envisioned.

Indeed, this new social order should not be limited to Western/European responses to liberalism and capitalism alone, but rather—as noted in Walter Mignolo's (2010) analysis of Aymara sociologist Félix Patzi Paco's work regarding Indian/indigenous conceptualizations of the "communal"—should include the views of those who continue to suffer under the expansion of Western civilization while recognizing that their perspectives in response to colonization may not fully overlap with communist/Marxist responses to capitalism. Mignolo (2010) writes:

> The communal system in Tawantinsuyu and Anahuac, as I imagine social organizations in China before the Opium War and the arrival of Mao Zedong, were not created as responses to liberalism and capitalism. They had to adapt and still are adapting to capitalist and (neo) liberal intrusion. (p. 147)

An inclusion of indigenous perspectives within revolutionary critical pedagogy should recognize that "the left of European genealogy of thought (and the same genealogy in modern/colonial states) doesn't have the monopoly to imagine and dictate how a non-capitalist future shall be" (Mignolo, 2010, p. 148). Instead, following the insights of Patzi Paco, Mignolo attests that indigenous systems do not have the same political pillar or economic management pillar as those of Western, capitalist systems or colonial systems and, therefore, take on a different perception of justice, collective rights, and change. A critical revolutionary pedagogy must actively engage these perspectives to truly create a future world that embraces all rather than a select few.

Of course, challenging epistemologies of empire by engaging indigenous perspectives also requires that we be cautious about *how* we engage with indigenous perspectives. In particular, Linda Tuhiwai Smith (2005) reminds us how researchers, academics, and project workers have always found "ways of 'taking' indigenous knowledge…[in a] systematic gathering of scientific data" that have proven dangerous to indigenous peoples (p. 2). Taking up indigenous perspectives has usually been as exploitative as the act of imperialism and colonialism itself; just as "Imperialism was the system of control which secured the markets and capital investments" of European and U.S. powers, research on indigenous knowledge and perspectives has been the accumulation of "Othered" information as a form of subjugation that defined indigenous as "backwards" and Western as "modern" (Smith, 2005, p. 21). Of course, central to the definition of "modernity" was colonization's reach into the Americas and the development of the U.S. As Quijano and Wallerstein (1992) explain:

> The modern world-system was born in the long sixteenth century. The Americas as a geosocial construct were born in the long sixteenth century. The creation of this geosocial entity, the Americas, was the constitutive act of the modern world-system. The Americas were not incorporated into an already existing capitalist world-economy. There could not have been a capitalist world-economy without the Americas. (p. 549)

In fact, creating "modernity" and "newness"—central to Westernization—involved also engaging four key concepts: "coloniality, ethnicity, racism, and the concept of newness itself" (Quijano & Wallerstein, 1992, p. 550). With this understanding in mind, it becomes crucial that, when engaging indigenous perspectives, we do not continue in the same exploitative manner as those who are responsible for the genocide of billions of indigenous people. We must challenge our concepts of "modernity" and recognize our European-based epistemologies in order to allow for complete reverence for all other local and global views.

Indeed, this is precisely why revolutionary critical pedagogy is so crucial for our increasingly diverse public schools.

As racially marked bodies in geohistorical space, we require another artisanship of pedagogical practices, what Walter Mignolo (2009, 2010) refers to as a geopolitics of knowledge and knowing. This entails a political and epistemic delinking from Western Eurocentric practices and from a zero-point epistemology in which knowing a subject maps the world for everyone else. The knower is never neutral, working from some God's-eye perspective in the snowy ranges of Mount Olympus; there is no Researcher's Stone to give us the universal code of neutrality. We are not scaling the heights of Point Omega here with Teilhard de Chardin. Rather, the knower is always implicated, geo- and body-politically, in the known. Developing another artisanship of pedagogical practices also means interrogating Eurocentered epistemologies as well as the production of decolonizing and decolonial knowledge through understanding our subjectivities as historical and biographical loci of enunciation. In other words, we need to engage in a geopolitics of knowing that will produce a geopolitics of knowledge that follows from a process of political and epistemic delinking from the grand Western episteme and cosmology. Arguing that "regions and people around the world have been classified as underdeveloped economically and mentally," Mignolo (2009) argues that we must take up the decolonial option that consists of "the unveiling of epistemic silences of Western epistemology and affirming the epistemic rights of the racially devalued" (p. 162). He maintains that it is not enough to change the conversation but to change the very terms of the conversation, that is, to move beyond disciplinary or interdisciplinary controversies and conflicts of interpretation. In other words, we need to call into question the very modern/colonial foundation of the control of knowledge and we do this by focusing on the knower (the enunciator or act of enunciation) rather than the known (the enunciated). This follows from Santos' (2007) assertion that all ignorance is ignorant of a certain knowledge and all knowledge is the overcoming of a particular ignorance (p. 229). The confrontation and conflict we witness among knowledge is actually the confrontation and dialogue among the different processes through which practices that are ignorant in different ways turn into practices that are knowledgeable in different ways (2007, p. 229). He makes an important distinction between simple ignorance (what he calls orthopedic thinking) and learned ignorance (2009).

We need to focus on the enunciation, that is, on the subject who produces and manipulates signs rather than on the structure of the sign itself. We need to understand, Mignolo (2009) asserts, the means by which we, as participants in the Western history of knowledge production (one that is theo- and ego-politically grounded), have moved from the formal apparatus of enunciation to frames of conversation to disciplines and to "super-frames" that he calls cosmologies—what he argues include the theological cosmology and the philosophy-science cosmology that both compete and collaborate with each other in order to "disqualify forms of knowledge beyond these two frames" (p. 164). History has shown us that certain knowledges (and I would add, systems of organizing our means of production) have defined people as human or as barbarians or somewhere along this thorny axis and thus we need to mount a pedagogical assault on the imperiality of modern/colonial loci of enunciations (disciplines and institutions) within the colonial matrix of power, which is a complex conceptual structure that guides actions in the domain of the economy (the exploitation of human [and animal] labor and the appropriation of land/natural resources), the government, the military, gender, sexuality, and knowledge/subjectivity. Mignolo (2009) invokes Frantz Fanon's sociogenesis as a reaction to phylogenetic and ontogenetic Western theories. Here Fanon reveals how the lived experiences of Blacks would always be formed by a particular framing of social and psychological dimensions manifested in the gaze of Whites. The Black body engages in necessary knowledge making "to decolonize the knowledge that was responsible for the coloniality of his being" (2009, p. 176).

Here I see an uncanny parallelism with the work of Canadian Marxist social theorist David McNally. McNally works from a premise that has occupied my work for several decades, namely, the notion that consciousness and language are not extra-natural or extra-bodily processes of becoming; they cannot be separated from the body, the sensuous body. In my book, *Schooling as a Ritual Performance* I talked about "enfleshment" and stated that the flesh also dreams. In other words, I am working with the assumption that we come into being through our communicative action with others, that is, through dyadic relations, and the transpersonal consciousness that we develop along this path is a substance/relation that is produced not by some abstract thought, some type of transcendental insight, but by our embodiment with others axiologically, aesthetically, politically, geopolitically, and in relation to the larger social totality where we are riven by class exploitation that is racialized and gendered. I do not exist for myself as an object that is located outside of the world of the flesh, the marrow, the bone. Communication born out of the experience of opposites, out of antagonisms structured in relation to the central conflict between capital and labor. There is a "withness" to knowing precisely because the experience of consciousness is always meaningful within the presence of another. In other words, consciousness emerges out of conflict between the ego experienced as a subject versus the ego experienced as an object; between the ego experienced as worthy of respect and praise and the ego experienced as bad, degenerate, and less than human; between the ego experienced as an active agent of history and experienced as a passive victim of oppression, betrayal, domination, or exploitation. We strive to become active beings who can effect the world around us, but capital has, instead, embalmed us (through the process such as alienation and reification) so that we experience ourselves as constantly empty, as never being able to fulfill the tear inside our self. We are placeless subjects having not been satiated by the determinations of bourgeois life. Critical pedagogy makes this conflict an object of knowledge. It is the power of critical reflection that separates the knowing subject from the object of knowledge so that the anguish and misery of everyday life can be examined; but critical pedagogy also enables the knowing subject to experience being the object of knowledge as the "Other" then becomes the knowing subject. That is, critical pedagogy enables the knowing subject and the known subject to coexist within the hydra-headed Medusan horror of capitalist exploitation. Critical pedagogy therefore functions as Athena's mirror shield that enabled Perseus to view Medusa through a reflection rather than directly; it protects the knowing subject from being consumed by the alienation of capitalism and the coloniality of being through a dialogical approach to reading the word and the world. It does so by challenging the knower in a way that does not take away her voice. Because to be voiceless, as my friend Henry Giroux frequently says, is to be powerless. In this way, the knowing subject can confront both the outer "Other" and the inner "Other" and thus discover the objective subject and the subjective object residing within.

Our identity is over time given continuity and coherence when we engage others not simply linguistically, as a set of linguistic relations, but as body-selves. The process of individuation—*Auseinandersetzung*—has as its most characteristic feature the encounter of oppositions (which in the capitalist world are really often distinctions within structural hierarchies that are metaphysically classified by the mind as oppositions) often experienced as antagonisms. This engagement—this dyadic relationship between self and other—gives form and substance to our sense of self. We don't just "language forth" our social universe, we "body forth" our social universe. Human consciousness is not the mere "reflection" of material processes and relations—as this would be a pre-dialectical stance—rather, consciousness and language are modes of my embodied being with others. Physical objects have culturo-technological meaning because they are embedded, as McNally (2001) notes, in networks of human meanings. Commodities have meaning according to the social relations and contexts that situate the individuals who interact with them. Every context is intercontextual, referring to other contexts of meaning. They interact, creating what is called a linguistic sphere. I have always been interested in what kind of bodies schools create. The body is integral to history and language. Consciousness, language, and culture are all vital aspects of our bodies.

We are "seeing bodies"—bodies that are the experiential sites of spaciality and temporality rather than the transcendental category of mind (McNally, 2001, p. 124). We can only overcome the fragmentary character of our experience of our fermenting subjectivity and the world through our interactions with others, rather than teachers viewing students as disembodied minds, apart from teachers and other students and the outside world. We need to instate the corporeal individual into our educational theorizing in and though the dyadic relationship between teacher and student, between the word and the world.

The dominant culture tries to drive socialist arguments underground but even in the homogenizing experiences of official culture, signs can never be rendered uniaccentual, we all struggle to accent signs differently. If the dialectic is about self-mediation, then theory and practice are already unified in the immanence of their self-unfolding (McNally, 2001). But many of the new avant-garde cadre of poststructuralists disavow the dialectic in favor of deconstruction. McNally (2001) makes the case that poststructuralist linguistics erases the laboring body, reproducing capital's myth of self-birth, the notion that capital can create itself without the mediation of labor (p. 230). Poststructuralists often suggest that language can create itself outside of bodies and material practices.

McNally (2001) describes the deconstructive efforts of poststructuralists such as Jacques Derrida as a form of linguistic idealism. In his critique of anti-fetishistic thought (like that of Marx), that palpates the farthest reach of linguistic meaning, Derrida devalues dialectical critique as useless by disavowing embodied human activity, by ignoring laboring human bodies and rejecting them as metaphysical illusions. When Derrida deals with issues of the economy, he is interested only in capital that begets capital—that is, in credit or fictitious capital. Likewise, in his critique of Saussure, he critiques the notion of a transcendental signified, a universal equivalent or what McNally refers to as meaning's gold standard (something positive that can exist outside of an endless reference of commodities to other commodities). There is nothing extra-linguistic for Derrida, since language suspends all reference to something outside of it. Similarly, for Derrida, money lacks a referent. It is driven by credit and speculation and lacks any material foundations. Derrida deals with fictitious or dematerialized money, money that can be produced without labor, that is, money as an expression of hyperreality. Capital in this view is nothing more than a self-engendering dance on a solipsistic path of self-fecundation. The real is folded into the representation. Derrida (and Baudrillard and others) assimilates the economy (the same one that is throwing people out of their homes and into the streets at present) into the post-structuralist model of language. Contrary to Derrida, McNally maintains that value is not a sign freed from its referent; rather, value expresses itself in material form. It must pass through laboring bodies and their history of struggle, through toiling subjects and practical human activity that takes place in an organic social universe of skin, hair, blood, and bone. And capitalism abstracts from these bodies, and commodifies them. The work of McNally implodes the limitations of poststructuralist thought in dealing with capitalist exploitation.

We must develop what Santos (2007) calls a new emancipatory common sense that is part of a decolonial project intended to serve as a guide for the construction of a non-capitalist, non-colonialist intercultural dialogue. According to Santos (2009), the theories and disciplines of the Western academy have, "on behalf of capitalism...theorized the universality of competition as opposed to cooperation, the economy of egotism as opposed to the economy of altruism, and buying/selling as opposed to the gift" (p. 112). Which brings us to ask: What are the antipodes of today's orthopedic educational discourse? My answer: The wager of revolutionary critical pedagogy. Santos (2009) distinguishes, after Nicholas of Casa, "learned ignorance" from "ignorant ignorance"; the former refers to a "learnedly not-knowing" that requires a "laborious knowing process on the limitations of what we know" (p. 114). It is "to know that the epistemological diversity of the world is infinite and that each way of knowing grasps it only in a very limited manner" (p. 115). The latter refers to a kind of ignorance "which is not even aware that it does not know" (2009, p. 114). Santos (2009) positions himself against what he calls "epistemological fascism" or the destruction of the concealment of other ways of knowing that could be described as "epistemicide." Instead, he calls for an "ecology of knowledge" that recognizes that "knowledge exists only as a plurality of forms of ignorance" (2009, p. 116). Santos argues that "the possibilities and limits of understanding and action of each way of knowing offers a comparison with other ways of knowing"—and what Santos calls an ecology of knowledge lies in such a comparison. He maintains that the superiority of a given way of knowing is assessed by "its pragmatic contribution to a given practice" (2009, p. 118).

Some astute critics of U.S. education might be tempted to look at critical pedagogy as a tradition that has made more of an impact on the publishing industry than on public education, and there would be some truth to this. Public education is in shambles, unable to fight off the corporate assaults on its ranks. What we need is something ambitious, but something that would mean changing the U.S. state from the bottom up. Something Venezuela has been able to do, although not without continued and often fierce opposition by the ruling class whose attempts at overthrowing President Hugo Chavez have been funded and supported by the U.S.

I am impressed by the new Organic Education Law which Venezuela's National Assembly passed unanimously shortly after midnight on August 14, 2009, following an extended legislative session. The fierce opponents of Chavez (which we call the *esqualidos*) claim the education law is unconstitutional, anti-democratic, politicizes the classroom, threatens the family and religion, and will allow the state to take children away from their parents for indoctrination. Of course these condemnations are part of a well-orchestrated campaign, which I am sure is highly funded by Washington. This law is important in that the Constitution requires it to uphold constitutional principles, which means that the state has the responsibility to ensure that all citizens have a high-quality education, free of charge, from childhood through the undergraduate university level. This concept of the "Educator State" (*Estado Docente*) is introduced in Article 5, which says the state must guarantee education "as a universal human right and a fundamental, inalienable, non-renounceable social duty, and a public service...governed by the principles of integrality, cooperation, solidarity, attentiveness, and co-responsibility" (Sugget, 2009). The law also requires "progressive annual growth" in education spending as a percentage of GDP. Article 6 lists nearly fifty aspects of the education system of which the state is in charge, including educational infrastructure, curriculum, and other administrative tasks, as well as specific duties that exemplify the principles of the education system established in Article 3. One of the key principles, in my view, is the one that advocates "equality among all citizens without discrimination of any kind." In fact, this new law mandates "equality of conditions and opportunities," as well as "gender equity," "access to the educational system for people with disabilities or educational needs," and the extension of educational facilities to rural and poor areas. Spanish is listed as the official language of the education system, "except in the instances of intercultural bilingual indigenous education, in which the official and equal use of their [native] language and Spanish shall be guaranteed" (Sugget, 2009). In addition to promoting "the exchange of social and artistic knowledge, theories, practices, and experiences," the law sanctions "popular and ancestral knowledge, which strengthen the identity of our Latin American, Caribbean, indigenous, and Afro-descendent peoples" (Sugget, 2009). Finally, Article 10 specifically prohibits speech and propaganda that promote hate and violence in classrooms or in the context of educational settings, including the news media. Article 3 also stresses a recurrent theme: "participatory democracy." This is clearly important and you can hear this echo throughout the new education act. Now Article 15 is controversial in the eyes of the opponents of Chavez, because it says that one of the basic purposes of education is "to develop a new political culture based on protagonist participation and the strengthening of popular power, the democratization of knowledge, and the promotion of the school as a space for the formation of citizenship and community participation, for the reconstruction of the public spirit" (Sugget, 2009). Yet there are plenty of references to the importance of "learning to peacefully coexist," learning to learn and teach simultaneously, "valuing the common good," the necessity for education to be "integral" as opposed to highly specialized or multilinear, "respect for diversity," and the importance of lifelong learning. The legal definition of the educational community has been significantly broadened to include families, community organizations, and wage laborers in addition to the formal educational workers. Article 20 states, "The educational community will be composed of all the fathers, mothers, representatives, students, teachers, administrative workers, and laborers of the educational institution...spokespersons of the different community organizations linked to the educational centers and institutions will also be able to form part of the educational community"

(Sugget, 2009). This new educational community is described in the article as "a democratic space of social-communitarian, organized, participatory, cooperative, protagonist, and solidarity-oriented character," and maintains that "Its participants will carry out the process of citizen education consistent with what is established in the Constitution of the Bolivarian Republic of Venezuela." Article 9 makes it clear that the communication media, including the television, radio, and press, are to be considered "essential instruments for the development of the educational process." Some public universities will continue to be run by the state and others, known as autonomous universities, will be funded by the state but run independently. But the law challenges the structural problems inherent in autonomous universities, mainly corruption by university administrators and the lack of transparency and democracy in budgeting decisions. In fact, many autonomous universities have worked with violent opposition groups by allowing violent demonstrators to store weapons, tires, and other protest materials and take refuge on university campuses. The state security forces are legally prohibited from crossing onto university campuses. There will be automatic university admission for all high school graduates who satisfy basic grade and behavioral requirements and wish to obtain a university education. The aptitude test that is currently used would be replaced by a diagnostic test aimed at assessing the academic strengths and weaknesses, career interests, and socio-economic conditions of the students, for the purpose of placing them in a corresponding university program. Approximately two dozen new universities across the national territory will be created, in order to help realize this goal. Well, the education act also deals with questions of labor rights, job security and benefits, and the training in "liberatory work." Article 15 states that the educational system must "develop the creative potential of each human being for the full realization of his or her personality and citizenship, based on the ethical value of liberatory work and active participation." There is also a stress on human rights and free speech. The law also maintains that education "should encourage an end to nuclear weapons in the world," it should fight racism, and develop in the students an "ecological consciousness to preserve biodiversity and social diversity" (Sugget, 2009). Now this is an excellent beginning, and fits the description that I have of the journey that I would like to see revolutionary critical pedagogy take in North America. But does it even have a chance?

The reaction to the law by the ruling classes in Venezuela is all too familiar—it reminds me of the reaction of Republicans here in the U.S. to the idea of a national healthcare system. They (especially the vile Teabaggers) see it as big government controlling the medical establishment (well, they should recognize that what already controls the medical establishment are the pharmaceutical companies, and the corporations and other for-profit organizations!). If this law is passed, the conservative forces in Venezuela believe that the country will be one step closer to a becoming a totalitarian communist society. You can see their eyes role to the back of their heads: Conspiracy! Conspiracy! The country will degenerate into an authoritarian regime that is redolent of fascist regimes of the past! Perhaps they will implant socialist microchips in the brains of every student. The classroom, they argue, should not be politicized! They reject the education act as a way of institutionalizing *populismo politiquero*. The schools will turn out automatons who will be mouthpieces for Chavez and the cause of socialism. Children will be taken from the homes and put into classes where they will have to chant in unison lines supporting the Bolivarian cause. They fear the community councils will train members in brainwashing techniques, forcing students to repeat "Cuban values" and will set up panopticon webs to keep all the schools under surveillance and to gain authoritarian control over local affairs. Well, if I am exaggerating their reaction, it must be acknowledged that I have captured a strong kernel of truth in their opposition to this bill.

If the opposition would look closely and fairly at this law, they will see that there is a section of the law titled, "Prohibitions of Political Party Propaganda in Educational Centers and Institutions" and Article 12 in this section clearly states the following: "proselytism or political party propaganda is not permitted in educational centers and institutions of the primary education system through any medium: oral, print, electronic, radio, informative, telephone, or audiovisual" (Sugget, 2009). In my view, this new education law, in effect, counters what the education laws of former pro-capitalist governments have achieved: the creation of passive, compliant, non-critical students who simply become instruments for the reproduction of the capitalist social order and the international division of labor. I believe that the socialist mission with which Venezuela's Bolivarian educators are involved is crucial for the development of a participatory democracy, not the democracy of empty forms that you so often find in the U.S., forms that eventually chain the people to the routines of bourgeois life. The pursuit of genuine democracy is what *Change Matters* is all about.

Am I saying that I want U.S. teachers to become Chavistas? Hardly. The obstacles we have to surmount in order to build real educational justice and equality will arise out of the contextual specificity of the U.S.—it will betray a distinctly U.S. character and culture. And it would be unrealistic to think we have the ideological conditions to mobilize the people toward a socialist alternative. We are still trying to work within Gramsci's war of position, finding a long and complex strategy for social justice across institutions of civil society. A war of maneuver is less likely, as there exists strong hegemony within the civil society. Most Americans believe capitalism is the best government available, even in the midst of the current economic crisis. So we are a long way off from suggesting viable alternatives to the current economic system. Which doesn't mean that it is not imperative to try. More than ever, it is essential to wage a war of position, even if it is long and protracted, which it surely will be. *Change Matters* is part of this war of position.

Whether this stellar collection of chapters in *Change Matters* represents the diverse perspectives embodied in topics such as The S.M.A.R.T. workshop (Sexual Misconduct Awareness and Response Training), a Vygotskian/Freirean approach to culturally sensitive teaching, or an engagement in participatory action research, they all get closer to the multimethodologies sought by the editors; contribute to a cogent research framework for social justice; trouble and disrupt normative versions of educational research, pedagogical practices, and policy making; and work (mostly with emerging methodologies that support research in English education) in developing a meta-framework for teaching social justice (one that encompasses reflection, change, and participation). The readers are invited to explore numerous approaches within the critical tradition: critical discourse analysis that utilizes critical race theory and Black feminist discourse; critical ethnographies of discourse; critically conscious analysis in literacy research; Deleuze and Guattari's nomadic science and rhizoanalysis; narrative analysis in sociocultural research; transformative data analysis, narrative autobiographical educational inquiry from feminist poststructuralist perspectives; the creation of social imaginaries based on difference; critical practitioner research; consensus models of decision making that emphasize local knowledge, multiple perspectives, and reciprocity; and using the lenses of critical ethnography, critical multiculturalism, and social critical pedagogy to analyze the experiences of youth—all of which are designed to contribute to diminishing human misery, ending linguistic apartheid, and building a more just world. Here we can join the editors and the authors in our refusal to abdicate our need for creating counter-stories that can break free from the licensed charter of neoliberalism that ridicules views not sanctioned by the corporate media, counter-stories and actions that will eventually congeal into a counter-public sphere. We need to fashion new cultural grammars that grow out of the life genres of the oppressed and that are designed to provide opportunities for subaltern groups to organize themselves around a unified political project of social justice, far away from the meek passivity of the victim role. I think it's important to reject the idea that subaltern groups naturally tend toward oppositional viewpoints since they often consent to the dominant values of the ruling class. But common sense is not all of one piece, it is usually an unstable constellation of alternative, oppositional, and hegemonic values (McNally, 2001). It is from within the messy terrain of the contradictory nature of common sense that a counter-hegemonic struggle must be waged. We need therefore to reject, as did Gramsci, spontaneism, or the notion that subaltern groups are spontaneously oppositional. Instead, there needs to be a systematic link of developing a critical pedagogy for a socialist alternative to capitalism that can invite subaltern groups to reexamine the terrain of their everyday lives. But since there is no outside to the dark physics of the capitalist commodity, we have to seek out redemption within the prison-house of this terrain, by means of an immanent critique and the development of a protagonistic socialist subjectivity. But in addition to immanent critique we also need a philosophy to guide us--a philosophy of praxis linked to a dialectics of self and social transcendence. Since the 1980s, we have tragically witnessed attacks on dialectical reasoning, not only from the pragmatists, the Althusserians, and the autonomists, but also poststructuralists and deconstructionists of various stripe. Many of these critics reject the very notion of self and social transcendence, believing it will only lead to the gulag. Yet liberation from capitalism and other antagonisms such as racism and sexism is not only immanent in spontaneous social struggles of the present. We must be able to transcend the present historical moment and reach out towards a different future. We have been left, regrettably, we multilinear or worse, non-economic, approaches to social change. We have enclosed ourselves within civil society and the public sphere falsely believing that these are the most productive arenas in which to struggle. We have forgotten about production relations altogether. This has been the tragedy of the left today. But the struggle continues. We need to turn our schools, our libraries and community centers, our churches and our factories into historical laboratories where we can foster and foment counter-hegemonic spaces of redemption and resistance, were we can create crucibles of possibility. There is no simple cautery for the destructive powers of capital. We refuse—and must continue to refuse—to beggar ourselves on war and violence against the "Other," and we must struggle hard to inaugurate a new age in our educational history. Matters will continue to change, and change will always matter. *Change Matters* speaks to this dual process in ways that need to be taken up by educators everywhere.

Note

Thanks to Jean Ryoo for her suggestions.

Bibliography

Debs, E. (n.d.) In Wikiquote. Retrieved from http://en.wikiquote.org/wiki/Eugene_V._ Debs.

Ebert, T. (2009). *The task of cultural critique*. Urbana: University of Illinois Press.

Ebert, T., & Zavarzadeh, M. (2008). *Class in culture*. Boulder, CO: Paradigm.

Foster, Hal. (1996). *The return of the real: The avant-garde at the end of the century*. Cambridge, MA: MIT.

Lebowitz, M. (Feb. 20, 2010). Socialism: The goal, the paths and the compass. *The Bullet*. Socialist Project. E-Bulletin No. 315.

McNally, David. (2001). *Bodies of meaning: Studies on language, labor, and liberation*. Albany, New York: State University of New York.

Mignolo, Walter D. (2009). Epistemic disobedience, independent thought and decolonial freedom, *Theory, Culture & Society 26* (7–8): 159–181.

Mignolo, Walter D. (2010). *The communal and the decolonial. Pavilion, 14*, pp. 146–155.

Peterson, B. (2009). Big city superintendents: Dictatorship or democracy? Lessons from Paulo Freire. *Rethinking Schools, 24* (1). Retrieved January 24, 2010, from http://www.rethinkingschools.org/archive/24_01/24_01_paulo.shtml

Quijano, A. & Ennis, M. (2000). Coloniality of power, Eurocentrism, and Latin America. *Nepantla: Views from south,* 1, 533–580.

Quijano, A. & Wallerstein, I. (1992). Americanity as a concept, or the Americas in the modern world-system. *International Social Science Journal 29*, 549–557.

Ranceire, J. (1991). *The ignorant schoolmaster: Five lessons in intellectual emancipation.* Palo Alto: Stanford University Press.

Santos, B.S. (2007). From an epistemology of blindness to an epistemology of seeing. In B. de Sousa Santos (Ed.), *Cognitive justice in a global world: Prudent knowledges for a decent life.* (pp. 407–437). Lanham and New York: Lexington.

Santos, B.S. (2009). A non-occidentalist West? Learned ignorance and ecology of knowledge. *Theory, Culture & Society, 26* (7–8), 103–125.

Smith, L.T. (2005). *Decolonizing methodologies: Research and indigenous peoples.* New York: Zed.

Sugget, J. (2009). Venezuelan education law: Socialist indoctrination or liberatory education? Retrieved from http://www.venezuelanalysis.com/analysis/4734

Contributors

Janet Alsup is associate professor of English education at Purdue University. Her specialties are teacher education and professional identity development, the teaching of composition and literature in middle and high schools, young adult literature and adolescent identity, and qualitative and narrative inquiry. She has published two books. The first, co-authored with Dr. Jonathan Bush, is titled *But Will It Work with Real Students? Scenarios for Teaching Secondary English Language Arts* (NCTE, 2003). Her second book, *Teacher Identity Discourses: Negotiating Personal and Professional Spaces* (Erlbaum/NCTE), was published in 2006 as part of the NCTE/LEA Research Series in Literacy and Composition and won the 2007 Mina P. Shaughnessy Prize. She is currently completing an edited book collection entitled *Young Adult Literature and Adolescent Identity across Cultures and Classrooms: Contexts for the Literary Lives of Teens*. Dr. Alsup regularly presents at the National Council of Teachers of English (NCTE) convention and is the current chair of the Conference on English Education (CEE). She has published articles in several major journals in her field, including *English Education* and the *Journal of Adolescent and Adult Literacy*.

Ralph Beliveau is on the faculty in the Gaylord College of Journalism and Mass Communication at the University of Oklahoma. He studies critical media pedagogy, rhetorical theory, and media criticism.

David Bloome is professor in the School of Teaching and Learning of The Ohio State University College of Education and Human Ecology. Bloome's research focuses on how people use spoken and written language for learning in classroom and nonclassroom settings, and how people use language to create and maintain social relationships, to construct knowledge, and to create communities, social institutions, and shared histories and futures. He is a former president of the National Council of Teachers of English and of the National Conference on Research in Language and Literacy. He is a former middle school and high school teacher. He is director of the Center for Video Ethnography and Discourse Analysis in Education in the School of Teaching and Learning at The Ohio State University, co-director of the Columbus Area Writing Project, co-editor of *Reading Research Quarterly*, and founding editor of *Linguistics and Education: An International Research Journal*. He is the co-author of five books and editor/co-editor of six books on language and literacy in education, and author or co-author of numerous journal articles and book chapters. Bloome's current scholarship focuses on: (1) the social construction of intertextuality as part of the reading, writing, and learning processes; (2) discourse analysis as a means for understanding reading, writing, and literacy events in and outside of classrooms; (3) narrative development among young children as a foundation for learning and literacy development in schools; and (4) the social construction of time in classrooms as it impacts definitions of knowledge and personhood. David Bloome's personal web page can be accessed at: web.mac.com/dbloome/iWeb/Bloome%20Web%20Site/Bloome%20Home%20Page.html

Laura Bolf-Beliveau is assistant professor and English education program coordinator at the University of Central Oklahoma. Her research studies how new teachers engage in social justice pedagogy.

Ayanna F. Brown is assistant professor of education in the Department of Education at Elmhurst College. Brown's scholarship reflects interdisciplinary studies of language, literacy, and sociology where she uses macro-level social issues to raise questions about pedagogy and social interactions. Her present research focuses on the relationship between racial literacy and discussions of "race" in secondary and undergraduate classrooms. Brown's work has been presented at national and international conferences and is presently in press.

Leslie David Burns is an Assistant Professor of Literacy and an English language arts teacher who has worked in rural, suburban, and urban schools across Kansas, Michigan, and Kentucky. He earned his Ph.D. in Curriculum, Teaching, and Educational Policy from Michigan State University in 2005 with specializations in English education and adolescent literacy. Dr. Burns' research focuses on equity, diversity, responsive pedagogy, and curricular relevance in contemporary schools. In addition, his scholarship explores issues related to standards for literacy and teacher education with an emphasis on the imperative for professional educators to participate in policymaking and reform at all levels. He has published research on curriculum, policy, identity development in education research, teacher education, the New Literacy Studies, and methods of adolescent literacy instruction. He chaired the Conference on English Education's Task Force for Political Action in Education Reform, serves on the National Council of Teachers of English Task Force for National Standards, and works as Program Chair of English Education at the University of Kentucky in Lexington.

Gerald Campano worked as a full-time classroom teacher for nine years and is currently associate professor in the Department of Literacy, Culture, and Language Education at Indiana University, Bloomington. His scholarly interests include urban education, practitioner research, and immigrant identities in the contexts of schooling. He is a Carnegie Scholar and 2009 recipient of the David H. Russell Award for Distinguished Research from the National Council of Teachers of English. Gerald loves spending time with his partner, Maria, and his friends and family. He also enjoys chilling with his canine rescue, Archie.

Stephanie Carter is associate faculty in the Department of Literacy, Culture, and Language Education at Indiana University, Bloomington, School of Education and also adjunct faculty in the African American and African Diaspora Studies Department at Indiana University. Her research and teaching interests include secondary education, discourse analysis, sociolinguistics, Black feminist theory, research on silence, research on whiteness, Black education, qualitative and ethnographic inquiry, and Black women's literature.

Marilyn Cochran-Smith holds the Cawthorne Endowed Chair in Teacher Education for Urban Schools and directs the Doctoral Program in Curriculum and Instruction at Boston College's Lynch School of Education. Professor Cochran-Smith is an internationally known scholar and frequent keynoter on issues related to teacher quality, teacher preparation, practitioner inquiry, and social justice. She is an elected member of the National Academy of Education and of the Laureate chapter of Kappa Delta Pi. Cochran-Smith was the 2005 president of the American Educational Research Association (AERA), and she received AERA's 2007 Research to Practice Award for her book *Practice, Policy and Politics in Teacher Education*. Dr. Cochran-Smith was also the inaugural holder of the C.J. Koh Endowed Chair at the National Institute of Education, Nanyang Technological University in Singapore in 2006 and served on NIE's International Advisory Panel in 2007. Dr. Cochran-Smith was co-chair (with Ken Zeichner) of AERA's National Panel on Research and Teacher Education, whose report, *Studying Teacher Education* was published in 2005 and received AACTE's Best Publication award. She also co-edited *The Third Handbook of Research on Teacher Education: Enduring Questions in Changing Contexts.* Dr. Cochran-Smith is a member of the National Research Council's committee on teacher education, which is sponsored by the National Academy of Sciences and was charged by Congress to study the state of teacher education in the U.S. Dr. Cochran-Smith is chair of Boston College's Evidence Team, which is part of the Teachers for a New Era project sponsored by the Carnegie Corporation of New York as well as co-editor of the Teachers College Press series on practitioner inquiry. Dr. Cochran-Smith has written eight books, four of which have won national awards, as well as more than 150 scholarly articles, chapters, and editorials. Her latest book, *Inquiry as Stance: Practitioner Research for the Next Generation*, co-authored with Susan Lytle, was published in 2009.

A. Jonathan Eakle is an associate professor and program director in Johns Hopkins University's School of Education. His research addresses conceptual and practical uses of literacies in classrooms and out-of-school settings, particularly in museums, adolescent learning, and content area reading education. Eakle's recent publications appear in *Reading Research Quarterly, Journal of Adolescent & Adult Literacy, Reading Teacher,* and *Reading Online,* among other venues. His co-edited volume about secondary school literacy published by the National Council of Teachers of English was recently nominated for the National Reading Conference's Edward B. Fry Book Award. For three years he coordinated international research reports for *Reading Research Quarterly.* Eakle's present projects include research of museum literacies in Mexico and the U.S., editorial service for national and international organizations, teaching graduate-level cultural studies and literacies classes, and supervising clinical practicum.

Bob Fecho is a professor in the Reading Program of the Language and Literacy Education Department at the University of Georgia, Athens. To date, his work has focused on issues of language, identity, sociocultural perspectives, practitioner research, and critical inquiry pedagogy as they relate to adolescent literacy, particularly among marginalized populations. He has published articles in *Harvard Educational Review, Journal of Literacy Research, Research in the Teaching of English,* and *English Education,* and articles he has written have garnered both the Richard A. Meade and Alan C. Purves awards. One of his books, *"Is This English?" Race, Language, and Culture in the Classroom* (Teachers College Press), tells of his experiences teaching across culture in an urban school and was awarded the James Britton Award for Teacher Research from the National Council of Teachers of English, along with receiving Honorable Mention for the 2004 Myers Outstanding Book Awards by the Gustavus Myers Center for the Study of Bigotry and Human Rights. Most recently, he was named the 2008/2009 Carl Glickman Faculty Fellow by the UGA College of Education for his distinguished work in research, teaching, and service.

Matt Ferkany is a visiting assistant professor of philosophy at Michigan State University. His recent published work discusses the politics and educational significance of a sense of self-worth. His other research interests include theories of personal well-being, moral psychology, philosophy of education, and environmental ethics.

Margaret Hagood is an associate professor of literacy in the Department of Teacher Education at the College of Charleston. She teaches undergraduate and graduate courses in early childhood, elementary, and middle grade literacies, focusing on sociocultural and poststructural theories relevant to new literacies. She researches middle school teachers' uses of new literacies and pop culture through the Center of Excellence for the Advancement of New Literacies in Middle Grades at the College of Charleston. She is the editor of *New Literacies Practices: Designing Literacy Learning* and has co-authored a text on using pop culture in content area learning in grades 4–12. She may be contacted at hagoodm@cofc.edu

Janette H. Hill is professor and head of the Department Lifelong Education, Administration, and Policy at The University of Georgia (Athens, Georgia, US). Dr. Hill has published extensively, with particular emphasis in the areas of online learning environments and community building in virtual environments. Her teaching interests include online learning, research methods, and adult learning. She has participated in diverse design projects, including a training project as a faculty fellow at NASA's Johnson Space Center and an exchange program as a Design Fellow at Douglas Mawson Institute in Adelaide, South Australia. Dr. Hill has presented her work and conducted workshops in the U.S. and other countries, including South Korea, Taiwan, and Tunisia.

Glynda Hull studies literacy development in the context of digital technologies and globalization. Her most recent work connects youth around the world via the Internet and explores how learning can be fostered across differences in language, ideology, and geography via social networking sites. This project is supported by a grant from the Spencer Foundation. Her publications include *School's Out! Bridging Out-of-School Literacies with Classroom Practice* (Teachers College Press) and *Many Versions of Masculine: Explorations of Boys' Identity Formation through Multimodal Composing in an After-School Program* (Robert Bowne Foundation). Hull received her PhD. at the University of Pittsburgh in 1983 and then joined the Graduate School of Education at the University of California, Berkeley, where she was named a Distinguished Teacher.

Korina M. Jocson is assistant professor of education in Arts & Sciences at Washington University in St. Louis. Her research and teaching interests include literacy, new media culture, and ethnic studies in education. For the past decade,

Jocson has collaborated with university programs, schools, and community-based organizations to promote literacy development among youth. She is the author of *Youth Poets: Empowering Literacies In and Out of Schools.*

Tara Star Johnson is an assistant professor of English education at Purdue University, jointly appointed in the Departments of English and Curriculum & Instruction. She is also affiliated with the Women's Studies Program. A former high school English and science teacher from west Michigan, Tara received her doctorate from the Department of Language and Literacy at the University of Georgia. Tara's research interests include the intersections among race, class, gender, and sexuality, specifically as they relate to teacher-student relationships. Her book *From Teacher to Lover: Sex Scandals in the Classroom* (Peter Lang, 2008) is a case study of how and why sexual misconduct happens by the educator. Currently Tara is studying the effectiveness of a professional development program called The S.M.A.R.T. Solution (Sexual Misconduct Awareness and Response Training) as one means of addressing the problem of sexual misconduct in schools.

Mary M. Juzwik is an associate professor of language and literacy in the teacher education department at Michigan State University. She teaches undergraduate and graduate courses in writing, discourse, and English education and coordinates the secondary English Education program. She is affiliated with the Rhetoric, Writing, and American Cultures program at MSU and is a principal investigator at the Literacy Achievement Research Center. Mary holds degrees in English from the University of Wisconsin, Madison (PhD), Middlebury College (MA), and Wheaton College (BA). She spent six years working as a middle and high school English teacher in a range of contexts in the U.S., including the Navajo Nation. Her current work focuses on classroom discourse in English language arts classrooms. Specific areas of expertise include English teaching in linguistically and culturally diverse contexts, narrative and rhetorical theory, dialogic instruction, writing theory and instruction, and Holocaust education. Mary received the National Council of Teachers of English Promising Research Award, the Ghoddousi Mentor Award, and the MSU College of Education Excellence and Innovation in Teaching Award. She has published articles, essays, reviews, and commentaries in journals including *Across the Disciplines, American Educational Research Journal, Applied Linguistics, College Composition and Communication, Educational Researcher, English Education, English Journal, Journal of the Council of Writing Program Administrators, Linguistics and Education, Teachers College Record, Teaching and Teacher Education,* and *Written Communication.* Mary is also author of a book, *The Rhetoric of Teaching: Understanding the Dynamics of Holocaust Narratives in an English Classroom.* More information about her work can be found at www.msu.edu/~mmjuzwik

David E. Kirkland is an assistant professor of English education at New York University's Steinhardt School of Culture, Education, and Human Development, in the Department of Teaching and Learning. His research focuses on urban youth popular culture, language and literacy, digital identities, and urban teacher education. Dr. Kirkland has worked closely with urban youth, particularly young Black women and men, to understand how they learn and leverage literacy between the competing poles of official and unofficial social situations and settings. His research has explored the spoken and written words that urban youth use to construct identities and articulate what he sees as "meaningful lives." From this perspective, language and literacy play an important role in youth culture and education. Dr. Kirkland has received many awards for his work, including the 2008 AERA Division G Outstanding Dissertation Award. He has also been a fellow of the Ford Foundation and NCTE's Cultivating New Voices. Dr. Kirkland is widely published and is currently completing a book, *A Search Past Silence*, which examines the literacy lives of young Black men. He believes that, in their language and literacies, youth take on new meanings beginning with a voice and verb, where words when spoken or written have the power to transform the world inside-out. Dr. Kirkland can be reached at: dk64@nyu.edu

Peter McLaren is a professor in the Division of Urban Schooling, the Graduate School of Education and Information Studies, University of California, Los Angeles. He is the author and editor of forty-five books and hundreds of scholarly articles and chapters. Professor McLaren's writings have been translated into twenty languages. Four of his books have won the Critics' Choice Award of the American Educational Studies Association. One of his books, *Life in Schools*, was chosen in 2004 as one of the twelve most significant education books in existence worldwide by an international panel of experts organized by The Moscow School of Social and Economic Sciences and by the Ministry of Education of the Russian Federation. McLaren was the inaugural recipient of the Paulo Freire Social Justice Award presented by Chapman University, California. The charter for La Fundacion McLaren de Pedagogia Critica was signed at the University of Tijuana in July, 2004. La Catedra Peter McLaren was inaugurated in Venezuela on September 15, 2006, as part of a joint effort between El Centro Internacional Miranda and La Universidad Bolivariana de Venezuela. Professor McLaren left his native Canada in 1985 to work in the U.S., where he continues to be active in the struggle for socialism. A Marxist humanist, he lectures widely in Latin America, North America, Asia, and Europe. His most recent book (co-authored with Nathalia Jaramillo) is *Pedagogy and Praxis in the Age of Empire* (Sense Publications). With Steve Best and Anthony Nocella, he has co-edited a forthcoming book, *Academic Repression: Reflections from the Academic Industrial Complex* (AK Press). In 2006, during the Bush administration, Professor McLaren made international headlines when he was targeted by a right-wing extremist organization in the U.S. and put at the top of the "Dirty Thirty" list of leftist professors at UCLA. The group offered to pay students a hundred dollars to secretly audiotape McLaren's lectures and those of his fellow leftist professors. Professor McLaren's work has been the subject of two recent books: *Teaching Peter McLaren: Paths of Dissent,* edited by Marc Pruyn and Luis M. Huerta-Charles (Peter Lang Publishing), translated into Spanish as *De La Pedagogia Critica a la pedagogia de la Revolucion: Ensayos Para Comprender a Peter McLaren,* (Siglo Veintiuno Editores) and *Peter McLaren, Education, and the Struggle for Liberation,* edited by Mustafa Eryaman (Hampton Press).

Janet L. Miller, awarded the 2008 American Educational Research Association's (AERA) Division B-Curriculum Studies Lifetime Achievement Award, is professor of English education and former director of research in the Department of Arts & Humanities at Teachers College, Columbia University, in New York City. She earned her PhD in curriculum theory and humanities education–English from The Ohio State University. Her research and teaching commitments focus on intersections of curriculum and feminist theories; constructions of teacher subjectivities within varying social and cultural contexts; and feminist poststructuralist forms of biography and autobiography as qualitative and narrative research. Elected as vice-president of AERA for Division B-Curriculum Studies (1997–1999), as secretary for Division B (1990–1992), and as president of the American Association for the Advancement of Curriculum Studies for two terms (2001–2007), she also served as managing editor of *JCT: The Journal of Curriculum Theorizing* (1978–1998) as well as program chair of the Bergamo Curriculum Theory Conferences sponsored by *JCT* during that time frame. In addition to numerous scholarly articles published in edited books and professional journals, she is the author of *Creating Spaces and Finding Voices: Teachers Collaborating for Empowerment* (1990), *Sounds of Silence Breaking: Women, Autobiography, Curriculum* (2005), and co-editor of *A Light in Dark Times: Maxine Greene and the Unfinished Conversation* (1998).

sj Miller is associate professor of secondary English education and director of the Master of Arts in Teaching English at Indiana University of Pennsylvania. sj earned a BA from U.C. Berkeley, an MA from the Hebrew Union College, and a PhD from the University of New Mexico and taught high school English in the Santa Fe public schools for ten years, working with suburban, immigrant and Native American youth. sj has published widely in journals and presented widely in state and national conferences on a variety of topics related to teaching young adult literature, multimodal applications of popular culture in secondary classrooms, innovative research methodologies, and matrixing English teacher identity in space-time. Most notably, sj won the 2005 Article of the Year Award from the *English Journal* for "Shattering Images of Violence in Young Adult Literature:

Strategies for the Classroom." sj co-authored *Unpacking the Loaded Teacher Matrix: Negotiating Space and Time between University and Secondary English Classrooms,* which received the Richard A. Meade Award from NCTE and co-authored *Narratives of Social Justice Teaching: How English Teachers Negotiate Theory and Practice Between Preservice and Inservice Spaces.* sj is the co-chair of the CEE (Conference on English Education) Committee for Social Justice, the co-president for NCTEAR (National Council of Teachers of English Assembly for Research), and is a consultant for the College Board, AP Grant Mentor, providing best practices to secondary Pre- and Advanced Placement English teachers. Most recently, sj helped draft the Beliefs Statement related to Social Justice in English education at the CEE policy summit. Current research interests are in unpacking how social justice manifests in preservice English teacher identity as teachers experience the larger matrix of the teaching world.

Lenny Sánchez is currently a doctoral candidate in Literacy, Culture, and Language Education at Indiana University, where he teaches as a future faculty fellow and serves as a school-university liaison. His teaching and research commitments include: urban education, practitioner inquiry, and critical pedagogy. In addition to examining school-university partnerships, Sánchez's current research addresses the complex ways elementary students engage in critical inquiry through participatory action research and ethnographic stances. He looks forward to furthering these research foci as he joins the faculty at University of Missouri as an assistant professor in Literacy Education.

Peter Smagorinsky, following his graduation as an English literature major at Kenyon College in 1974, was credentialed to teach English at the University of Chicago. He taught English at Westmont, Barrington, and Oak Park & River Forest High Schools from 1977 to 1990, coaching track and basketball as well. He has taught in the English Education programs at the University of Oklahoma (1990–1998) and University of Georgia (1998–present) since receiving his doctorate from the University of Chicago in 1989. He has written and presented widely in state, national, and international publications and conferences on a variety of topics. These include literacy across the high school curriculum, the teaching and learning of the English curriculum, the dynamics of small group and whole class discussions of literature, the composition of nonverbal texts across the high school curriculum, the discourse of character education, and related topics. His writing has appeared in a variety of journals aimed at both teachers and researchers. He has won a number of awards from the University of Georgia, the National Council of Teachers of English, and the American Educational Research Association for his teaching and research. For the National Council of Teachers of English, he chaired the Research Forum, co-edited *Research in the Teaching of English,* co-chaired the Assembly for Research, served as president of the National Conference on Research in Language and Literacy, was a member of and chaired the Standing Committee on Research, and was a trustee of and chaired the Research Foundation. With a recent grant, he designed and is teaching Service-Learning in English Education, a course in which each student provides twenty hours of mentoring, tutoring, and coaching for a student in an alternative school.

Mariana Souto-Manning, PhD, is associate professor of early childhood education at Teachers College, Columbia University. From a critical perspective, she examines the sociocultural and historical foundations of early schooling, language development, and literacy practices. She studies how children, families, and teachers from diverse backgrounds shape and are shaped by discursive practices, employing a methodology that combines discourse analysis with ethnographic investigation. Her work can be found in journals such as *Early Child Development and Care, Early Childhood Education Journal, Journal of Early Childhood Research, Journal of Early Childhood Literacy, Journal of Research in Childhood Education*, and *Teachers College Record*. She was awarded the American Educational Research Association (AERA) Language and Social Processes Early Career Award in 2008 and the AERA Early Education and Child Development Early Research Career Award in 2009.

Arlette Ingram Willis received her PhD from the Ohio State University. She is currently a professor at the University of Illinois at Urbana-Champaign in the Department of Curriculum and Instruction, the division of Language and Literacy. Her publications include teaching and using multicultural literature in grades 9–12: *Moving beyond the Canon* (1998), *Reading Comprehension Research and Testing in the U.S.: Undercurrents of Race, Class, and Power in the Struggle for Meaning* (2008); three co-edited books: *Multiple and Intersecting Identities in Qualitative Research* (with B. Merchant, 2001); *Multicultural Issues in Literacy Research and Practice* (with G. Garcia, R. Barrera, and V. Harris, 2003); and *On Critically Conscious Research: Approaches to Language and Literacy Research* (with M. Montovan, H. Hall, C. Hunter, L. Burke, and A. Herrera, 2008); and numerous articles, book chapters, book reviews, and monographs.

APPENDIX A

Teacher Education Activities/Assignments

sj Miller

Stage: Critical Reflection

In this stage, teacher educators can create a classroom environment where participants are willing to open up to critical reflection of themselves and others. This means critically reflecting on one's past and present as they relate to one's habitus. By unveiling possible prejudices and actions that might be interpreted as oppressive toward self and others, students prepare themselves to advance through the other stages.

Activities to facilitate critical reflection:

REFLECT

- Have students describe their belief systems and principles and ask them how they came to terms with them.
- Discuss what critical reflection means.
- Have students consider a time when they were oppressed or have oppressed others and how they would have handled it differently today.
- Ask students to consider what social justice means to them.
- Ask students to consider what social justice looks like in the schools they've attended.
- Have students construct a vocabulary of terms that are related to social justice teaching: oppression, power, prejudice, hegemony, privilege, disenfranchised, marginalized, ally, agency, social action, empowerment, safe.

- Ask students to reflect on state and national standards and ask what they would change about them and why.
- Discuss the First Amendment and reflect on the apparent contradictions in schooling. and how they might affect a classroom space.

Reconsider

- Have students identify how an important issue related to social justice ties into a national issue and then reconsider how to be proactive about it in school.
- Have students bring in stories from the field related to social justice and ask peers how they might have responded differently to the situation. Ask peers to write on what they gained from the session.
- Explore texts, short stories, prose, poetry, drama, music, film, art, mixed media, and speeches that can illuminate some aspect of social justice.
- Revisit the national and local standards for English and review how social justice aligns with them.

Refuse

- Support students in their disagreements by asking them to back up their perspectives with concrete examples. Challenge their thinking by providing multiple points of view. Ask students if there are particular ideas that they disagree with and invite them to share.
- If students are resistant to sharing, allow for that space. Refusal is a position—invite them to explore their resistance.
- Invite students who refuse to unpack some of the reasoning for their positions. Explore (through mixed-media projects) those who historically stood up for others or wrote about or performed about social injustice.
- Invite students to explore their concerns about standards, to critique them, and make rationales for changes.
- Affirm students' counter views, encourage them to understand how to create a defensible argument, invite critique, and provide multiple opportunities to critically reflect on topics.

Reconceptualize

- Have students diagram or map out the school and look at its organizations. Ask students to reconsider how the school could be designed differently so that it would be for the betterment of the student body and faculty.
- Consider how to develop lesson or unit plans and assessment that explore social justice through texts, short stories, prose, poetry, drama, music, film, art, mixed media, speakers, community events, and speeches.
- Ask students to carefully consider where the line is crossed into coercive dimensions—and reflect on what oppression must look like for it to be oppressive—i.e., what is the critical line between oppression and hurt feelings?
- Discuss the impact of the standards movement on schools. Revisit NCATE's stance on professional dispositions. What kind of message does this convey to the students?

- Discuss personal symptoms of burnout and create a contingency plan when it begins.
- Develop skills to identify root causes of frustration. Identify triggers and be aware of what causes them.
- Encourage discussion about current injustices and give students space to voice them.

REENGAGE

- Be honest about the spaces that have more inclusive teaching environments and support teachers in going after what they desire.
- Help students consider the pros and cons of teaching and help them see the bigger picture of their lives.
- Offer them curricular and social support that might help sustain them when times are tough.

Stage: Acceptance

In this stage, students begin to own how the ways their habitus evolved and has affected who the person is today. In this stage individuals begin to understand how power, prejudice, privilege, and oppression manifest in society and are able to see their participation in various hierarchies. During this stage, misconceptions about roots of various forms of prejudice are unveiled: how and where they manifest, how they secure their dominance, how they are internalized, and how that affects behavior.

Activities to facilitate acceptance:

REFLECT

- Have students discuss what acceptance means and what that would look like in schools. Ask them if they see any contradictions.
- Ask students to consider how they felt when they were oppressed or when they oppressed someone else. What was that like?
- Ask students to write a script that shows how they have manifested misunderstandings about any forms of prejudice that they have encountered.
- Ask students to role-play scenes that involve something unjust, i.e., discrimination or bullying in school based on actual or perceived looks, social class, age, sexual orientation, ability, national origin, language, and ethnicity, against someone and then describe how to problem solve the situation.
- Ask students to investigate a community issue and look at the root causes of the problem.
- Ask students to bring in actual scenarios that happened in the field, discuss them in class, ask for feedback, and develop a strategy to reengage.
- Review the concept of inculcation and reflect on how that plays out under the First Amendment.
- Review NCATE's professional dispositions and consider how to make inroads for social change in light of current discourse.

- Ask students to review how their principles can affect their teaching.

RECONSIDER

- Have students research some aspect of an issue they dealt with or deal with in the field, and ask them to discover something new about the topic.
- Ask students to reflect on ways they can develop a disposition about accepting others who have opinions that may be socially unjust.
- Ask students to reflect on ways they can develop a disposition with their own classroom students about accepting others who have opinions that may be socially unjust.
- Have students create a spatial map that shows what an ideal community looks like.
- Collectively debate about the standards movement.
- Reconsider how particular bias may affect how one teaches.

REFUSE

- Support students in their reasoning about their concerns over acceptance. Provide opportunities for students to reflect on their perspectives, understand where they come from and what barriers affect their desire or ability to accept the issue at hand.
- Ask students to make meaning of their rationales for their refusal to accept something. Help them strategize their understandings and support them in their development.
- Ask students to consider how they might respond to a student who struggles with accepting people or ideas. Troubleshoot and role-play scenarios.
- Have students script scenarios about how they might respond if a student does not respect their or another's point of view.
- Debate over the importance of respect. Ask questions such as: Is respect important. Can you have a safe atmosphere without respect? Is respect a social contract and if so, between whom?
- Consider how the current educational system does or does not respect teachers or students.

RECONCEPTUALIZE

- Revisit what social justice means and explore additional ways to support students in finding spaces that enact social justice.
- Have students journal about their burgeoning awareness of what being a social justice educator means.
- Have students interview other teachers in the school and ask them about the positive and negative aspects of the school.
- Have students review the English and history curriculums in their school districts and consider what they can do to enhance teaching about social justice.
- Ask students to review how to change a prejudice they may have.

REJUVENATE

- Help students identify a mentor with whom they can talk openly.

- Remind students that stress can be part of the teaching profession and that students need to develop healthy detachment from situations where they may have little or any control.
- Have students identify peers and colleagues who advocate for social justice. Encourage them to ask someone to coffee or lunch.

REENGAGE

- Encourage students to consider ways to help them stay true to their principles to social justice even when others may marginalize them.
- Encourage students to attend events that help stabilize and affirm their belief systems.
- Encourage students to consider a motto that they can keep to help them move forward.

Stage: Respect

In this stage, students begin to develop compassion, empathy, sympathy, and an understanding about how peoples' lives have been oppressed and even disenfranchised by disrespect of any aspect of habitus. In this stage, students are likely to want to amend wrongs and may even feel remorseful for their unknowing or knowing participation in oppressing others. It is important to keep a watchful eye on this and turn the grief into something proactive for the individual. Respect can also be toward the self.

Activities to facilitate respect:

REFLECT

- Collectively reflect on what is unjust in society, schools, and families and facilitate dialogue amongst peers.
- Discuss the meanings of respect. How is respect earned/lost? Is it important?
- Have students reflect on times when a former or current teacher used respect positively and negatively. What did that look or feel like?
- Review the standards movement and reflect on how to pay homage to what needs to be done in schools as it aligns with students' principles.
- Discuss if prejudices have a place in a classroom. Discuss if it is okay to have prejudice. When is it problematic? When is it beneficial?

RECONSIDER

- Review the First Amendment again, but this time ask how it is/isn't and can/can't be embodied fully in schools. Ask to reconsider how to address certain social justice issues when First Amendment rights are suspended in schools.
- Research discrimination policies in the school district and state where you teach and then help make informed decisions about whether or not you can or should teach in that district or state.

- Ask students to reconsider what it means to be a social justice teacher in a school district that doesn't support teaching for social change.
- Have students journal about how they want to see respect manifested in their classroom.

REFUSE

- Speak candidly with students about what respect means and help them consider what lack of respect means in the context of the discussion. Review with them instances when there was lack of respect for them and when they have lacked respect for others. What brought them to those moments? How did it affect the outcome?
- Explore myriad instances where students have observed a lack of respect for others. What caused or led to those experiences? What could have been done to affect the outcome?
- Ask students to write about moments where they felt they deserved respect but weren't rewarded it.
- Review the standards movement and reflect on how to pay homage to what needs to be done in schools as it aligns with students' principles.

RECONCEPTUALIZE

- Have students identify an idea to reconceptualize relating it to social justice, then prepare a presentation for class, and open it up for discussion and feedback.
- Revisit what it means to be a social justice educator and align it to what is or isn't being enacted in their schools.
- Ask students to sketch out a plan for fostering more respect of student differences in your classroom.
- Propose how to revisit respecting norms.

REJUVENATE

- Form and create ally groups where students can go to for support.
- Consider ways in which students can regroup after tough days of teaching (exercise, massage, candles, movies, reading, TV, dinner, walking, talking, etc.).
- Have students create a plan for taking days off. What would that look like? How would they know when it is time to take time off?
- Remind students that they cannot be super-heroes but they can make a significant difference in what they do on a daily basis (even though it may not immediately be self-evident).
- Ask students to check-in with themselves about what is/isn't working in their classrooms and change it.

REENGAGE

- Remind students to reflect on what is important to them about teaching and support them in how they can be their best in their schools. They should ask themselves: What do I need to feel happy here?

- Suggest to students to do random acts of kindness.
- Discuss how personal dispositions are supported in their schools and focus on the positive.

Stage: Affirmation, Solidarity, and Critique

In this final stage, students begin to understand the universality of power, oppression, prejudice, and privilege. They begin to see connections between self, and other and develop a global context for social movements. Students may begin to form alliances with each other and/or consider how to develop them in their own classrooms or schools. They also have a matured consciousness that will enable them to continue to critique current and future manifestations of anti-socially just behavior.

Activities to facilitate affirmation, solidarity, and critique:

REFLECT

- Collectively discuss the meanings of affirmation, solidarity, and critique. What do they each look like? How have they manifested in their lives?
- Have students research organizations that are in the community, state, or nation that support different issues, write them, gather information.
- Help students build a resource pool of like-minded friends, teachers, and community members and meet once a month to discuss social justice issues.
- Have students research a school site and conduct a survey about the campus climate. Then consider how to enact change.
- Craft a pedagogy and share aloud while inviting feedback.
- Ask students to describe instances when they have enacted, embodied, and/or been an ally for social justice.
- Collectively reflect on the current positive and negative aspects to our current democracy.
- Make evident the paradoxes in democracy and have a debate about how they affect and effects teaching and schooling.
- Ask students to revisit times when they were poorly critiqued. What does a good critique look like?
- Ask students to review their principle and ask how they have changed?
- Ask students to describe what it means to be an ally in a school.

RECONSIDER

- Have students role-play scenes that demonstrate what a teacher can do to affirm students.
- Discuss instances when students felt threatened or oppressed in school and reconsider what a teacher could have done differently to make the situation better.
- Have students switch lives with someone in your class for a day—work out the arrangements and then take a walk in their shoes.
- Revisit the paradoxes and obstacles that are evident in democracy and consider ways to build that into lesson and unit plans.

- Revisit students' pedagogies and reflect on what can be shifted.

REFUSE

- Foster a discussion about refusing or being unwilling to adapt to circumstance. Could there be negative consequences?
- Explore with students how they can form counter-sites for spaces of empowerment. What would those sites look like? How might those manifest?
- Have students build a library of counter-arguments (different kinds of mixed media and text) that present opposing and nonconforming points of view.
- Remind students that refusal is a position, and that from that stance, much can be learned. Assure them that one must be well informed on any position in order to be conversant.
- Practice with students on how to be professional with discourse when taking counter points of view.

RECONCEPTUALIZE

- Ask students to consider what the clubs in the schools they work in might need and then do the research to begin that club.
- Encourage students to meet with other like-minded teachers and identify gaps in instruction related to social justice and then develop a plan that can be strategically mapped out and implemented over time.
- Imagine how students can take on more of a leadership role in their own schools and then create a focus group with students and identify what's missing from the school (clubs, safe spaces, policies, etc.).
- Revisit the curriculum and reflect on what community links can be made to the school.
- Revisit students' pedagogies and reflect on what can be shifted.
- Ask students to describe instances when they have enacted, embodied, and/or been an ally for social justice.
- Collectively reflect on the current positive and negative aspects to our current democracy.
- Make evident the paradoxes in democracy and have a debate about how they affect and effect teaching and schooling.
- Ask students to revisit times when they were poorly critiqued. What does a good critique look like?

REJUVENATE

- Encourage students to join an organization that has personal meaning.
- Encourage students to do something positive for the environment.
- Remind students to take a day off here and there.
- Ask students to consider volunteering their time.

REENGAGE

- Encourage students to form heterotopias. [1]

- Encourage students to move into higher education after some time (after they have spent at least three years teaching, since that is a minimum qualification for most university positions in English education).
- Encourage them to join national organizations, attend conferences, and present research with the National Council of Teachers of English, International Reading Association, American Educational Research Association, or the Shepard Symposium on Social Justice.
- Encourage them to subscribe to national journals in their field like the *English Journal*, *English Education*, *Journal of Adolescent and Adult Literacy*, *Reading Research Quarterly*, *Social Justice*, *Teaching Tolerance*, and the Teacher's College Press catalog.
- Invite students to create community links to their classrooms so that they can begin to develop a larger networking community.

Note

1.   Heterotopias are a "real" place, where there is a "sort of mixed, joint experience" or a "counter-site" occupied and created by those who contest the dominant sites (Foucault, 1986, p. 24), so that teachers can refer to the skills that they have learned to embody as a tool of resistance against larger and more dangerous sociopolitical agendas.

Bibliography

Foucault, M. (1986). Of other spaces (J. Miskowiec, Trans.). *Diacritics, 16*(1), 22–27.

Sample Pedagogy Assignment

Throughout the semester we will write, revise, and revisit our pedagogy for the classroom three times: at the beginning of the semester, at midterm, and for our final exam. Your task is to describe in detail your pedagogy which should include how you will approach teaching, reading, and writing and how you will manage your classroom. Your pedagogy should be student centered and focused in English language arts. In order to do this write-up, you might ask yourself, "what are my belief systems?" and "how do those belief systems create my pedagogy?" When constructing your pedagogy, be sure to draw upon course readings, discussions, and field experience.

Expectations/Assessment for Each Pedagogy: Minimum of two pages but should not exceed three pages. Papers must be typed with 10 or 12 pt. font (preferably Arial or Times), spacing 1.5–2 in. Use proper in-text citations, as per the most recent edition of MLA or APA guidelines. Create a works cited page. Create a cover page. When describing your pedagogy, be succinct and explicit and include answers to the questions at the top of the paper.

First Emergent Pedagogy

We consider this a draft of what your final pedagogy will be. As such, consider this task seriously but also recognize that you will have another opportunity to revise your ideas at midterm.

Second Emergent Pedagogy

This draft should reflect changes from your first emerging pedagogy. You may use aspects of the first draft in this version and include any changes. Along with this draft, you must submit a secondary reflection that addresses the following:

- Identify each change that occurred from draft one to draft two and specifically reference what impacted that change, i.e., texts, theories, conversations, class discussions, teachings, etc.

Final Emergent Pedagogy

This final draft is still an emergent pedagogy. We believe that even after *x* number of years teaching of pedagogies can shift over time and in different spaces and are never final or complete. This draft should reflect changes from your midterm emergent pedagogy. You may use aspects of that draft in this version and include any newer changes. Along with this draft, you must submit a secondary reflection that addresses the following:

- Identify each change that occurred from draft one to draft two and specifically reference what impacted that change, i.e., texts, theories, conversations, class discussions, teachings, etc.

- Develop an assessment rubric with clear criteria that we will use to evaluate you on the lesson plan that you will be teaching for your final exam. Consider that your assessment rubric must clearly contain criteria that show how your pedagogy is enacted in your lesson plan. For example, if you believe in student-centered discourse then your lesson must show that.

Sample to follow.

Assessment:
3% of overall portfolio grade.

Note

Emergent pedagogy assignment was developed by sj Miller and Linda Norris (2007) for use in methods.

Index